CONSTRUCTING SOCIAL WORK PRACTICES

Constructing Social Work Practices

Edited by
ARJA JOKINEN
KIRSI JUHILA
TARJA PÖSÖ

Ashgate
Aldershot • Brookfield USA • Singapore • Sydney

© Arja Jokinen, Kirsi Juhila and Tarja Pösö 1999

All rights reserved. No part of this publication may be reproduced, stored in a retrieval system, or transmitted in any form or by any means, electronic, mechanical, photocopying, recording or otherwise without the prior permission of the publisher.

Published by
Ashgate Publishing Ltd
Gower House
Croft Road
Aldershot
Hants GU11 3HR
England

Ashgate Publishing Company
Old Post Road
Brookfield
Vermont 05036
USA

British Library Cataloguing in Publication Data
Constructing social work practices
   1. Social service
   I. Jokinen, Arja II. Juhila, Kirsi III. Pösö, Tarja
   361.3'2

Library of Congress Catalog Card Number: 99-72851

ISBN 1 84014 984 1

Printed in Great Britain by
Antony Rowe Ltd, Chippenham, Wiltshire

Contents

PART I : SOCIAL WORK AND SOCIAL CONSTRUCTIONISM

1. Introduction: Constructionist Perspectives on Social Work Practices
   Arja Jokinen, Kirsi Juhila and Tarja Pösö 3

2. Social Construction in Social Work and Social Action
   Malcolm Payne 25

PART II: PRACTICES OF ENCOUNTER

3. Using Narratives in Social Work Interaction
   Elisabet Cedersund 69

4. Examining the Artfulness of 'Risk Talk'
   Susan White 87

5. Doing 'Delicacy' in Institutions of Helping: A Case of Probation Office Interaction
   Eero Suoninen 103

6. Speaking of Emotions in Child Protection Practices
   Hannele Forsberg 116

7. Masculinity Discourse in Work with Offenders
   Sally Holland and Jonathan B. Scourfield .... 13˜

PART III: DISCURSIVE STRUGGLES

8 The 'Social Construction of Child Maltreatment': Some Political, Research and Practice Implications
  Nigel Parton — 153

9 Constructing Child Welfare Practice in Ontario, Canada
  Evelyn Khoo — 173

10 Constructing Juvenile Delinquency: The Socio-Legal Control of Young Offenders in Israel, 1920-1975
  Mimi Ajzenstadt — 193

PART IV: PRACTICAL RELEVANCE

11 Financial Counseling at Norwegian Social Offices: Lessons for Constructing Social Work Practice
  Michael Seltzer and Svein Alve — 217

12 A Model for Constructivist Social Work Practice: The Product of a Clinician-Researcher Dialogue
  Jaclyn Miller and Mary Katherine O'Connor — 238

13 Speaking Up and Speaking Out: A Dialogic Approach to Anti-Oppressive Practice
  Danielle Turney — 257

14 Negotiating Constructions: Rebridging Social Work Research and Practice in the Context of Probation Work
  Kirsi Juhila and Tarja Pösö — 274

Notes on Contributors — 304

PART I:
SOCIAL WORK AND SOCIAL CONSTRUCTIONISM

1 Introduction: Constructionist Perspectives on Social Work Practices

ARJA JOKINEN, KIRSI JUHILA AND TARJA PÖSÖ

Social work is defined by many and in many different contexts. Parallel to clients and social workers, research and science are central constructors of social work. Descriptions of social work are, however, constructed in many other contexts as well. At times, it is a 'popular' topic in the media. Public policy defines tasks for it, formulates expectations of it and evaluates it as part of the local or national welfare agenda. In organisations providing social work education and in the development discussions and disputes related to education, social work and the qualifications of social workers are given varying contents. Employer and employee organisations are crucial definers as well, not to mention various client organisations and movements. We must also remember cultural differences. In different countries, in the contexts of different welfare states and welfare traditions, social work and its tasks are constructed in different ways. Moreover, the heterogeneity of culture inside individual countries brings local nuances into the spectrum of definitions.

Is social work, then, 'disappearing', becoming a jumble of fragmentary practices, as has been stated in certain discussions on the modern and the post-modern? According to some, there is no clear position or task for social work in the uncertainty of the post-modern world. Together with the modern welfare state, social work has entered a crisis. It can no longer justify its position by calling upon universal expert knowledge based on research. There exist many, even conflicting, knowledges and truths, all of which are exposed to criticism. Thus, social work is opened up for a multiplicity of interpretations. It may be defined in a great number of ways, both by people outside it and by people inside (Clarke, 1995; Howe, 1994; Parton, 1994 and 1995).

The present book, based on social constructionism, starts out from the claim that despite the multiple and fragmented definitions, social work can be observed, studied and analysed. *The observation must be based on concrete practices of social work, which are defined as social work or which in some other way cause the existence of social work. To increase the understanding of these multiple practices is the first goal of our book.* In our study, we avoid a normative evaluation of social work practices, since we do not hold the key to defining 'good' social work. Instead, we have at our disposal research tools for studying what happens in the social work practices, as the various case studies in the book will show. Whenever we are dealing with societal activity such as social work, the requirement often placed to research is its utility. *Can research based on social constructionism be applied in social work, can it bring about change? The second goal of the book is to present answers to this question.* Before moving on to these themes, however, we will describe the conversations leading to the genesis of this book, and particularly of this introductory chapter.

The Chain of Conversations as a Context

No scholarly text can be born in vacuo, nor can it be the end-point of any chain of events. In constructionist terms, research can be structured as consequent, parallel or overlapping conversations. The texts comment on other texts and integrate elements from them. In addition to texts, face-to-face meetings of researchers also constitute activity where research is constructed. Moreover, research practices – especially in applied research such as social work – interact with other societal conversations and often also with social work carried out in the field.

Every scholarly text contains several elements – conversations or parts of conversations familiar from other contexts – since 'new' is always constructed in a communicative relationship to 'existing'. In their new context, however, 'old' elements are no longer visible as clearly defined loci in the text, or as neat references. Rather, they may be understood as the resources for working the new text, only receiving their significance in the context of their presentation, and consequently the significance may differ considerably from that presented in other contexts. It is impossible to locate all conversational links in an individual text, yet in the following we will attempt to trace one series of conversations which was crucial for the genesis of the present text. We will study conversations as something which proceeds temporally and finds a spatial location.[1] The function of this study is, on the one hand, to construct a historical context for the text to facilitate the reader's orientation, and on the other hand, to illustrate the analytical basis of our method of work. Even though we are constructing a narrative on the basis of our own activity, it is as well to bear in mind that local research (in this case, research carried out at Tampere) is always intertwined with a wider debate, without which it could not exist.

In 1995 we edited a book in Finnish on the union of social work and constructionism. We justified the utility of a constructionist frame of reference emphasising the practices of social work as follows:

> General definitions (of social work) often create difficulties for a researcher approaching social work from the direction of practices. They do not seem to pull together the endless multiplicity of social work practices, which appear to escape categorisations coming from the outside, whether they are interpretations produced inside the discipline or science, tasks defined by administration or legislation, societal function, professional ethics, or something even more general than these. When starting out from empirical work, you are likely to catch something else. In this case, it is difficult or even impossible to begin your research report by asking the question, "What is social work?", but the question, "How should we study social work?", becomes even more pressing. Thus, one possibility – not unheard-of, but little applied in Finnish research – of grasping social work is to emphasise the priority of empirical research (Jokinen, Juhila and Pösö, 1995, p. 11).

In our book, we built up a constructionist angle on social work by studying social work practices as social problems work. The concept originates from James A. Holstein and Gale Miller (1993; Miller and Holstein, 1991), who used it to describe the processes of defining and solving social problems occurring in the local practices of human service organisations. The concept linked the constructionist research tradition, attached to social problems (Spector and Kitsuse, 1987; Kitsuse and Spector, 1973), to organisational practices in a way which made it possible to study social work in a more data-oriented manner than the 'conventional' social work research. Especially in the context of Finnish social work debate, the study of social work practices as local social problems work opened up a new approach, which helped scholars who appreciate empirical qualitative research (i.e., us) in structuring both the methodological and substance issues related to social work research. The various chapters of the book (in addition to ourselves, the writers included Hannele Forsberg, Jaana Jaatinen and Irene Roivainen, all social work researchers and colleagues familiar to us) studied various linguistic everyday practices of social work, especially with a view to how categories of social problems and clienthood are produced in and through them. Our data included interviews with social workers, encounters between workers and clients and conversations between workers. The topics addressed included child abuse, homelessness and alcohol problems. We justified the relevance of our study by saying that constructionist analysis makes visible things and processes which are otherwise regarded as self-evident.

The book project was purely national in scope, even though, naturally, it received impulses from international literature on research methods and social work. Its reception was varied. In particular, a number of social work researchers criticised the constructionist approach for concentrating on work practices and face-to-face interaction, thus leaving aside a study of the societal conditions of the work. Moreover, they suspected that the researchers 'over-interpret' social work and transform random chains of events into an unrealistic 'theory' of social work. In addition to adverse criticism, our book also awakened curiosity and expectations which encouraged us to continue. In the aftermath of the book we conceived the idea of determining whether the union of constructionism and social work would find a wider interest. We knew of the existence of researchers interested in this topic in other countries, but as far as we knew, there was no extensive network for them. With the aim of building at least a partial network, we began to plan an international symposium[2], which was then implemented under the name 'Constructing Social Work Practices' in Tampere, Finland, on 13-15 August, 1997. The symposium announcement was as follows:

> Social constructionism aims to study reality as socially and linguistically constructed in everyday practices of different kinds. Recently, institutional practices such as social work have been the focus of this approach. Therefore, a seminar on social constructionism and social work is well motivated and actual, and also provides a welcome forum for scholarly exchange and cooperation in this field. In this seminar, we want to look at the relationship between social constructionism and social work from the point of view of social work research and teaching, as well as of daily social work practices.

The main financier of the symposium was NorFa (Nordic Academy for Advanced Study). The partners also included the 'Language, Interaction and Social Care in the Nordic Welfare Systems' research network, the Department of Social Work and Social Policy at the

University of Tampere and the Swedish School of Social Science at the University of Helsinki. About 70 actors from the field of social work, especially researchers, but also teachers, postgraduate students and social workers from ten countries met in Tampere. For three days, the symposium discussed social work and constructionism, which proved a broad topic with several dimensions. On the one hand, the consensus was that there already exists a considerable body of research on the topic, but on the other hand, new research challenges seemed constantly to present themselves.

This book contains a number of papers given in the 'Constructing Social Work Practices' symposium. The structure of the book grew from a dialogue with the texts submitted for publication, resulting in our naming the main chapters of the book as follows: Social Work and Social Constructionism, Practices of Encounter, Discursive Struggles, and Practical Relevance. All of the articles selected interpret and define social work and constructionism, and their mutual relationship, from one of the above angles. One consequence of this demarcation was that not every interesting paper could be accepted for publication.

In writing this introductory chapter we conducted yet one conversation with the texts included in the book. Our analytical tool was to interpret them from certain angles: we used the texts as our resources, we integrated elements from them into the entity of the introduction. The issues we are highlighting below – the encounters between clients and social workers or social change – are not the main topics of any of the texts, but in their way, each of them also addresses these issues. The method of conversation was strongly two-directional: the idea for highlighting these themes was born out of our reading the texts, but at the same time, we also made the themes visible in them. The other side of the coin is, of course, that our opening chapter does not introduce the other texts on their own terms: each of them presents one complete and independent interpretation of the relationship between social work and constructionism, and our text does not claim to do justice to these interpretations.

8   *Constructing Social Work Practices*

Researching Social Work Encounters

Social Work as Encounters between Social Workers and Clients

What do we mean by claiming that social work can be grasped in social work practices? We shall specify this starting-point and present that social work is constructed as social work particularly in *the encounters between clients and social workers*. This starting point contains a certain, if loose, definition and understanding of social work. According to this, the three crucial elements of social work are clients, social workers and the encounters between them. In strictly constructionist terms, even a loose pre-definition constitutes a problem. How do we know, in observing a practice, that we are dealing with a client-worker relationship? Don't the words 'client' and 'social worker' in themselves constrain our manner of understanding what is happening in the situation; i.e., that there is one helping, supporting or controlling the other? Do these concepts contain a set interpretation of the nature of the client-worker relationship; for instance, as regards its hierarchical nature? Is the word 'client' too strong a label? All these questions are justified. However, we cannot speak of matters without naming them or without somehow limiting the area to be scrutinised. Thus, a loose definition of social work is necessary. However, what is essential from the constructionist angle is that the concepts of client and social worker, as well as the encounters between them, are linked to as few as possible advance definitions concerning their content or form, for concrete contents and forms are essentially only constructed in the practices of encounters.

Encounters between clients and social workers take place in many different arenas. The client and the worker may be present in the same space and speak to one another, i.e., the encounter is face-to-face. An encounter may also take place when one of the partners is physically not present; when social workers discuss clients among themselves or write case reports, when clients describe their experiences as clients in different contexts, etc. In an even broader sense, the partners may be thought to encounter one another also indirectly, for instance, in legal discourse which defines the persons in need of help or control by social workers, or in textbooks on social work which advises on the construction of a good client-social worker relationship.

'Client' and 'social worker' are not self-evident categories; rather, they receive their content in each individual encounter, as is pointed out by

Malcolm Payne (1991). The use of language, whether oral or written, holds a crucial role in constructing these contents, even though the systematic observation of the linguistic aspects of social work is fairly recent (Baldock and Prior 1981; Rojek et al 1988). In the articles of this book the client and the social worker come into existence through speech and writing in many types of encounters. At times, the speakers and writers are the persons involved, at other times these categories are produced by other speakers and writers. The texts and speeches draft many different versions of clients and social workers and their mutual relationships. The versions are also linked to each other, and these links are also looked for in various chapters.

Arenas of Encounters

The face-to-face encounter between the social worker and the client is the most clear-cut arena of encounter in the sense that the partners are present to define their status as client and social worker for themselves and for the other. The defining process is strongly interactive. These encounters, which take place in many different organisations, are studied by many writers of this book from different angles. The encounter between the social worker and the client in the everyday work of the social welfare office is the topic of Elisabet Cedersund's article. She is particularly interested in the narratives constructed by clients of the welfare office in speaking of their financial needs and the causes leading to them, as well as in the roles given to these narratives in the interaction between the worker and the client. In her analysis, Cedersund shows that it is the construction of narratives which lets clients participate in the creation of their 'case'. Narratives are often presented in a form which requires the worker to present solutions to the client's problems, i.e., to take the position of a helper. The subtle dynamics of interaction between the social worker and the client is studied by Eero Suoninen, who deals with encounters in the probation office. He shows that the interaction is not simply a matter of sending and receiving messages, but a complicated search for a shared understanding, as words have many meaning potentials. Suoninen's analysis shows that social workers mark certain topics as delicate and thus avoid 'directly dictating speech'. This, in its turn, enables the handling of morally sensitive issues, for instance, without endangering the 'saving face' of either party or their mutual cooperation relationship.

The topic of Hannele Forsberg's article is the verbalising of emotions in the face-to-face encounters of child protection clients and social workers. By comparing the conversations between clients and workers in two child protection organisations with different basic orientations (social welfare office and family support centre) she shows how conversations may define the clients either as victims of their suppressed emotions or as actors who actively process their emotions. In the former, the elements of the interpretation are looked for in the past, while in the latter interpretation, the focus is on future-oriented constructions. Thus, the tasks of the social worker are also defined differently in the two conversations: they are either analysing the causes of the emotional problems or constructing solutions. The task of the social worker and its relationship to the construction of the client image is also searched for by Michael Seltzer and Svein Alve, in encounters between indebted clients and social workers acting as financial counsellors. Seltzer and Alve note that the mainstream publicity in Norway defines excessively indebted persons primarily as persons with 'not enough self-control'. In encountering such persons, social workers attempt to mediate between two worlds – that of the indebted and that of the debtors – and to facilitate the contact between the two, which has often broken down. In a similar vein, Jaclyn Miller and Mary K. O'Connor's article emphasises the wide spectrum of potentially existing possibilities in the encounters between clients and social workers. They call for a continuous, bold, inquiring and respectful search by the social worker for new and alternative ways of interpreting the client's narratives and of re-constructing them as well, together with the client.

There exist numerous *arenas where social workers encounter their clients through speaking of them without the presence of the clients concerned.* Susan White describes the arena of *a meeting between childcare social workers*, where the workers encounter and also construct an individual client (or client family) by talking about them. In their talk, they re-create themselves as assessors of the need for the deficiency of child protection; this may be concluded from the ways in which their speech constructs deviation, risks, certainty and uncertainty. The clients encountered through the talk are, in their turn, defined as targets of assessment and eventual measures. *Social workers' talk to or with researchers* is also an arena of encounter without the presence of the clients. Kirsi Juhila's and Tarja Pösö's study on the assessment practices related to the suitability of community service is an example of this, based on conversations between researchers and social workers. In these conversations, the workers construct not only the general characteristics of a client suitable for community service (regularity, commitment, life control, attitude towards criminal lifestyle), but also the means which they as social workers possess for finding out about those characteristics.

Interviews are another form of talking to researchers. Sally Holland and Jonathan B. Scourfield have conducted a study partly based on interviews with probation officers. In addition to interviews, their data includes various files and reports on clients, which form a part of the staple workload of the workers. *Files and reports are an important arena of encounters in social work; in them, workers report on and describe their individual clients without a significant participation by the clients.* In their data, Holland and Scourfield identify three different discourses defining the masculinity of the clients, which are characterised 'as traditional (boys will be boys), new (explicitly challenging masculinity) and mainstream (implicitly challenging masculinity)'. In the interview arena, where the workers produced reports for the researchers, emphasis was placed on the discourses which challenged traditional masculinity either explicitly or implicitly. In contrast to this, daily practices, the various documents written by workers, were dominated by the traditional discourse.

Our book studies *the encounters between social workers and their clients also in arenas where the actors and definers are not social workers or clients*. The focus of Nigel Parton's article is the report 'Messages from Research' produced by the UK Department of Health. This is an administrative text which assesses, criticises and produces visions for British child protection work, partly on the basis of existing constructionist research into social work. In this textual encounter, i.e., on the pages of the report, child protection workers and their clients are brought to an encounter first, by criticising the past and present work practices, and second, by attempting to create space for new and more constructionist encounter practices in child protection. Similarly, Mimi Ajzenstadt's article on young offenders is based on texts which define encounters in social work 'from the outside'. Her data includes official reports, private correspondence, newspaper articles and articles published in professional magazines. These arenas of textual encounters discuss the preferred attitudes towards young offenders. In these texts social workers are described as one of several groups of actors (together with psychologists, medical doctors and educationalists) with the task of normalising their young clients and of integrating them as productive members of society. Evelyn Khoo is also interested in the task written and defined for social work and social workers in a body of texts. She has studied the mainstream theories on childhood. According to her, these theories repeat the interpretation where childhood is seen as a universal process with progressive stages. The theories 'prescribe' professional intervention if these progressive stages fail to appear. In the practices of child protection, in the physical encounters between clients and workers, this 'theoretical' interpretation is partly reproduced, though partly also brought under criticism.

The above analyses based on texts which define social work 'from the outside' emphasise a critical approach; the researchers show how polemic the definitions of clients, social workers and their mutual relationships presented in the texts are. However, *texts may also bring social workers and clients to visionary encounters*. We are dealing with the visionary when talks and writings sketch the outlines of social work which is good and worth striving for. Such outlines are searched for by Danielle Turney, basing her work on philosophy and social sciences and writing of an anti-oppressive social work practice which is sensitive to people's needs regardless of their social status.

Thus, there are many arenas for encounters. In studying social work practices it is possible to focus on one or several of them. The relationship between definitions produced in different arenas is an interesting topic reflected on by most of our contributors. It is particularly studied by Malcolm Payne in an extensive chapter dealing with social work and social constructionism. He writes on the social construction of the social work cycle. On this comprehensive cycle he places 'the client-worker-agency cycle, the political-social-ideological cycle, and the agency-profession cycle'. The first of the three deals with the face-to-face encounters between the client and the social worker. The second contains broader societal debates where social problems are constructed. The third cycle consists of professional conversations dealing with knowledge in social work. These cycles interact continuously with each other; their influence on each other is multidirectional. According to Payne, our picture of social work is fuller if we look at it on all three cycles. However, it is also possible to concentrate on one cycle alone, in which case the other two will act as framing contexts. Payne's construction brings us smoothly to our next topic: how do we analyse encounters in social work?

How to Analyse Encounters?

Constructionist-oriented research into social work practices emphasises the facts that practices – both of social work and of research – interpret social reality and that the use of language is a basic element. The fact that use of language is not only seen to reflect the existing reality, but also to actively construct it, has manifold consequences for practical research. The focal point in constructionist research is formed by the many processes of language use (both oral and written), in and through which social reality – including social work – is constructed (Burr, 1995; Gergen, 1994; Shotter, 1993)[3]. In his article, Malcolm Payne gives a detailed description of this linguistic turn, so significant even for social work research.

The studies by Elisabet Cedersund, Hannele Forsberg, Susan White, Eero Suoninen, and Michael Seltzer and Svein Alve, focusing on the analysis of face-to-face encounters, utilise data primarily collected by tape-recording conversations between either the social worker and their client or several social workers among themselves; the conversations have been transcribed down to the level of detail considered useful by the researcher(s). In three studies, data was also collected by the method of (participatory) observation, in which cases the tapes only form a part of the data. In the study by Sally Holland and Jonathan B. Scourfield the data consists of interviews with social workers and of documents. Kirsi Juhila and Tarja Pösö use as their data both tape recordings of conversations between clients and social workers and joint conversations between researchers and social workers recorded through ethnographic notation. The studies by Nigel Parton and Mimi Ajzenstadt are based on existing textual data: Parton constructs his analysis around an administrative report in the form of a case, while Ajzenstadt has gathered a historical corpus of data containing several kinds of documents.

Thus, sets of empirical data can be of many kinds, but so can the ways in which data is analytically organised. Thinking in constructionist terms, sets of data in themselves do not tell the researcher anything, but instead, the researcher highlights certain aspects in them and at the same time attempts to organise them in a sensible way. In the organisation, various methodological instruments can be made use of. Elisabet Cedersund approaches the interaction between client and social worker by means of narrative analysis. Susan White analyses the rhetorical means which social workers use in their meeting when assessing and justifying the child protection needs of their client families. Eero Suoninen's discourse analytical study, which draws upon conversation analysis, focuses on aspects of speech which analysis often disregards as 'insignificant' (such as stammering, hesitations, pauses, conversational fillers) and studies their communicative function in a professional encounter. Sally Holland and Jonathan B. Scourfield identify various discourses which interpret masculinity in their data and reflect on their use in different contexts.

Narrative analysis, rhetoric, discourse analysis and conversation analysis, as well as various combinations of them are methodological approaches allowing a very detailed analysis of the processes of language use. A researcher making use of them is primarily connected with certain local sets of data: applied to social work, s/he asks how the client and the social worker encounter each other in a given arena. Without such a connection, the detailed analysis of language use is not possible. However, none of the texts in this book deals exclusively with local data, but at the least they all make observations on the links between the local and wider debates inside organisations, professions or society at large. The social work cycle sketched by Malcolm Payne (described in the chapter above) is thus more or less in use.

The ethnographic approach offers concrete tools for combining the local level and a wider debate, especially when dealing with topics related to the professional culture and organisational operation environment of social work. The comparison between two child-protection organisations presented by Hannele Forsberg is one such tool. In showing the existence of two different local cultures, she also proves that situational conversations are linked to the organisational context of work. Kirsi Juhila and Tarja Pösö's manner of 'framing' situational client-worker encounters with reports produced by the workers in order to make individual episodes understandable to researchers, is another concrete ethnographic tool. In themselves, the reports by the workers do not explain local situations, but in their special way they describe the professional and organisational culture shared by probation officers.

The societal contextualisation of data on local encounters, in its turn, is particularly crucial for the studies by Susan White, Nigel Parton, Mimi Ajzenstadt and Michael Seltzer and Svein Alve. According to Susan White, child protection work is entwined with ritualised narratives which reproduce child welfare policy discourses prevalent in UK in the 1990s. Parton starts out from this same policy, which he names the 're-focusing of children's services' debate. Parton makes the debate understandable by placing it in the arena of conversations related to societal transformation, within the crisis of organised modernity. The arena of political and societal encounter is also strongly present in Mimi Ajzenstadt's article, in which she shows both how the medical welfare model became the mainstream discourse in Israeli practices related to young offenders from the 1920s onwards, and how this model was directly linked with the project of constructing a Jewish society. Michael Seltzer and Svein Alve in their turn read debt counselling situations through the general debt crisis in Norway and through financial activity impacting individual households.

In addition to the above studies, based on analyses of local encounter data, a number of contributions are more *theoretical or reflective or search for new types of activity models*, rather than being strictly empirical, even though they, too, are connected with the practice of social work. By means of theorising born out of a cross between hermeneutic and constructionist research, Danielle Turney constructs a model of anti-oppressive dialogue for the interaction between social worker and client. Evelyn Khoo uses an ideal type constructed from the practice of child protection to illustrate the diversity of cultural and professional dilemmas inevitably encountered in actual cases of child protection work. Jaclyn Miller and Mary K. O'Connor utilise experiences they have gained elsewhere to create a new helping model for social work, based on constructionist ideas.

The constructionist frame of reference does not lead to one single manner of conducting research; rather, we are introduced to a broad spectrum of possibilities. The methodological choices and solutions of our contributors are a proof of this: in studying the encounters between social workers and clients in the different arenas of social work, they utilise different sets of data and various possibilities for combining and analysing data.

Social Work Encounters and Change

Reconsidering and Reconstructing Encounters

Should we attempt to evaluate the encounters between social workers and clients in different arenas, in addition to studying and making them visible? Where could we go for evaluation criteria? As we know, the expectations placed on social work come from many different directions. The expectations always contain some kind of understanding about high-quality social work. Thus, social work and social workers have often been criticised by various groups, as expectations and quality criteria are deemed not to have been met. When this happens, social work is seen through a normative filter believed to be capable of distinguishing high-quality social work from work deficient in quality.

The constructionist approach, which starts out from the practices of social work, does not utilise such a filter. *Constructionism does not embody a normative definition of good social work.*[4] Instead we can see that *the evaluation of encounter practices as well as their reconsideration should be based on empirical research*, not on an activity defined on the basis of advance criteria for 'good' social work. When starting with practice, it is easy to see that normative definitions coming from the outside do not meet the multiplicity of practical social work or the unexpected, context-bound consequences of actions. This opens up an opportunity for understanding change. In our opinion, even though constructionist research focuses on analysing practices, change is incorporated as a topic of research. When social work is studied as an activity which constructs social problems in different encounters, the object of study is – as presented by Gale Miller and James A. Holstein (1991) – at the same time the construction of the means, resources and valuations needed for change. Social work as social activity defines not only social problems, but also the manner of managing, changing or eliminating them, and they also become objects of study. Thus, constructionist research is in a very basic manner interested in the rhetorical construction of both problems and change.

In a nutshell, our understanding of change is as follows: since the categories of 'client' and 'social worker' receive their contents in the various arenas of encounter, the changes in the categories also take place locally on the same arenas. Changes in the arenas of encounter may have an effect on each other, but they are not causally related. For instance, changes in an administrative report or legislative text do not automatically lead to changes in the face-to-face encounters between client and social worker, but such changes could become integrated as parts of the encounters, or parts of local change. A detailed study of practices gives cues of potential change and its direction. It is up to the individual researcher to decide whether, in addition to analysing, s/he will also adopt the position of an active debater or critic. All of these are needed in the forum of social policy.

Constructionist research into social work may be considered basic academic research, but it may also be considered critical or applying research. These elements may also be combined in one single study, in its successive stages. Different research weightings lead to different practical relevancies. Basic academic research studies encounters and makes their practices visible without taking a direct stand on the need for or direction of change related to practices. However, such research can also offer material for a reconsideration of encounters. In showing how encounters produce different versions of clients and social workers it simultaneously shows that choices made in encounter situations have a practical significance. Critical constructionism may adopt the task of challenging dominant discourses, for instance, and of increasing multiplicity. The supremacy of a given version may be challenged by making visible its process of gaining hegemony and excluding other versions. Applied social work research studies particularly the uses of results from constructionist research for encounter practices.

Practical Relevancy of Social Constructionist Research

The present collection of articles contains both basic academic research and critical and applying research. Particularly the texts by Susan White, Eero Suoninen, Hannele Forsberg, and Kirsi Juhila and Tarja Pösö contain many elements of *basic academic research.* They analyse in detail the various face-to-face encounters in social work, showing how a number of choices is continuously made during the conversations, not dictated by factors external to the situations. On child protection conversations between social workers and on analysing these, White writes as follows: 'These data demonstrate that social work is a profoundly moral enterprise for which few rational-technical tools exist. They (practitioners) make choices about whom to believe often based on the moral adequacy of the account offered'. Eero Suoninen highlights the production of delicacy in professional encounters as an 'essential part of the communicative act itself and an essential quality of professional skills', with the function of 'the pedagogical maintenance of morally special issues'. Hannele Forsberg's results concerning the two different ways of speaking about emotions also reveal local choices. Similarly, Kirsi Juhila and Tarja Pösö's analysis of interviews assessing the suitability of community service shows how both the suitability and unsuitability are constructions produced jointly by the clients and the social workers. All four studies clearly show

how changes or different choices are or could be possible in these encounters; they, too, are constructed through speech acts.

The *critical direction* in constructionist research is represented, among others, by Nigel Parton, who writes: 'For one of the potential attractions of social constructionism as a contribution to social work research and practice is as a method of critique, where particular attention is paid to the politics of subjectivity and the ways in which meanings, cultural codes and knowledge production are entangled in the construction and maintenance of unequal power relations'. According to Parton, such critical emphasis is lacking from the way in which the British child protection policy has adopted some constructionist principles as part of its agenda. Similarly, Mimi Ajzenstadt, Evelyn Khoo, and Sally Holland and Jonathan B. Scourfield present ideas leaning towards critical constructionism. All of them deal with the gaining of hegemony of certain discourses (the medical-welfare discourse in dealing with deviant youngsters, the discourse universalising the development stages during childhood in child welfare, and the traditional masculine discourse in probation service) and reflect on the possibilities of challenging them.

Malcolm Payne calls for a strongly *applying* constructionist research into social work. Since social work is an activity striving for a change, constructionist research should be able to offer tools for practical work. Elisabet Cedersund's text outlines such tools. After studying the ways in which clients speak of their financial problems through narratives she shows that narrative analysis can also be used as a method of social work. The joint production of several alternative narratives may have an emancipatory function for the clients. Emancipatory social work is also stressed by Michael Seltzer and Svein Alve, as well as Jaclyn Miller and Mary K. O'Connor. The former search for the change agent in the social worker, who in their opinion should attempt to de-stabilise the dominant 'help to self help' ideology which makes the client's situation even more difficult. The latter two focus on developing the worker-client relationship as emancipatory as possible. Danielle Turney present similar ideas in writing on ethically informed constructionism with the essential element of opposing hegemonistic discourses and bringing out alternative voices.

Creating Voices and Silences

The practical relevancy of constructionist research is reflected on all the contributions from the viewpoint that conversation is the centre of change and language the mediator of change. The articles all express a strong concern over who constructs the change through language. Nearly all of the contributors write about *whose voice is heard in social work encounters, what this voice is allowed to say and how far it is allowed to be heard.* These questions are dealt with in detail from several angles.

The constructionist viewpoint emphasises that speaking and writing are processes which are open to interpretation and produce social reality. For instance, gathering information on the client's situation is an active series of successive choices, as is shown by Susan White. Encounters also bear traces of the institutional, ideological and juridical status of social work. Evelyn Khoo describes this process of mediation by taking up a topical issue: the construction of a child client as the target and partner in social work. In her article she illustrates how the voice of the child client or its absence are linked not only with the unique interaction in the client-worker encounter, but also to the broader societal role, situation and interpretations of social work and the position of the child. When child clients are ignored or made secondary in relation to adult clients, both of these acts are ideological stands. Therefore, social work practices can reveal the ideology of social work both as regards the structurisation of interaction and the principal administrative directions, as is pointed out by Nigel Parton and Mimi Ajzenstadt.

Change in social work is essentially based on 'struggles' between voices – between speakers and that which is being said. Social work activity requires a starting-point, an interpretation of the situation of the person or group currently worked with. This interpretation may be understood as a narrative in the manner of Elisabet Cedersund. The essential thing is, who tells the narrative, and in what situations are narratives believed in. Power can be seen, among other things, in who defines certain narratives as important and others as less important or uninteresting. From this viewpoint, the construction of a narrative is continuously linked with the possibilities of emancipation or oppression. Oppression is linked to the silencing of narratives, emancipation to listening to them and giving space to a change of narrative. For instance, Sally Holland and Jonathan B. Scourfield observe 'struggles between voices' from the angle of how discourses which structure masculinity in different ways contribute to constructing the object of work, i.e., the interpretation of men who have committed crimes, of the causes of these acts and of responsibility. Thus, interpretations have consequences for the manner of doing 'change work' with the clients. Danielle Turney's concern over the enabling of change in social work has a similar basis: different ways of speaking and conducting conversations construct different social relationships between clients, workers and other social actors. According to Turney, the crucial question in social work is the kind of dialogue taking place in social work: the nature of oppression occurring in social work is that certain aspects are repeatedly not allowed to surface in conversations or they are excluded. Emancipatory social work, in its turn, supports itself on a dialogue where voices are not suppressed, but there is a continuous sensitivity for noticing and hearing them. Turney emphasises that the ethical basis of social work is in dialogue, and it must be continuously re-constructed in an ethically sustainable manner. Jaclyn Miller and Mary Katherine O'Connor also develop a dialogical model of social work which strives to pay attention for the client's voice. In a way, Eero Suoninen carries on this theme and makes it more concrete by showing how the 'negotiation' of meanings occurs in live interaction and how seemingly insignificant conversational acts may have a bearing on whether the client's voice is heard.

On the basis of the above it is not surprising that silence is something of concern for many of the contributors. If voices are important as the basis of change in social work, then silence on the structural level of practice is one of the greatest obstacles to change. That is why it is important to acquire sensitivity for *how silences are compensated for or remedied in social work encounters*. This is discussed, among others, by Hannele Forsberg. She has observed what happens in a worker-client encounter when the client does not express emotions which would be expected of her/him in the situation. It is possible that 'emotions are filled in', i.e., the social worker begins to work in such a manner that the expected emotions surface in the interaction as a result of the worker's acts and – above all – as the worker's speech.

Encounters in social work have consequences: they construct certain things as possible which may then become real in situations outside the encounter. This is related to the social worker's responsibility. It is typical of constructionist research to study responsibility primarily as something related to the 'inside' of the encounter – as has been done above –, but *some of our contributors study the worker's responsibility also as something reaching to situations outside the encounter*. One of them is Susan White, who stresses that social workers are responsible for acting so that issues which are problems for the clients are made visible. She reminds us that social workers may be accused of mistakes and failures. This could happen, for instance, when a social worker bypasses something in a client's life situation – such as physical assault – and thus silences it. The workers must assume responsibility for their mistakes, and this responsibility should also be studied as a topic of constructionist research. Michael Seltzer and Svein Alve in their turn feel concern over the worker's responsibility of placing themselves on the client's side against predominant social ideology which stigmatises clients and paralyses their resources for activity. Kirsi Juhila and Tarja Pösö place workers and researchers together to study social work and after that ask the question as to what happens to the researcher's voices by the time the social worker's speech has become so familiar that the researcher can no longer regard it as an object of study.

The topic of responsibility has wider links to the core of criticism towards constructive social work research. It is often criticised precisely because it is not sufficiently serious about the fact that social work deals with problems which are at the extreme of the social and human spectrum, such as assault and starvation. Are there situations, problems or concerns in social work which are above linguistic definitions, i.e., exist as material facts without an interpretation by a defining agent? All of our contributors answer more or less in the same manner: the social worker has no tools with which s/he could with certainty find out about the totality of the client's life and its misery as such, separate from meanings and use of language. However, social workers strive to lessen the social difficulties in life, and as a basis of their work they require someone to talk with, in order to make the definition of problems and construction of change possible. Social work always requires a minimum of two actors. This also links social work strongly with the dynamics of interaction and encounter, and consequently issues related to problems, change, responsibility and mistakes are permeated by the interpretative nature of the actors. Social constructionism shows that responsibility, mistakes and failure are bound to actors and situations, and it may sensitise us to the moral links and consequences in them. These issues are not unknown to researchers, as is seen in the articles in this book.

The topic of change is a suitable conclusion to this introductory chapter for, as Malcolm Payne fittingly says: 'Everything we do has an impact: that is what social construction offers us. We, ourselves and people whom we call clients, take part in social processes which make a difference'. To use a different turn of phrase, we could also say that change is not a transition from one state to another, but rather, it is active movement simultaneously going on in different arenas, the direction of which is continuously re-defined by actors in speech and writing during various encounters. Thus, encounter is movement – movement is change.

Acknowledgements

As described in the first paragraphs of this chapter, this book, too, was created as a result of many different encounters. We are also aware that after the symposium in 1997, many contacts, research teams and workshops have been organised among researchers in the field. Thus, the links between social work and social constructionism are being forged in many arenas – one of them being presented to you here. That this book was made possible is due to the contributors, the publisher and the financial contribution by NorFa, all of which receive our gratitude. The editing process was made possible through the Academy of Finland's project 'Institutions of helping and their activities as everyday practices', within which we have carried out our work.

Notes

1   However, using a temporally proceeding narrative is only one of several potential modes of presentation, since past things can never be described plainly, 'as they were'. In the constructionist frame of reference, remembering is understood as a pragmatic activity carried out in and from the present. In other words, remembering always has a certain function (Edwards and Potter, 1992; Middleton and Edwards, 1990).
2   In addition to ourselves, the organising committee consisted of Hannele Forsberg, Irene Roivainen and Ilmari Rostila from the Department of Social Policy and Social Work at the University of Tampere, and Harriet Strandell and Inger Siiriäinen from the Swedish School of Social Science at the University of Helsinki. The symposium secretary was Virpi Keso.
3   Emphasising the importance of the use of language does not, however, signify that non-linguistic practices (such as taking children into custody) are regarded as negligible for social work. Instead, an attempt is made to highlight the fact that practices such as taking into custody are intertwined in many

ways with linguistic processes: discussions between parents, children and social workers, and discussions between workers, as a result of which the problems of the family or the child have become defined as requiring child-protection measures. Moreover, social workers also need to justify their interventions verbally. (cf. Pösö 1993).

4 Our position on the idea of purely 'constructionist social work' linked to certain pre-determined criteria of 'good' social work is reserved. Such links would lead to constructionist social work being defined as, for instance, having multiple voices, open, and dialogical. Not infrequently one also sees the constructionist frame of reference linked with solution-oriented social work in a straightforward manner, with the result that the 'only correct' purpose of encounters between social workers and clients is to construct problem speech into solution and resource speech. Critics, on the other hand, claim that for constructionist social work 'anything goes', since the ways of defining problems and risks are always relative constructions. Without dealing in any more detail with this debate we simply state that in this introduction we consider constructionism as primarily a research approach rather than a theoretical framework or method for social work practice.

Bibliography

Baldock, J. and Prior, D. (1981), 'Social Workers Talking to Clients: A Study of Verbal Behaviour', *British Journal of Social Work*, vol. 11, pp. 19-38.
Burr, V. (1995), *An Introduction to Social Constructionism*, Routledge, London.
Clarke, J. (1995), 'After Social Work?', in N. Parton (ed) *Social Theory, Social Change and Social Work*, Routledge, London, pp. 36-60.
Edwards, D. and Potter, J. (1992), *Discursive Psychology*, Sage Publications, London.
Gergen, K. (1994), *Realities and Relationships: Soundings in Social Construction*, Havard University Press, Cambridge.
Holstein, J. and Miller, G. (1993), 'Social Constructionism and Social Problems Work'. In J. Holstein and G. Miller (eds), *Reconsidering Social Constructionism*, Aldine de Gruyter, New York, pp. 151-172.
Howe, D. (1994), 'Modernity, Postmodernity and Social Work', *British Journal of Social Work*, vol. 24, pp. 513-32.
Jokinen, A., Juhila K. and Pösö T. (1995), 'Tulkitseva sosiaalityö', in A. Jokinen, K. Juhila and T. Pösö (eds), *Sosiaalityö, asiakkuus ja sosiaaliset ongelmat. Konstruktionistinen näkökulma*, Sosiaaliturvan keskusliitto, Helsinki, pp. 9-31.
Kitsuse, J. and Spector, M. (1973), 'Towards a Sociology of Social Problems', *Social Problems*, vol. 20, pp. 404-419.
Middleton, D. and Edwards, D. (eds) (1990), *Collective Remembering*, Sage Publications, London.

Miller, G. and Holstein, J. (1991), 'Social Problems Work in Street-level Bureaucracies. Rhetoric and Organizational Process', in G. Miller (ed), *Studies in Organizational Sociology*, Jai Press Inc, Greenwich, pp. 177-199.

Parton, N. (1994), 'Problematics of Government, (Post)modernity and Social Work, *British Journal of Social Work*, vol. 24, pp. 9-32.

Parton, N. (1995),'Social Theory, Social Change and Social Work: an Introduction', in N. Parton (ed), *Social Theory, Social Change and Social Work*, Routledge, London, pp. 4-18.

Payne, M. (1991), *Modern Social Work Theory. A Critical Introduction*, MacMillan, Hong Kong.

Pösö, T. (1993), *Kolme koulukotia. Tutkimus tyttöjen ja poikien määrittelykäytännöistä koulukotihoidossa*, Acta Universitatis Tamperensis, ser A, vol. 388, Tampere.

Rojek, C., Peacock, G. and Collins, S. (1988), *Social Work and Received Ideas*, Routledge, London.

Shotter, J. (1993), *Conversational Realities*, Sage, London.

Spector, M. and Kitsuse, J. I. (l987), *Constructing Social Problems*, Aldine de Gruyter, New York.

2 Social Construction in Social Work and Social Action

MALCOLM PAYNE

Strands of Thinking in Social Construction

Social construction is a complex of ideas, and a number of strands of debate offer ideas relevant to social work. They may be divided into sociological and social psychological sources. These two areas, of course, overlap and influence each other, but their origins and connections are distinct. Both display a characteristic epistemology; that is, an account of how knowledge is created and used. Social construction's particular contribution is to assert the *priority* of social relationships in the formation of knowledge and explain how those relationships contribute to knowledge formation. A related set of ideas, constructivism, argues that objective knowledge can only be understood in relation to the means of knowing. This leads to a concern for perception, cognition, interpretation and neurological means of knowing rather than for the contribution of social relations to knowing.

The first part of this paper outlines the complex of social construction ideas. In the second part, I consider how these ideas have been used in social work and social action, before going on to examine the problems and potentialities of social construction ideas for social work theory and practice.

Sociological Social Construction

Sociology contains four well-known sources of social construction ideas. The first is the theoretical work about the sociology of knowledge of Berger and Luckmann (1967). They are concerned with explaining and demonstrating general social processes by which knowledge comes to be legitimated within society. After outlining their analysis, I examine three other sociological uses of social construction: the social construction of social problems, phenomenological and related sociologies and the social construction of human categories.

Berger and Luckmann's 'Social Construction of Reality'

Berger and Luckmann (1967) start by reviewing the history of the sociology of knowledge and then distinguish between intellectual knowledge and the everyday knowledge that guides our behaviour. This is a useful starting point for social workers who must use intellectual ideas to guide them in everyday interactions with other human beings. Knowledge is related to social context, because interpretation about the same reality varies in different social circumstances. We take for granted that our surroundings are an ordered reality, and that reality is an *intersubjective* world; that is, it is shared with others. As a result, our meanings correspond to or connect with meanings that others attach to the world. We treat our realities as routine until we are presented with a complexity. We have many face-to-face interactions with others. These provide us with constant detailed evidence of the other so that we create a conception of them. Some of the conception will be typifications; that is, we fit them into categories according to the type of person they are.

Our understandings about reality and our typifications are expressed in a number of systems of *signs*. These are contained in gestures, body movements and possessions that we see. Language, a system of vocal signs, is the most important sign system in human relations. It is our main reference system for everyday life. To use it to any effect, we have to use it according to agreed rules that we have learned and these have to be more or less the same rules that other people have learned. Language is used in themes which transcend the mere words used and symbolise, that is, stand in place of, complex ideas about the world. This allows us to express complex ideas and thoughts, in religion or philosophy. Knowledge is socially distributed, that is different people and groups of people have different knowledge for different purposes.

Knowledge becomes *institutionalised*. This happens because much human activity is habitual, and we develop recipes of knowledge, like 'how to use the telephone', to reduce the complexity of coping with everyday life. These habits of behaviour and thought are shared with others, who use the same short-cuts, and so the typifications of the world that arise from the habits are shared. Institutions imply a history of developing knowledge in a particular way and social control in the group being built up so that agreed forms of behaviour and knowledge can be developed. Institutionalised behaviours thus form a shared social world, outside the people themselves: it is *externalised*. *The social world is a human product.* People in a shared social world, acting as a collectivity, interact with their own creations, thus treating it and behaving as though the social world which they created is an external, objective reality. Thus, *society is an objective reality* to people who are behaving in relation to it; it is *objectivated*. However, as this objective reality interacts with us, it begins to form us in accordance with its reality. Thus, *people are social products* of the society which they created as an objective reality; the reality is *internalised*. The social reality can be *legitimated* by a series of explanations and justifications, referring to the historical and cultural circumstances in which the knowledge was institutionalised. Language is the fundamental basis for the legitimation of the objectivated social world. Much knowledge forms sediments and traditions, on which new realities are built. Particular forms of behaviour become conventional and these are acknowledged as roles. As these become associated with particular individuals they come to typify the roles that they undertake, and themselves become types.

If meanings are widely shared, the scope of any legitimated, objectivated social world may be very broad. Legitimation produces new meanings which make the total institutional order plausible to participants in any part of the social relations involved. Individuals must also find that successive events in their life make sense, that is, they are plausible. Legitimations are only required when passing on the institutionalised order to another generation or group, because the people who first create the institution have themselves constructed it and do not require legitimation. Legitimation explains and justifies the institutional order by transmitting values, then maxims and wisdom, then a set of theoretical systems and then a symbolic universe into which all these fit. The symbolic universe forms a more or less consistent total world into which knowledge fits. The symbolic universe orders history and biography and contains social mechanisms, such as rules, mythologies, heresies and taboos, which invoke forms of social control to ensure compliance with the constructed social order.

Reality becomes internalised through social structures for socialisation, which control and filter interactions with the outside world to confirm the accepted reality. General socialisation takes place through families and education in childhood. Later socialisations into specialist roles and statuses are subsequently built on this. Socialisation mainly involves 'significant others' who will have much more influence than the 'chorus', so social patterns are organised to make sure that significant others 'sing from the same hymn sheet', and this supports existing groups and discourages significant cross-group contacts. This leads in turn to stratification and social division in societies.

Berger and Luckmann's (1967) work is the formative account of sociological social construction ideas, drawing on broad sociological thought, including Marx, Durkheim and particularly G. H. Mead. Its basic approach is to see individuals in dialectical relationships with the legitimated social structure of reality in the society which surrounds them.

The Social Construction of Social Problems

An important use of social construction ideas occurs in American sociological work on what are called 'social problems'. Some writers (e.g. Kane, 1996, p. 178) regard this as unrelated to other forms of social construction theory because the essence of social construction theory to them is the process of building shared structures of understanding as part of cultural or micro-social interpretation. I think this is a mistaken distinction, since the essence of the social construction approach to social problems is a process of 'claims-making' within political life. Although this is not concerned with culture or social interpretation, but with more public social processes, it nonetheless deals with similar social processes but in another arena. Rubington and Weinberg (1995) identify social construction as one of seven perspectives on social problems. The social construction perspective argued that other perspectives failed to explain how particular conditions or widely varying kinds in societies came to be seen as a 'social problem'.

The work of Spector and Kitsuse (1977) is based on the process of 'claims-making'. They argue that social problems are a process by which claims about a condition in society are made. Social problems are '...*the activities of groups making assertions of grievances and claims with respect to some putative conditions*' (Kitsuse and Spector, 1973, p. 296, emphasis original). Interest groups have to organise to promote their claims. They do so on grounds of material interests (for example, that they are disadvantaged by some consequence of the conditions) or on moral grounds (that is, that the condition is having undesirable effects on society). The study of social problems, therefore, involves explaining the '*emergence and maintenance of claim-making and responding activities*' (Kitsuse and Spector, 1973, p. 296, emphasis original). Spector and Kitsuse (1977) propose a four-stage process: social problem definition and issue creation, official recognition of the problem, group dissatisfaction with established procedures and rejection of established procedures and attempts by groups to replace them with their own procedures. Different *interests*, particularly those who might gain in support from a problem being recognised, the availability of *resources* and *legitimacy* of groups trying to make claims are crucial elements.

Table 2.1 Debates about social construction views of social problems

Critique of social construction views	Social construction response
The social construction position only represents a view, which anyway is widely accepted, that definitions of social problems are subjective.	The social construction position shifts the area of debate and research to accounting for claims and the way in which they are made.
The social construction focus on claims-making ignores the importance of dealing with the harmful realities of social problems.	Objectivist study of social problems has not produced a theory of why they arise. Also, we only see problems as 'real' and 'harmful' if there has been a successful 'claim'.
'Ontological gerrymandering' (Woolgar and Pawluch (1985) There is a hidden assumption in social construction views. The existence and maintenance of objective social conditions (about which claims are studied) is taken for granted.	*Strict* social construction position focuses only on the claims and views about them: the objective conditions are irrelevant and unknowable. *Debunkers* use social construction to describe mistaken or exaggerated claims (and so therefore take for granted that they know what the true state of reality is). *Contextual* social construction focus on claim-making but accept that knowledge about the social context and objective information can help explain how claims arise.

Source: Best (1989).

This position has been attacked, and Best (1989) reviews the debate (see Table 2.1). A crucial contribution made by Best is to identify strict and contextual social construction positions. Strict social construction seeks to exclude reality and self-consciousness from the construction process and is concerned only with the linguistic and intersubjective development of constructions. Contextual interpretations of social construction include reality and human self-consciousness as contexts for construction. He also usefully points out that some writers use the term 'socially constructed' of some social issue when they want to express doubt about the reality and validity of claims which are made about it. This does not really reflect an acceptance of many of the ideas about social construction discussed here.

An influential application of the social construction theory of social problems is the idea of 'moral panics'. Cohen (1972) studied seaside conflicts between 'mods' and 'rockers' in Britain during the late 1960s. He found that the press 'over-reported' minor incidents in exaggerated language, thus raising public concern about a potential social threat. In turn, this has a strong effect on particular parts of society, especially law enforcement agencies. Politicians and legislators respond to the escalating concern and public action groups develop to press for further action, creating 'folk devils' for the society to oppose. This pattern is widely recognisable in various countries and has led to more development of the theory. Goode and Ben-Yehuda (1994) relate these processes to the social construction view of the development of social problems: a moral panic might be seen as a relatively extreme and speedy construction of a problem.

Social Construction, Phenomenological Sociology and Postmodernism

The third area of the sociological view of social construction is, perhaps, a series of connections, rather than an explicit usage of social construction directly. However, social construction relates to, and is informed by a whole set of ideas such as phenomenological sociology (Schutz, 1962), symbolic interaction (Blumer, 1969), ethnomethodology (Garfinkel, 1967a) and labelling theory (Becker, 1963; Lemert, 1972). Related to these, social construction is often represented as part of post-modernist views of the world.

A number of interpretations of social construction treat it as inherently a post-modernist form of explanation. For example, McBeath and Webb (1991) explore constructions of social work in Britain, pointing to a trend towards interpreting social work not as a unity but as having a diversity or dispersed character. Laird (1993a), discussing social work education, treats social construction as an aspect of the post-modern movement, primarily because its relativism relates to pluralism, eclecticism, uncertainty, ambiguity and paradox. It rejects one certain reality in favour of many interpretations of reality. Dickens and Fontana (1994) regard postmodernist analysis as concerned with the analysis of signs, symbols and language particularly to demonstrate how social institutions and power relations operate, and the criticism of the principles of objectivist or positivist knowledge as the basis for knowing. Some, particularly social psychological, views of social construction focus on language and power, and social construction is typically aligned with relativist rather than objectivist views of knowledge formation.

Perdue (1986, pp. 165-7) suggests that symbolic interaction theories propose that reality is socially constructed and that that social reality is a matter of the shared *definition* of social realities. The original development of these ideas, particularly by Mead, in Chicago in the 1920s and 1930s was concerned to reject determinism, and particularly the kinds of explanations offered by behavioural psychology. Craib (1997) argues that Mead's symbolic interactionism assumes internal dialogues in which the 'I' or self plays an important role. This kind of conception is probably inconsistent with psychological social construction. Social construction differs from many of these forms of sociology in that its concern is with collective products of thought and talk shared by many, rather than being concerned with the interaction of the social and the individual (Pilgrim and Rogers, 1993). Many such pluralist theories are traced (e.g. by Perdue, 1986, Franklin, 1995) to Kant's philosophy. He argued for the existence of two dimensions of reality: the outside world (the starry sky above) which can be studied scientifically and human reasoning about the outside world (the moral world within).

The Social Construction of 'Human Categories'

The fourth area of social construction in sociology derives primarily from feminist scholarship and, to some extent, work on social patterns of 'race' and ethnicity (Smaje, 1997). The character of this work is to demonstrate that identifiable biological attributes, such as sexual differences between men and women and differences in skin colour, culture and ethnicity between particular social groups, are not the cause of social relations between groups possessing these different characteristics. Instead, femininity or 'race' come from social ideas about human relationships which are attributed to the reality of identifiable biological or cultural difference.

Social construction has had an important role in analysis of sexuality, partly through the pioneering work of Foucault (1979). The main focus of this work denies the essentialism of claiming that sexuality (that is, behaviours and beliefs about bodies and their differences) derives solely from sex (that is, the anatomical sexual characteristics of bodies), and claims that sexuality is understood within historical and cultural milieux (Weeks, 1992; Vance, 1989). Social construction, specifically Berger and Luckmann's position, has also influenced feminist theory (Farganis, 1994), because it allows for placing events in historical and social contexts. Farganis suggests that postmodernist and feminist theory have in common that they both try to include wide ranges of people, rather than concentrating on elites and marginalising women and oppressed groups in society. Conventional economic, political and social explanations are not sufficiently inclusive, particularly for complex modern societies that include many different ethnic and social groups. Both forms of theory reject the universalising of explanations, and tie knowledge to its historical and cultural origins. Both reject objectivity in social explanation, relying on pluralist conceptions. Both give great importance to the role of language. However, feminist theory is grounded in the women's movement. It therefore has a project and a purpose and rejects the denial of social purpose that is associated with postmodern theories. While postmodern theories allow existing oppressive systems of knowledge to be rejected, they do not push forward the political objective of feminism.

This has been a particular issue in mental health. Watters (1996) argues, for example, that much of the literature on Asian mental health in Britain has sought to identify patterns which differentiate Asians (treated as a homogenous group) from others. Ahmad (1996) argues that in health care we focus on 'race' differences rather than socio-economic or service provision issues to explain why people from minority ethnic groups do not use health care services fully. Carter and Green (1996) summarise these arguments as 'race-thinking', when serious criticisms may be made about the use of the term 'race' in accounting for differences.

This fourth area of sociological debate connects most closely to social psychological ideas of social construction, since they are at least partly about how external social relations create internal characteristics, or the 'self' of particular individuals. One of the origins of such ideas lies in work such as Kelly's personal construct theory (Granvold, 1996).

Social Construction and Social Psychology

Social psychological ideas of social construction focus mainly on the formation of the personal psychological characteristics of individuals and groups, in particular 'the self' and personal identity. More conventional 'objectivist' psychology proposes that people and recognisable groups such as communities or families have a consistent self which can be perceived and, at least to some extent tested for. Such conventional views say that we, as individuals and the groups we can identify, have an essence. Thus this view is essentialist: things possess an essence of their own. The social construction view says that consciousness and self emerge from the meanings and practices in social relations (Wetherell and Maybin, 1996). These are formed in a cycle in which we experience and build upon social practices as children by acquiring competence in communicating as this is expected in our culture and through dialogue and narrative begin to express our conception of our self in relation to others. That conception is formed through our use of language and in power relations with others.

At the extreme, this position means that social construction ideas question the existence of internal personality structures that we conventionally suppose to exist. Instead, the self and the personality are the product of interactions and relationships between people. You only perceive your 'self' in the reactions of others to your behaviour towards them and those reactions are formed by their perceptions of their self which they only perceive in your reaction to them. Our selves and personalities, therefore, cannot be within us, but are outside our 'selves', deriving from everyday human relationships. Moreover, they constantly change and develop in every interaction that we take part in. Thus, to understand our psychology, we must study the discourses which take place between us and others. That is, we must look not only at how we act and how another acts, but also at how the actions intertwine with each other. Hence, discourse analysis becomes a crucial part of the study of social construction.

Social construction takes these ideas further. As we examine discourses among people, the only evidence we can have for them is our perceptions of the communications between people. Much of that communication takes place in language and other 'signs', such as those identified by Berger and Luckmann, and even action or behaviour must be described in language and is understood and interpreted by linguistic symbols. Therefore, we need to understand how language is used to interpret and explain behaviour, either privately and internally or publicly and externally. As the sociological concepts of social construction say that we regard as real shared explanations of social phenomena, so social construction ideas in social psychology examine our explanations of behaviour. It is assumed that we form 'narratives' to explain behaviour and social events in a way which fits our expectations and current understandings, and discourse analysis explores these narratives.

Social Construction and Epistemology

The epistemology of social construction is inherent in my account of these analyses of social construction. It applies these ideas at a higher level of abstraction as a metatheory, which argues that social construction implies that knowledge is created and maintained in particular ways. Knowledge becomes not a set of understandings about reality, but a set of constructions, shared for the moment among people within a particular social group.

The sociological view of social construction proposes that knowledge of social matters is formed by social processes which legitimate shared ideas about the world. The social psychological view proposes that identity and personality are external to ourselves, contained in a constantly shifting discourse or narrative interpretations of perceptions of the interactions. These ideas obviously place knowledge within social actions and interactions: it only exists through social processes and it is constantly maintained and supported or changed and adapted through those social processes. This must mean, in turn, that general, intellectual knowledge does not exist. We can only accept knowledge as useful in relation to the social situations from which it arises. All knowledge is specific to particular cultures and particular points in history. This leads Burr (1995) to identify the following four characteristics of social construction:

1. It has *a critical stance towards 'taken-for-granted' knowledge*, because we must always interrogate the social processes which have constructed the knowledge
2. Knowledge is *historically and culturally specific*, because all knowledge arises from and is interpreted within particular social processes.
3. Knowledge is *sustained by social processes*, because it is created by daily social interactions.
4. *Knowledge and social processes go together*, because a piece of knowledge presses us to act in particular ways, the ways in which we act imply and rely on particular forms of knowledge.

Craib (1997) has recently attacked this formulation. He argues that all sociology and most social theorists fundamentally take these positions. Being opposed to taking knowledge for granted cannot be allied to anti-positivism, since such a position can equally well be applied in positivist research. However, he argues, these four epistemological principles do distinguish the 'new' social psychology from conventional psychological epistemology. He regards the crucial distinctive features of social construction as compared with mainstream sociology as *anti-essentialism*, that is, against the view of '...the person having some definable and discoverable nature...' (Burr, 1995, p. 6), and *anti-realism*, which '...denies that knowledge is a direct perception of reality' (Craib, 1997, p. 4).

Craib (1997) suggests that social construction as an epistemology, a way of knowing, is only a partial form of knowledge. He asks what you would say about someone who comes into your office and says: 'I am a social construct.' Such a person seems psychotic: it is like saying 'I am a machine'. They claim to have nothing about themselves at all, and yet they are there saying something about themselves, so they are conscious of themselves. He makes the point that the idea of social construction implies that:

- something (A) is constructed

- something (B) does the construction

- something (C) is worked on by (B) to produce (A).

He argues that social psychological, or what the social problems theorists call 'strict', interpretations of social construction neglect this third element. Thus, social construction becomes part of an interpretation of the world which suggests that the Western world is developing destructively, is losing traditional social sanctions and controls, is descending into crisis. Human beings respond to this by creating their own interpretations and satisfactions, and create and recreate their 'selves' to respond to and gain satisfaction from this fragmenting world. He says, however, that this denies the feelings of failure, loss, self-destruction and powerlessness that we all feel, and thus denies the full complexity of our world. Individuals cannot be in full control and creating and recreating their world, because alternative realities constantly invade. Sociological and social psychological views of social construction, in Craib's view, claim to replace all other forms of explanation with this study of social processes. But because the 'strict' interpretation of social construction denies the importance of having a real aspect of the world to work on in forming its construction it forms only a sociological reinterpretation of other knowledges. Thus social workers dealing with the social problems of the city or the personal problems of their clients are dealing with a social reality which may be partially, but probably not wholly, reconstructed in a different form.

Constructivism

These epistemological ideas can be linked to constructivism. This term is used interchangeably with social construction in much of the social work literature (e.g. Thyer, 1994, in the same article) and some of the sociological literature with social construction, possibly in analogy with the form 'positivism', with which it is often contrasted (e.g. Gray, 1995). However, distinctions are properly made. Dean (1993, pp. 57-8) defines constructivism as '...the belief that we cannot know an objective reality apart from our views of it' and social construction as stressing '...the social aspects of knowing and the influence of cultural, historical, political, and economic conditions'. Franklin (1995) similarly associates constructivism with a cognitive, developmental psychological approach and social construction with linguistic, cultural and narrative processes. In making these distinctions, both note the importance to constructivism of each individual's biological and neurological evidence that our physical systems for observing things outside ourselves constrain and determine our knowledge of external worlds. Social construction, on the other hand, emphasises the fluidity of assumptions and categorisations of the world, and how they are affected by our interchanges with others in a social context which has a history and culture.

Social construction treats knowledge as outside the person, being formulated in a shared language and understanding between two people in a relationship. Constructivism treats knowledge as inside the person, being formed though perceptions, cognitions, interpretations and formulations of the world as it is presented to us in our interactions with it. In both cases, as in Berger and Luckmann's (1967) social construction of reality and phenomenological sociology generally, the concern is not only with formal scientific and intellectual knowledge. The epistemology can be and is applied to that, but here the focus is more on everyday knowing, that is the perceptions of reality that form our daily behaviour and relations with each other.

Summary

A range of interpretations of social construction from a number of different sources can be identified, and a related concept, constructivism, which is sometimes confused with it in the social work literature. All these are relevant to social work and social action to some extent, as also are the criticisms of the various approaches. I have sought to argue that social construction is not one concept but a complex of ideas. There are different emphases and different interpretations of social construction. The emphases that I have distinguished are those concerned with relativist epistemology, with the processes of issue formation in societies and with the understanding of interpersonal interactions. I have distinguished two interpretations. Strict social construction interprets all knowledge as formed and therefore only accepts the processes of knowledge formation as a legitimate object of study and analysis. Contextual or 'soft' social construction accepts the existence of the social context within which knowledge is formed and the reality of legitimated knowledge as continuing and consistent elements of the social world being studied.

I have characterised the typical analysis of social construction processes as reflexive or recursive. That is, it is a series of cycles of mutually influencing factors, leading to a progression in the formation of ideas. There is an implication here that I want to make explicit: that is that construction within one spiral may imply destruction elsewhere. So, if a social worker has a view (construction) of families that they are ideally formed of two heterosexual parents with children, she is likely to respond adversely to a lesbian couple who seek to adopt a child. This destroys the conventional conception of social work that it should start from 'where the client is', be accepting of difference and behave in an anti-discriminatory way, and begins to create an adjusted form of social work. We must distinguish this kind of destruction from *deconstruction* which is an analytical tool, derived originally from the study of literature, which analyses texts to identify underlying meanings which demonstrate power relations and social and linguistic discourses.

I have suggested, in summarising some of Craib's arguments, that the use of social construction in social work requires the inclusion of reality and self-consciousness. This is because social work activity does not merely seek to explain and account for but to interact and change the context of social constructions. It must take account of 'reality', even if it is socially constructed, which is the conventional world of the people that a social worker deals with. A strict interpretation of social construction cannot, therefore, be valid within social work thinking.

Social Construction Ideas in Social Work and Social Action

In this section, I argue, first, that the different emphases within social construction thinking form different arenas or focuses of analysis and that the two interpretations of social construction relate to the inclusion of those different levels in social construction analyses. Second, I argue that social construction concepts have been explicitly applied in debates of direct concern to social work and social action and have in fact been used within social work and social action, at these different levels and using both interpretations. Later, I want to move on to the possibilities and disadvantages of social construction as a model of and a theory for practice in social work.

Different Levels of Analysis

Social construction can be conceived of as a cyclical process (Glesnes, 1996); it is recursive or reflexive. That is, interactions from different parties to events influence each other, continuously promoting readjustments which in turn re-influence the parties. Sibeon (1981) in one of the earliest uses of social construction to analyse social work, argues that an important aspect of social construction analysis for social work is its capacity to deal with the interactions of a micro- and macro-analysis. Some formulations of social construction, particularly in social psychology, are primarily concerned to document, describe, analyse and account for these processes at the micro-level. These operate at a micro-focus of analysis, which is largely relativistic and because of its micro-focus is able to be a 'strict' form of construction. Applied to social work, these forms of social construction help us to understand within social work how social workers and clients interact and form their behaviour in relation to one another. Other formulations of social construction are not limited to this arena of analysis, and examine cycles of construction which form agreed social constructs of greater stability, which change more slowly. These forms of social construction are more about persistent social constructs of wider application such as gender, disability or mental illness. Applied to social work, they contribute to shared conceptions about the structure and organisation of society such as social agencies and occupational groups or professions such as social work. Finally, we have noted that some forms of social construction are primarily concerned with how knowledge and understanding is created throughout society. Therefore, social problems are identified and political and social interactions forming the context in which agencies and professions construct their activities and social workers and clients operate at the micro-focus. We can thus conceive of a series of social construction cycles operating with different focuses in different arenas.

Social construction of social work cycle

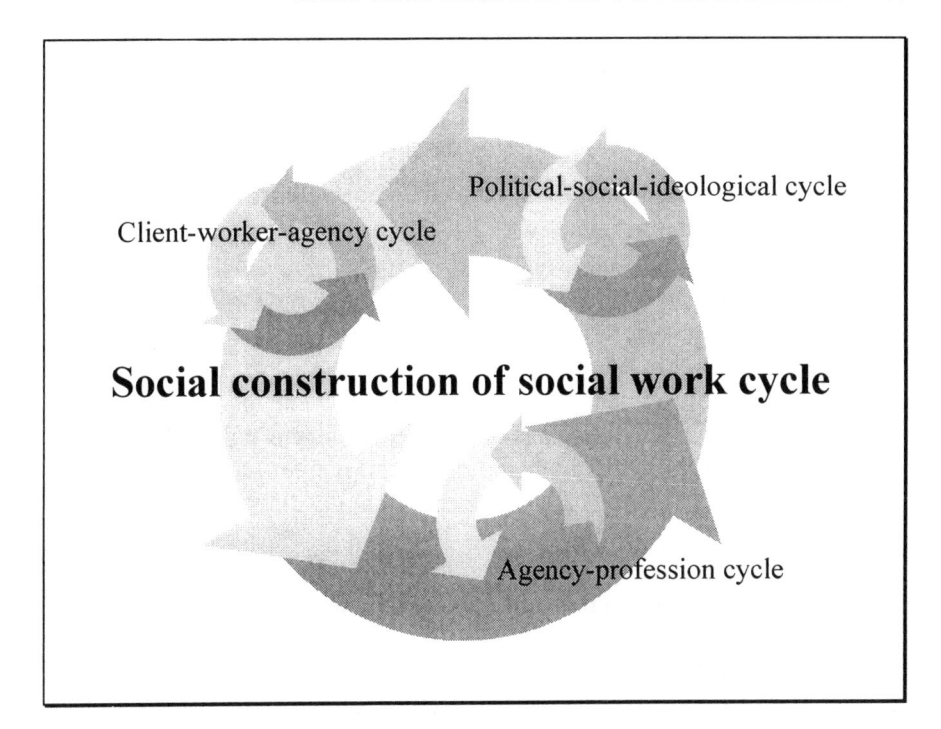

Client-worker-agency cycle
Political-social-ideological cycle
Agency-profession cycle

Figure 2.1 Cycles of Social Construction in Social Work

In Figure 2.1, all these cycles are brought into play together focusing on various aspects of the social work. The broader cycle of construction shows how the context and political construction of social concern influences how clients and workers construct their activities to form practice and practice theory and this in turn influences how agencies and professions construct themselves, which in turn reinfluences the context. The cycle can equally be conceived as working in the other direction and from any starting point, so that the context might construct agencies which construct practice. Social construction implies that the cycles would operate in both directions simultaneously, forming a continuous process of mutual influence.

Three points may be made about this conception of social construction in social work. First, a complete view of the construction of social work requires a broad focus on all the arenas of construction and how they interlock. Second, however, any particular cycle may be analysed with a more limited focus without reference to other arena for particular purposes. Third, again however, because the elements interlock, other elements in the main cycle form taken-for-granted contexts when we focus on one of the smaller cycles. This relates to the distinction between 'strict' and 'contextual' social construction. Strict construction focuses on construction in a cycle at one particular focus, usually a microfocus. Contextual construction, on the other hand, at least takes into account, and may include in the analysis, different levels of analysis which may interlock with the present focus.

Social construction analyses which apply one or the other focus to cycles of construction are both valid forms of social construction analysis, using the same epistemology of rejecting objectivist analysis and focusing on social contributions to knowledge formation. However, a crucial element of difference is the level and type of evidence used in analyses of social construction. These are fundamentally different in the policy-making and political focus, in the focus of broad shared formation of social ideas and structures and in the micro-focus of interpersonal practices.

Social Construction in Debates of Concern to Social Work

Social work literature and debates cover a wide range within each of these focuses. Here I examine the use of social construction in some examples (it is not intended to be comprehensive) at each of the three focuses. First, I consider social construction ideas in some important social concepts used within social work. Second, I explore some significant social work practice theories, and their relationship with social construction ideas. Some direct uses of social construction in practice prescriptions may also be identified. The third focus is concerned with social construction directly applied to social work organisation and professional construction.

Social Construction in Social Concepts Relevant to Social Work

Several concepts important to social work are widely seen as socially constructed. For example, Cohen (1985) argues that the idea of 'community' is a symbolic construction. We maintain a symbolic conception of people with whom we have something in common and those whom, as a result, we exclude from that commonality. This symbolism leads to an idealisation of the boundaries between us and the other, strengthening our self-identity. We believe that this commonality and exclusion of the other was easier in earlier societies, that we are equal with people whose interests we share and we attach importance to the commonality between us. This symbolisation is apparent in social policy, for example in the way we idealise the possibility of mutual support from families and neighbours. Commonality is more important in some, more naive, views of feminism or anti-racist work than the differences between women or minority ethnic groups in different positions. White (1995) has shown, for example, contrary to feminist assumptions, that women social workers are unable to use commonality of women's experience with their clients in feminist practice, because of the differences in their class position and official and professional power.

Family and childhood are particularly important arenas of social work action. Social construction analyses seek to understand how shared conceptions of a social situation expressed in linguistic usage, are created within social welfare practices. Leira (1989) for example, identified different models of motherhood in the everyday practices of social welfare agencies in different Nordic countries. Parton (1985) analysed how conceptions of childhood and child abuse varied over history and responded to social changes and power relations through a 'politics' of child abuse. McBeath and Webb (1991b) analysed official British guidance on child abuse to explore professional discourses about the nature of social work action.

Disability is another area where similar influence may be identified. Riddell (1996) identifies social construction as one of the important ways of theorising disability. A social construction perspective '...questioned the "reality" of impairment and suggested that, rather than residing in the individual, disability should be understood as a negative label applied by some people to others with the effect of enforcing social marginalisation' (Riddell, 1996, pp. 85-6). The social model of disability has promoted the view that disability is created by the organisation of society for able-bodied people, rather than by the impairment that the disabled person suffers from. However, these views have been criticised. For example, Soder (1989) argued that uncritical acceptance of symbolic interaction theories in social work and education training led to attitudes which might justify the destruction of specialised provision and the rejection of the idea that there is any difference between disabled people and others.

Social construction ideas are associated with mental health and illness, particularly arising from the work of labelling theory and Foucault's (1965) work. He argues that expert discourses of diagnosis and treatment found in the language of doctors and other mental health professions reflect social constructions of behaviour as mental illness, bound up with discourses concerned with moral regulation and the general ordering of society. Although writers such as Szacs (1971), argue that mental illness is a myth or social construction, they treat the behaviour which is said to be mental illness as behaviour which exists, but they regard it as non-problematic. Foucault has influenced sociology to treat all behaviour as subject to analysis. Pilgrim and Rogers (1993) regard social construction ideas as particularly influential in accounting for and stimulating research which shows that women and minority ethnic groups are oppressed within the mental health system. Since social work is closely associated with psychiatry in its history and, in many countries, social workers have an important role in psychiatric services, these uses of social construction ideas have been influential.

Social construction is also an important aspect of debate about ageing. It is a continual counterpoint to Bytheway's (1995) discussion of ageism. He analyses how old age has been conceived differently in different societies, how ageism has been constructed through different theories of old age and ageing. Power relations, language and social institutions influence perceptions and interpretations of ageing.

Two crucial aspects of these uses of social construction have played important parts in the analysis of social work as a participant in social relations which construct important aspects of society. Both Rojek et al. (1988) and Pugh (1996) focus on how language in social work represents and constructs power relations. Pugh, in particular, emphasises how it represents and creates identity. He argues that much social work practice stresses linguistic communication as a medium of action in social work. However, its role in creating and maintaining the relationships and objectives of social work activity is often ignored or underplayed.

A wide variety of this work in essence uses social construction ideas to promote pluralism. Here, we can see a connection with the 'debunking' use of social construction in the sociology of social problems. The pluralism implied by 'construction' statements in feminist and anti-oppressive literature also includes an element of a critique of the power relations which lie behind the construction. Thus, male power in constructing female experience, white power in constructing black experience and State power in constructing the experience of the oppressed is often implied by a 'construction' statement.

Social Work Practice Theories and Prescriptions

Table 2.2 contains, in the first column, an analysis of a range of social work practice theories. In each case, I have indicated in the second column aspects of that theory which are particularly relevant to social construction ideas, and in the third aspects which seem particularly rejecting of social construction.

The first group of theories, the traditional therapeutic theories of social work, use many aspects of understanding which are relevant to social construction. The most importance of these are the focus on language, symbolic interpretation and a degree of reflexiveness whereby emotions and behaviour are understood to respond to social influences and affect 'the social'. However, these theories have two underlying assumptions which bring them into conflict with social construction. First, their interpretation of social influences on behaviour is primarily one-way: the social influences the personal, but the personal does not influence the social. In psychodynamic and systems theory, the system and the person *is*, and must be understood and changed. In behavioural work, both the social and the personal are regarded as constructions which are incapable of being known, and behaviour is the only acceptable area of study and action. Curiously, this places the behavioural understanding of people's actions, which of course includes linguistic behaviour, as outside the person, in the same way that social construction sees understanding of the world as being outside the person. However, while this might suggest a relationship, behavioural work is the classic case of the other problem that these theories present. That is, second, these theories assume the reality and consistency of personality and the person as the crucial actors in the social world. People's consciousness and humanity present a reality which has an impact on an external reality. The purpose of these theories is to understand and change the real person and their interaction with a real environment, and the interpretations of language and behaviour through symbolism are representations of that reality, not evidence of social formations in themselves.

The second group of theories are much more related to, and in many senses can be said to include sociologies and psychologies of social construction. However, the work which has had an impact on social work has not been of this character. Traditional social psychology and communication theory, while they focus on human interrelations and language, do so from an objectivist epistemology. In these traditions, we are studying human relationships and communications as aspects of human behaviour and evidence of human nature. Humanist and existential work accepts social reflexivity but is wholly concerned with the person and its character.

Table 2.2 The receptiveness of social work practice theories to social construction explanations

Practice theory	Elements receptive to social construction	Elements rejecting social construction
Psychodynamic theory	Focus on language, interpretation of symbols, developmental psychology of incorporation of social experiences in mental structures.	Determinist, biological epistemology.
Crisis intervention	Focus on personal interpretation of events as 'crises'.	Focus on the reality of emotional reaction.
Task-centred	Focus on externally-generated, explicitly shared definitions of problems and social events.	Concrete, objectivist prescriptions and action. Not necessarily related to understanding and knowledge.
Cognitive-behavioural	Focus on cognition and not emotion or drives as the basis for action.	Determinist, objectivist epistemology.
Systems and ecological	Different levels of attention to micro, meso and macro systems.	Acceptance of realities of social structures.
Social psychological/ communication	Focus on social determinants of behaviour; importance of perceptions and communication.	Objectivist epistemology (but in dispute); focus on outward forms and consequences of behaviour.
Humanist and existential	Pluralist and personally constructed epistemology; includes symbolic and linguistic social constructions.	Personalist; does not require shared constructions of reality.

Social and community development	Focus on socially-constructed conceptions of localities or interests.	Objectivist epistemology of target problems.
Radical and Marxist	Focus on hidden meanings of social experience and structures for oppressed classes.	Materialist, realist epistemology of social structures.
Anti-discriminatory	Oppressions and inequalities seen as socially constructed. Oppressed groups' perspectives may construct prescriptions.	Materialist epistemology; usually structural.
Empowerment and advocacy	Focus on how people are socially disempowered.	Objectivist construction of prescriptions.

Source: Payne (1997).

The third group of theories, derived from reformist and Marxist social thought present the alternative position. They focus on how the individual is constructed by the societies in which they exist, and they are dialectical and dialogical in character: that is, people are constructed from their interactions with the society which surrounds them. However, much of this thinking assumes the immutability of the society: it is an actuality which enforces oppressions of all kinds on the people affected by it.

Direct Applications of Social Construction in Social Work

There are a number of direct applications of social construction ideas in writing about social work theory and practice. An early important usage is Smith's (1975, 1982) work on loss and bereavement. It is particularly useful because most work in bereavement is psychological and even psychodynamic in character. That is, it sees loss and bereavement as an internal psychological response to a life event. Smith proposes, instead, that it is at least partly conditioned by social expectations. Thus, people behave as they do because social definitions of loss require them to experience events in certain ways, and behave in ways which are considered to be socially appropriate. We can see that responses vary in different societies, and have varied at different times in history. Death and dying disrupt a shared social reality which needs to be reconstructed again. Understanding this, Smith argues, can allow social workers to respond much more appropriately to different bereavement situations in a range of cultures, rather than trying to impose a consistent psychological interpretation on disparate social responses. Smith's work provides an exemplar of how a careful application of social construction ideas can be used to re-form a fundamentally psychological analysis of a phenomenon into a social analysis in a way which can be intellectually stimulating and practically useful. This conversion of social work thinking from a psychological to a social focus is, I argue later, one of the significant advantages of using social construction in social work thinking.

Social construction is relevant to broader therapeutic models which are sometimes used in social work. Important bases for this in American therapeutic practice are strength-based models, such as that of Saleebey (1992) and solution-focused practice (e.g. White and Epston, 1990; de Shazer 1985, 1988). These are all approaches which are concerned with concentrating on and reframing specific elements in the client's situation. Laird (1995) argues that these therapeutic models may extend to broader community work practice concerned with empowering people to respond to wider social issues. Here, approaches to the analysis of power relations and changing perceptions and influences of stakeholders in particular social situations where we seek change might arise from social construction ideas.

The origins of the perspectives used are diverse, but most of this work is concerned with gender divisions within the family or ethnic diversity. It calls on the sociology of knowledge, the epistemological debate, but probably reflecting the American mainstream social work emphasis on therapeutic work, social psychological accounts of social construction applied to therapy and counselling, rather than specifically social work (e.g. Anderson and Goolishian, 1992; Howard, 1991; McNamee and Gergen, 1992). The main emphasis is on the construction of self, particularly in families of origin and minority ethnic communities (e.g. Greene et al., 1996; Real, 1990), on eliciting and analysing narratives (Laird, 1989) and on reconstructing clients' narratives to benefit their construction of self and their problem-solving capacities.

Some uses of social construction in practice theories are more constructivist in character. They call on personal construct theory (PCT) and family therapy but particularly on cognitive theories of behaviour and of personal and social development (Franklin, 1995, pp. 400-1). They are much more concerned with internal constructions of the outside world and distinguish between internal constructions and external reality. Granvold

(1996), for example, sees constructivism as a development of cognitive practice, which is classically concerned with presenting clients with the conflict between their perceptions and external reality. Fisher's (1991) book uses constructionist epistemology to formulate an idea of social work in which people interact upon each others' constructions of each other and the environments which surround the created shared constructions of the world within which they work. This is applied to social workers' interactions with clients. He argues that this makes it easier to explain and account for conflicting interests within the social work process. For example, where an elderly person is looked after by a carer, workers must respond to the interests of both client and carer, even though their interests and interactions are complex and ambivalent. It enables social work to focus on the social expectations and interests of the people involved, rather than seeing what they do in terms of their behaviours, attitude and emotions. Fisher usefully explores how power relations are involved in the construction of social roles within the occupational group and in relation to clients.

Understanding Social Work Organisation and as a Profession

The third focus, on the construction of social work organisations and social work as a profession, takes in two related areas of work. First, linguistic social psychological views of social construction have been used to try to account for the organisation of and social practices within social work. Second, there are accounts of social work and its formation which include social construction in their formulation.

The linguistic view of social construction is also represented in studies of social work organisations. There is a long history of sociological studies of social work organisations which are designed to illuminate hidden aspects of the bureaucracy. More recently, similar analysis has moved to explore the micro-level. Pithouse (1987), for example, studies interactions between social workers and their supervisors, in which the worker creates narratives of their cases, and the supervisor judges them on the commitment and level of activity revealed in the story. Stenson (1993, 1994) has explored how the language and discourse in social work interviews discloses the clash of collective discourses which exist between the parties in which the worker attempts to govern and regulate the client's behaviour through educative and other processes. Cedersund (1992), similarly, explores the content of social work interviews in welfare bureaucracies as a process in which a relatively routinised pre-structuring of interactions with the public in accordance with bureaucratic assumptions takes place. Sipilä (1989) shows how the apparatus of public social services narrow the scope of professionals understandings of clients' life-worlds by turning them into clients and turning their social experiences into legal and regulatory categories. He argues that social workers need a common cultural understanding and interpretation of clients' experiences. Eräsaari (1994) demonstrates how the management of space in various welfare offices reflect professional, gender and power relations, analysing video recordings of interactions, and offers narratives of how she investigated processes. Kivinen (1994) studies the stages by which children became clients of social welfare offices, through a process of notification, examination of their circumstances and acceptance into clienthood. Similarly, I have analysed clienthood as a process rather than a state (Payne, 1993) in which people follow pathways, becoming, moving through and ceasing to be a client. Jokinen and Juhila (1997) and Rostila (1995, 1997) treat social work as a process of negotiation between client and worker in constructing conceptions of the problems faced by clients. Bull and Shaw (1992) also argue that social work may usefully be examined by exploring the kind of causal explanations that workers use to justify or explain their activities.

Looking more broadly at policy in the welfare services, there have also been research developments. Samson and South (1996) argue that social policies are not just an account of public policies for social purposes or the processes by which they are formed. 'They are also symbolic gestures, channelled through the legislative process and amplified in political rhetoric' (Samson and South, 1996, p. 3). They are both symbolic of attitudes to social problems and also of particular ways of responding to those problems. In their analysis, we must understand and explore a range of social constructions of symbolic importance in society to see how those constructions affect the implementation of social policy in welfare services. Relevant constructions include the policy research process, policy thinking among opinion-formers and actors in policy-making processes, planning and bureaucratic processes and attitudes to crucial value concepts such as citizenship, health, rights, and inequalities.

However, social construction perspectives in social policy have also been aligned with post-modernist perspectives, and a substantial debate has recently grown up disputing the validity of these kinds of explanation in social policy. Taylor-Gooby (1994, 1995), for example, has argued strongly, for example, that post-modern theories such as social construction claim that universal themes of social policy such as rational planning, welfare services bureaucracies, equality and social justice are obsolete, being replaced by a plural interest in diversity and choice. He argues that post-modern theories represent an ideological smokescreen supporting market liberalism and tending towards inequality, poverty and regulation of oppressed groups. However, the trends towards fragmentation and dissolution of class structures arising from economic competition because of globalisation of markets is at best only a partial trend, and many other developments need to be considered.

De Maria (1992) argues that the dialectical and dialogue-based element of radical practice requires focusing on contradictions in students' and clients' experience. This means using values in a 'multi-prescriptive' way, rather than expecting them to represent just one viewpoint, and develop 'radical storytelling' as part of the process of exploring possibilities in people's lives and overcoming barriers to progress. In similar vein, I argue (Payne, 1996) in relation to social work values that they must be seen as incorporating their opposites and leading from and to a discourse about their area of concern, rather than presenting prescriptions for action.

Social construction has been influential in social work education as well as social work practice. An important review of social construction ideas in social work education appeared in Laird (1993). Its main focus is that social work education and practice must acknowledge multiple realities. Also, there must be increased collaboration between worker and client and students and lecturer implied by the denial of the status of objective knowledge, critical consciousness implied by sensitivity to narrative and language and an emphasis on the process of acquiring and interpreting knowledge. The teaching approach is based on personal journals, the critical analysis of narratives from different points of view, an emphasis on experience, the study of power relations and by reducing inequalities between lecturer and student.

Social construction has also become a protagonist in social work's epistemological debates, because it has become equated with the anti-positivist movement of the 1980s and 1990s. Social work has sought 'scientific' status for its knowledge base since the days of Mary Richmond (1917), who stressed the scientific base of social diagnosis. Germain (1970) presented the history of social work theory as a struggle to develop a more scientifically defensible system of thought. Its success in achieving this came under attack in the 1960s through an attack on the psychodynamic theory base of social work from behavioural psychology and through empirical studies of the effectiveness of social work practice at that time in achieving its intended outcomes. This led to the creation, through the 'empirical practice movement' (Reid 1994), of models of practice, such as task-centred work, which rely on a positivist evidential base. There has been a consistent current of practice writing, based on behavioural and more recently cognitive psychology, seeking to promote a throughly empirical or evidence-based practice. This has occasionally been resisted on the grounds that most social services agencies include social work in broader aspects of service and with wider social objectives than can be measured, or that human variability made the use of scientific method inappropriate. In the early 1980s, after an opening shot fired by Heineman (1981) in what Bloom (1995) has called the 'great philosophy of science war', a number of writers (e.g. Ruckdeschel and Faris, 1982; Imre, 1984; Atherton, 1993; Witkin, 1991a) set out to argue for more subjectivist methods. They have been described as social constructionists and have argued for the empirical methodology of social construction to be applied in social work (e.g. Witkin, 1991b). The argument is that a wide range of methods of enquiry are appropriate and acceptable (Pieper, 1989). Therefore, scientific method should lose the status it has gained as the only one offering a high standard of validity, although it is particularly useful for identifying causal relationships between factors in a situation. Positivist methods are criticised for being unable to question their own assumptions and value positions and for being concerned with number rather than meaning (Haworth, 1991; Wakefield, 1995).

Finally, I turn to my own work. I used the idea of social construction as an organising concept in my book which surveys social work theory, and this means that I am often cited as a social constructionist (e.g. by Franklin, 1995; Gray, 1995). I used the concept, in the first edition (Payne, 1991), in two different ways. It is first introduced as part of an argument that theory is not an unchanging given of social work practice, to be learned and applied. Instead, I argue that workers construct and reconstruct their theory as they practice, and that that construction takes place between them and their client in the context of the social agency in which they meet. Each of these three contributors to social work theory is formed by the pathways that they follow, to the point at which their interaction takes place. Thus the worker is formed by training, experience and occupational role. The client is formed by expectations of the service within their community, and the pathways opened up or closed off by the places which sent them to the agency. In its turn, the agency is created by social, political and managerial requirements within its history. This aspect of the argument is at the micro-level. At the meso-level of professional formation, my second use of social construction argues that a range of social factors forms the profession of social work, not merely internal professional debate and theory.

This account of the formation of the profession is dealt with more extensively in my *What is Professional Social Work?* (Payne, 1996) and a separate paper 'Why social work? Comparative perspectives on social issue and response formation' (Payne, 1998). In the former, the profession is depicted as part of a series of interlocking networks of theories, agencies, professional organisational structures, educational structures and practices, policies and law. These are in constant negotiation with other parts of the networks, and, because they interlock, the different networks support or detract from each other. In doing so, they strengthen or weaken the position of social work as an occupational group. The latter paper argues that social work becomes established as a social response to issues through a series of stages in which problems and responses to them become symbolised in public perceptions through social and political processes.

The basic argument remains similar in the second edition of the theory book (Payne, 1997), but is rather more extensively explained and is related to postmodern theory. My more recent work is concerned to examine sources of different forms of social work knowledge biases. My approach to this is through the analysis of everyday documents (such as job descriptions: Payne 1997a) used in social work, the processes and sources of knowledge formation (such as official guidance: Payne, 1997b) and, in the future, formal sources of social work knowledge.

Social Work, Social Action and Social Construction: Their Links and Conflicts

So, while I have argued that social construction ideas are present in social work to some extent, mainly recently, and are certainly relevant to and consistent with much of social work's existing thinking, the main groups of social work theories do not include it very strongly. Two questions arise from this account of the inhospitable climate of existing social work theories to social construction thinking. First, I have argued that social construction ideas have relationships with the social psychological and humanist group of theories. If this is so, why have they not had a wider impact on social work? Second, I have argued that feminist thinking and Foucaultian work have been important contributors to social construction ideas, as they have been to radical and anti-oppressive thinking. So why has radical and anti-oppressive practice not developed a strong element of social construction? I deal with each of these questions in turn, in order to develop an argument that the weakness of social construction in social work is its weakness in providing a theory of action for incorporation into practice. One reason for the weakness of influence from social construction in social work may be that social construction is a relatively recent and arcane form of theorising, still controversial in its own areas of origin, which has still to have an impact.

While this may be true, there is a much more important issue. All of these areas of social psychological theory, communication theory and humanist ideas have a weak presence in formal social work theory. They are widely acknowledged as relevant and interesting, even motivational, but they have not originated substantial and sustained theories of practice. They are the basis of the accusation that social work is 'woolly-minded' and unclear in its objectives. They are often the foundation of fads and 'trendy and fringe therapies' rather than theories which form the foundation of consistent practice in mainstream social agencies. The reason for this, in my view, is that they are substantially perspectives on the world, rather than theories of action. Rogers's espousal of empathy, warmth, genuineness and acceptance as bases for effective social and counselling relationships is acknowledged as an accurate representation of the requirements for successful practice. However, this tells the worker how to *be* and the associated theories are extremely relativistic: they promote the client's personal and social development according to their own wishes. They assume that insight and opportunity are what is required to achieve this and do not prescribe what the worker is to do to achieve any more exacting outcomes. More defined and socially relevant outcomes are, however, a basic requirement of social work carried out within and on behalf of the state in formal agencies. While communication theory offers evidence and detailed analysis of human behaviour and interaction upon which social workers may impose their own objectives, it does not say anything about what communication objectives might contribute to individual or group well-being – it is objective-neutral.

If we extend this argument to social construction and related ideas, we can see that it presents the same problems. While it is an interesting and relevant set of explanations, it fails to offer a theory and prescriptions for *action*. It seeks to account for and explain social relations rather than propose a form of action to achieve changes. Indeed the status of change in social construction is itself dubious. The basis of social construction is a constantly changing cycle of human and social interrelations. While this offers an interesting and useful explanation and reflects the complexity of how people experience the world, it implies that change will be a constant process, with multiple influences. Thus, a professional group such as social work cannot claim to have the *crucial* professional impact which leads to a significant social outcome: it can only be one among many. This may be a good representation of people's experience of the world, but it is not a good basis on which to seek social resources to maintain a superstructure of agencies and a profession. Moreover, any outcomes achieved cannot be *maintained*. They will always be subject to future continuing changes. Again, this may be a reasonable representation of the world, and it may be better to present social work as joining in a constant process of change for a period, pushing it in one particular direction. Social construction might provide a technology for such an approach. But it is inconsistent with our Western society which wants clearly defined results.

Turning to the failure of social construction's influence on radical approaches to social work, I noted above the significance of social construction as the basis for radical ideas in feminism, disability studies, mental health and many of the important areas of action in which social work operates. However, radical practice, although reformed by these sets of ideas, seems little influenced in its basic mode of explanation, which is fundamentally materialist. The objective of radical practice is to *change society*, not to recognise and work with the mutual interactions of society and person. Moreover, the objectives of feminist and anti-oppressive thought are to recognise the diversity and value of alternative modes of thought and human experience. However, the view is in many respects essentialist: that is, the essence that gender creates in us or the essence of cultural experience of minority ethnic groups must be valued and worked with. Social construction ideas in this arena have made us aware of the cultural and experiential relativity that we must all deal with. Nonetheless, forms of practice deriving from these ideas have a project: we must change society to recognise the diversity, we must respect the rights of minorities, we must seek justice and equality between different groups. These projects do not come from the social construction analysis, however its value in understanding it is acknowledged. They come from the underlying Marxist and critical theory origins of radical practice.

Social construction, then, presents a problem for radical and anti-oppressive social work because it is objective-neutral. It offers no fundamental purposes to be pursued. Although it provides some relevant modes of understanding, it does not apply that understanding to a purpose or purposes. This is a particular problem for social action approaches to social work, as opposed to more therapeutic views of social work, because these specifically seek to engage people's participation in identifying desired social changes and acting in a concerted way towards achieving them. Social construction offers a hope that such participation has the possibility of achieving social change because it presents the possibility that all participation in social constructions will have an impact. However, its epistemology in the strict form of social construction argues that such change is constant and insubstantial: a change cannot be achieved and maintained.

To summarise this section, therefore, I have argued the value of social construction ideas for social work. I have shown how it relates to social work values and social work objectives. However, I have also argued that it fails as a theory of action and purpose. Not only does it fail to offer possibilities for action and purpose, it inherently sets it face against action and purpose.

Is incorporating social construction in social work and social action hopeless, then? Is its theoretical character inappropriate to purposive action? In this conclusion I want to argue, first, that social construction has the capacity to be a new-style social work theory. Second, I argue that it will need to be developed in particular ways to achieve a useful contribution.

The Advantages of Social Construction in Social Work

The first advantage that social construction offers to social work as a theory is that it is principally a *social* theory, rather than a psychological one. It focuses outside personal identity at interpersonal and social behaviour and this is where social work also has its main focus. It is strange that social work has never developed a satisfactory social theory of this kind.

Moreover, the second advantage, unlike other social theories which are available, it offers a system of analysis which is potentially strong at the interpersonal level as well as at the level of more general social or professional explanation. One of the problems of social work theories which are predominantly social, such as systems theory or Marxist radical theory, is that their explanatory framework does not offer a clear interpretation of interpersonal behaviour: other theories have to be imported to achieve that.

The third advantage is the strong links which social construction ideas have with existing social work practices. There are two points about this. First, detailed analysis of language and interpretation of the symbolic meaning of behaviour is well-accepted and integral to many other understandings of social work, so that many of the methods used in social construction are not unfamiliar to social workers. They therefore might be more easily adopted within the current frameworks of social work practice. The second point is that the fact that these aspects of social analysis are already present in social work suggests their importance to the work that social workers have to do.

There is, however, a danger in the way in which many areas of analysis which are important to social construction are already present in social work.

That is, social workers might reinterpret social construction ideas into already well-understood paradigms. The confusion between constructivism and social construction and using constructivism as an adjunct to cognitive and behavioural therapies is an example. This reinterprets social construction as another form of interpersonal therapy, which focuses upon processes of communication and perception, rather than the social and interpersonal character of processes of constructing knowledge and understanding of the world.

A fourth advantage of social construction ideas as a contributor to social work practice is its focus on reflexive, dialogic forms of interaction. Existing social work theories are either therapeutic in character or concerned with broad social change. Therapeutic theories tend to assume an identifiable problem which a client has, and which social workers contribute to changing. This model of practice has been under attack because it fits badly with modern assumptions of participation, consumerism and human rights. Theories of social action, concerned with broader social change in communities or societies through community and social development have similarly developed models of action which propose a dialogue between participants and workers. Advocacy and empowerment imply responsive, reflexive and dialogic modes of interaction with clients and users of services, rather than workers representing the power of the State or dominant groups in society helping the disadvantaged. Social construction ideas have the capacity to offer a model of analysis for assessment and a basis for action in negotiation of understanding and action and in reconstructing narratives and interpretations of the social world. Social construction also presents forms of explanation which fit well with social work values of self-determination, and they refuse to 'blame the victim'. Similarly, the social construction view of social problems and the idea of moral panics avoids focusing on people or social groups who are problems, but instead looks at the processes that make them so.

Related to this, the fifth advantage of social construction ideas is their emphasis on openness to change. Many theories of social work, such as psychodynamic or radical perspectives, stress the resistance of people and social structures to change. People in these perspectives are determined by their world. In other perspectives, such as humanist or existentialist approaches to social work, the individual is assumed to be free to achieve desired personal growth, and the difficulties of the surrounding world are rather underestimated. Yet social work requires its practitioners to be able to achieve change, while recognising that the possibilities are restricted. Social construction ideas fit this requirement closely. They present people as both a product of and as capable of creating their environment. Moreover, they provide a mode of analysis for seeing how apparently established understandings of the world were created and for finding points of intervention and leverage to change those understandings. So social construction provides a good analysis both of capacity to change and also resistance to change, which social workers can use in practice.

So, modern social work in its increasing concern with reflexive, dialogic and participative practice is more ready for social construction ideas to have a strong impact than it has ever been. There is a sixth aspect of social construction ideas which also make them a crucial contributor to modern theoretical needs within social work. That is, their interaction with post-modern analyses, which reflect the ambiguity and fragmentation of the social relations and institutions which social workers must deal with and within which they operate. Social workers must increasingly deal with a complex and disputed world. Moral and social assumptions are no longer undisputed and established social institutions. They are constantly debated and re-formed to deal with new complexities in a much more fragmented society. Social workers must negotiate within uncertain and disputed worlds. Social construction ideas give them a means of analysis to do so.

To go further, we must also acknowledge that Western models of positivist knowledge-creation do not fit well with alternative models of knowledge that we find in Eastern societies. Western social work is particularly individualistic. It seeks to create individuals who are independent, who 'stand on their own two feet', as the British saying goes. Eastern social work seeks to create interdependency among people. In African tribes and in Chinese and Indian families the wish is not to create a privatised, individualistic social work service which provides therapy for clients with problems. Instead, work should develop within family and community structures, which must be harnessed and involved in dealing with problems. We can see this in Eastern and African critiques of Western social welfare and in the widespread adoption of social development in developing countries in preference to the Western model of welfare (see Payne, 1997, for a more detailed analysis of many of these trends). If we acknowledge that our formation of social work must respect these alternative conceptions of the way in which we should construct our activity, then we need theories which allow for the negotiation of assumptions and conceptions of the world and the purposes which we seek to undertake.

Social work also has something to offer to the development of social construction ideas. It is an ideal arena for the study and analysis of social interactions and constructions. It is an occupational group integral to the claims-making process within social problem formation. Because of its therapeutic activity and its participation in social action towards social change, it provides opportunities for access to a wide variety of processes of social change at every level of society. Because of its relatively uninstitutionalised professional status, it provides an ideal arena for the study of social processes of construction and negotiation of social institutions of occupational groups and professions.

The Future for Social Construction in Social Work

In this conclusion, I want to build on what has gone before. I have reviewed some aspects of the complex of social construction ideas in the social sciences and shown that they are applied in social work and social action at different levels and within different ('strict' and 'contextual') interpretations. I argued that the difference between the interpretations lies in the extent to which account is taken in analysis and research of arenas within which the analysis is not operating. 'Strict' social construction tries to take in each of the arenas; 'soft' or 'contextual' social construction excludes or takes for granted other arenas of analysis. I also argued that 'strict' social construction is clearly based in sociological and social psychological interpretations of construction and is extremely relativistic, whereas 'contextual' social construction views are more concerned with different individuals' interpretations of reality, and contain significant elements of constructivism.

I moved on to argue that social construction has practical uses for social workers and connects well with ideas which have been found useful to social work. Including elements of social construction in social work has immense potential for social work.

However, in looking at various criticisms of social construction, I identified some problems in achieving an influence for social construction in social work. One problem is the need for social work to be active in its stance towards the world. The social worker must act, not merely analyse. Craib's (1997) analysis suggests that an actor cannot take a completely holistic social construction view, it must always be partial and therefore will always take a contextual social construction position. Social workers must be able to move round the circle of different arenas of construction, acting perhaps only in one but bearing in mind the others and being able to shift focus to another arena where it is relevant.

I also identified the problem of purpose. That is, because it requires action, social work must have a project. It must aim to achieve something. That achievement may be at the more general level of social action, or it may be for individual change. Whichever it is, it will imply purposes in the other arena. If we seek personal changes, this implies a view of the social world. If we seek social action, this implies a view about how individuals are or should be. This presents a problem for social construction ideas because they are sometimes taken to imply that there can be no general social project: social construction must be continually renegotiated. However, I think this conception of social construction is a false one. What we must do, again, is identify the processes of social construction which provide the context for the actions which we undertake for the purposes that we seek. Social work objectives in a formal sense are constructed within the circle of construction around professional and agency activities, and in the circle of construction of social and political purposes, but I have shown how these interact with the personal and interpersonal arena. Where we focus in social construction now is in a context where social constructions are continuing in other arenas. We must take these into account and respond to them.

This conception of social work also has the benefit of including within every social work activity action within different arenas in a way that most other social work theories have found difficult to respond to. We have traditionally said, within social work, that action at the interpersonal, community and social levels interact and are mutually relevant – we have never had a theory adequate to show us before how this might work. This is one of the crucial contributions of social construction ideas to social work. Another crucial asset of social construction is its research approach, based in detailed ethnographic and other analysis of actual social interactions and everyday evidence of patterns of social construction. Other formulations of social work practice which have been successful have always had the capacity for rich insights into the detail of, in the past mainly psychological, human experiences. Social construction is the first sociological theory which offers the kind of detailed methodology and analysis which will support those rich insights into social interactions as well as psychological understanding.

It is also clear, however, that social construction ideas, as presently formulated, have weaknesses in offering a theory of practice for social work. They seek at present mainly to analyse practices, but not to offer prescriptions. If they are to be successful as a theory of practice, social construction ideas must allow social workers to use them in action for a purpose, not merely to analyse what has happened. At the very least, social construction must set forward ideas on three aspects of social work practice.

First, it must provide a model and method of assessment, so that social workers may analyse and categorise the complex social situations that they face. This is necessary to put them in a position to take action in the future. Social construction's methodology must be adapted and systematised to form an assessment model.

Second, it must provide concepts for practice action. There are beginnings of such concepts in narrative reconstructions, contrasts, solution and strength-focused work are beginning to develop. To achieve an impact for social construction, we need to develop a systematic formulation of many of these ideas into a model of practice.

Third, it must provide for the analysis and consideration of purpose within social work. This would allow the moral and social processes which form social work's social context and direction form a daily aspect of the practice of constructing and reconstructing our activities with clients, groups and communities around us and in social action for broader social change. One of the important aspects of social construction is that it offers an integral analysis of power and influence within social processes which connects daily practice to a broader analysis of social justice which informs the moral basis of much social work action. Social construction thus enables us to include a purposeful response to moral and justice issues in our daily work, but to recognise and respond to how our priorities and objectives are constantly in play in the social processes which go on around us. Through using social construction ideas, we can be constantly aware of the part we are playing, not only in helping the people we are working with, but how we are participating with them in a wider endeavour, to participate in social change. Our participation may be at the small scale, but social construction ideas offer us the tremendous motivation of knowing that every action and every participation in social processes creates social movements. Everything we do has an impact: that is what social construction offers us. We, ourselves and people whom we have called clients, take part in social processes which make a difference. What other form of social work theory offers us that?

Bibliography

Ahmad, W. (1996), 'Consanguinity and related demons: science and racism in the debate on consanguinity and birth outcome' in C. Samson and N. South (eds), *The Social Construction of Social Policy: Methodologies, Racism, Citizenship and the Environment*, Macmillan, London, pp. 68-87.

Allen, J. A. (1993), 'The constructivist paradigm: values and ethics', *Journal of Teaching in Social Work*, vol. 8, no. 2, pp. 31-54.

Anderson, H., and Goolishian, H. A. (1992), 'The client is the expert: the not-knowing approach to therapy' in S. McNamee, and K. J. Gergen (eds), *Therapy as Social Construction*, Sage, Newbury Park, CA, pp. 25-39.

Atherton, C. R. (1993), 'Empiricists versus social constructionists: time for a cease-fire', *Families in Society*, vol. 74, no. 10, pp. 617-24.

Becker, H. (1963), *Outsiders: Studies in the Sociology of Deviance*, Free Press, New York.

Berger, P. L. and Luckmann, T. (1967), *The Social Construction of Reality: A Treatise in the Sociology of Knowledge*, Penguin, Harmondsworth (original USA publication, 1966).

Berlin, S. B. (1996), 'Constructivism and the environment: a cognitive-integrative perspective for social work practice', *Families in Society*, vol. 77, no. 6, pp. 326-35,

Best, J. (1989), 'Debates about constructionism', in E. Rubington and M. S. Weinberg (eds) in *The Study of Social Problems: Seven Perspectives*, Oxford University Press, New York, pp. 341-52.

Bloom, M. (1995), 'The great philosophy of science war', *Social Work Research*, vol. 19, no. 1, pp. 19-23.

Blumer, H. (1969), *Symbolic Interaction: Perspective and Method*, University of California Press, Berkeley, CA.

Brower, A. M. (1996), 'Group development as constructed social reality revisited: the constructivism of small groups', *Families in Society* vol. 77, no. 6, pp. 336-44.

Bull, R. and Shaw, I. (1992), 'Constructing causal accounts in social work', *Sociology*, vol. 26, no. 4, pp. 635-49.

Bytheway, B. (1995), *Ageism*, Open University Press, Buckingham.

Carter, B. and Green, M. (1996), 'Naming difference: race-thinking, common sense and sociology', Samson, C. and South, N. (eds), *The Social Construction of Social Policy: Methodologies, Racism, Citizenship and the Environment*, Macmillan, London, pp. 57-67.

Cedersund, E. (1992), *Talk, Text and Institutional Order: a study of communication in social welfare bureaucracies*, Linköping, Department of Communication Studies, Linköping University, Linköping Studies in Arts and Science 78.

Cohen, A. P. (1985), *The Symbolic Construction of Community*, Routledge, London.

Craib, I. (1997), 'Social constructionism as a social psychosis', *Sociology*, vol. 31, no. 1, pp. 1-15.
de Maria, W. (1992), 'On the trail of a radical pedagogy for social work education', *British Journal of Social Work*, vol. 22, no. 3, pp. 231-52.
de Shazer, S. (1985), *Keys to Solution in Brief Therapy*, Norton, New York.
de Shazer, S. (1988), *Clues: Investigating Solutions in Brief Therapy*, Norton, New York.
Dean, R. G. (1993), 'Teaching a constructivist approach to clinical practice', *Journal of Teaching in Social Work*, vol. 8, no. 1/2, pp. 55-75.
Dickens, D. R. and Fontana, A. (1994), 'Postmodernism in the social sciences', Dickens, D. R. and Fontana, A. (eds), *Postmodernism and Social Inquiry*, UCL Press, London, pp. 1-22.
Efran, J. S. and Clarfield, L. E. (1992), 'Constructionist therapy: sense and nonsense', in S. McNamee, and K. J. Gergen (eds), *Therapy as Social Construction*, Sage, London.
Eräsaari, L. (1994), 'The reproduction of silence in street-level bureaucracies: three narratives', in S. Hänninen, (ed), *Silence, Discourse and Deprivation*, STAKES: National research and Development Centre for Welfare and Health, Helsinki, pp. 81-107.
Farganis, S. (1994), 'Postmodernism and feminism', in D. R. Dickens and A. Fontana (eds), *Postmodernism and Social Inquiry*, UCL Press, London, pp. 101-26.
Fisher, D. D. V. (1991), *An Introduction to Constructivism for Social Workers*, Praeger, New York.
Foucault, M. (1965), *Madness and Civilisation*, Random House, New York.
Foucault, M. (1979), *The History of Sexuality: Volume 1, An Introduction*, Allen Lane, London.
Franklin, C. (1995), 'Expanding the vision of the social constructionist debates: creating relevance for practitioners', *Families in Society*, vol. 76, no.7, pp. 395-406.
Garfinkel, H. (1967a), *Studies in Ethnomethodology*, Englewood Cliffs, Prentice-Hall, NJ.
Garfinkel, H. (1967b), 'Studies in the routine grounds of everyday activities', *Studies in Ethnomethodology*, Englewood Cliffs, Prentice-Hall, NJ.
Glesnes, I. (1996), I owe this emphasis on the circularity of social construction processes to Inger Glesnes, a colleague from Bergen.
Goode, E. and Ben-Yehuda, N. (1994), *Moral Panics: The Social Construction of Deviance*, Blackwell Cambridge, MA.
Granvold, D. K. (1996), 'Constructivist psychotherapy', *Families in Society*, vol. 77, no. 6, pp. 345-57.
Gray, M. (1995), 'The ethical implications of current theoretical developments in social work', *British Journal of Social Work*, vol. 25, no. 1, pp. 55-70.

Greene, G. J., Jensen, C., Jones, D. H. (1996), 'A constructivist perspective on clinical social work practice with ethnically diverse clients', *Social Work*, vol. 14, no. 2, pp. 172-80.
Haworth, G. O. (1991), 'My paradigm can beat your paradigm: some reflections on knowledge conflicts', *Journal of Sociology and Social Welfare*, vol. 18, no. 4, pp. 35-50.
Hay, C. (1996), 'Narrating crisis: the discursive construction of the "winter of discontent"', *Sociology*, vol. 30, no. 2, pp. 253-77.
Heinemann, M. B. (1981), 'The obsolete scientific imperative in social work research', *Social Service Review*, vol. 55, no. 3, pp. 371-97.
Howard, G. S. (1991), 'Culture tales: a narrative approach to thinking cross-cultural psychology, and psychotherapy', *American Psychologist*, vol. 46, pp. 187-197.
Imre, R. W. (1984), 'The nature of knowledge in social work', *Social Work*, vol. 29, no. 1, pp. 41-5.
Jokinen, A. and Juhila, K. (1997), 'Social work as negotiation: constructing social problems and clienthood', *Nordisk Socialt Arbeid* 1997, vol. 17, no. 3, pp. 144-52.
Kane, A. E. (1996), 'The centrality of culture in social theory: fundamental clues from Weber and Durkheim' in S. P. Turner (ed), *Social Theory and Sociology: The Classics and Beyond*, Blackwells, Cambridge, MA, pp. 161-80.
Kitsuse, J. I. and Spector, M. (1973), 'The definition of social problems', *Social Problems*, vol. 20, no. 4, pp. 407-419, reprinted in Rubington and Weinberg (1995), pp. 294-301.
Kivinen, T. (1994), 'Becoming a client in child welfare – production and reproduction of what?' in S. Hänninen (ed), *Silence, Discourse and Deprivation*, STAKES: National research and Development Centre for Welfare and Health, Helsinki, pp. 114-27.
Laird, J. (1989), 'Women and stories: restorying women's self-constructions', in M. McGoldrick, C. M. Anderson, and F. Walsh (eds), *Women in Families: A Framework for Family Therapy*, Norton, New York, pp. 427-50.
Laird, J. (ed) (1993), *Revisioning Social Work Education: A Social Constructionist Approach*, Haworth, New York, *Journal of Teaching in Social Work*, vol. 8, no. 1-2.
Laird, J. (1995), 'Family-centered practice in the postmodern era', *Families in Society*, vol. 76, no. 3, pp. 150-62.
Leira, A. (1989), *Models of Motherhood: Welfare State Policies and Everyday Practices: the Scandinavian Experience*, Nordiska Institut för samhällsplanering, Oslo, Report no. 89.7.
Lemert, E. (1972), *Human Deviance, Social Problems and Social Control* (2nd ed.), Englewood Cliffs, Prentice-Hall, NJ.
McBeath, G. B. and Webb, S. A. (1991), 'Social work, modernity and post modernity', *Sociological Review*, vol. 39, no. 4, pp. 745-62.

McBeath, G. B. and Webb, S. A. (1991b), 'Child protection language as professional ideology in social work', *Social Work and Social Science Review*, vol. 2, no. 2, pp. 122-45.

McNamee, S. and Gergen, K. (eds) (1992), *Therapy as Social Construction*, Sage, London.

Neimeyer, R. A. and Stewart, A. E. (1996), 'Trauma, healing, and the narrative emplotment of loss', *Families in Society*, vol. 77, no. 6, pp. 360-75.

Parton, N. (1985), *The Politics of Child Abuse*, Macmillan, London.

Payne, M. (1991), *Modern Social Work Theory: A Critical Introduction*, Macmillan, London.

Payne, M. (1993), 'Routes to and through clienthood and their implications for practice', *Practice*, vol. 6, no. 3, pp. 169-80.

Payne, M. (1996), *What is Professional Social Work?*, Venture, Birmingham.

Payne, M. (1997), *Modern Social Work Theory* (2nd ed.), Macmillan, London.

Payne, M. (1997a), 'A suitable job' *Professional Social Work*, August 1997, p. 13.

Payne, M. (1997b), 'Government guidance in the construction of the social work profession', Adams, R. (ed), *Crisis in the Human Services*, University of Lincolnshire and Humberside, Hull.

Payne, M. (1998), 'Why social work? Comparative perspectives on social issue and response formation', *International Social Work*, vol. 41, no. 4, pp. 443-453.

Perdue, W. D. (1986), *Sociological Theory: Explanation, Paradigm and Ideology*, Palo Alto, CA, Mayfield.

Pieper, M. H. (1989), 'The heuristic paradigm: a unifying and comprehensive approach to social work research', *Smith College Studies in Social Work*, vol. 60, pp. 8-34.

Pilgrim, D. and Rogers, A. (1993), *A Sociology of Mental Health and Illness*, Open University Press, Buckingham.

Pithouse, A. (1987), *Social Work: the Social Organisation of an Invisible Trade* (2nd ed.), Ashgate, Aldershot.

Pugh, R. (1996), *Effective Language in Health and Social Work*, Chapman and Hall, London.

Real, T. (1990), 'The therapeutic use of self in constructivist/systemic therapy', *Family Process*, vol. 29, pp. 255-72.

Riddell, S. (1996), 'Theorising special educational needs in a changing political climate' in L. Barton, (ed), *Disability and Society: Emerging Issues and Insights*, Longman, London, pp. 83-106.

Rojek, C., Peacock, G. and Collins, S. (1988), *Social Work and Received Ideas*, Routledge, London.

Rostila, I. (1995), 'The relationship between social worker and client in closing conversations', *Text*, vol. 15, no. 1, pp. 69-102.

Rostila, I. (1997), 'How to start to talk about money: developing clienthood in interaction in a social welfare office', *Scandinavian Journal of Social Welfare* 6, pp. 105-18.

Rubington, E. and Weinberg, M. S. (1995), 'A sociological review of the perspectives', in Rubington, E. and Weinberg, M. S. (eds), *The Study of Social Problems: Seven Perspectives*, Oxford University Press, New York, pp. 356-63.

Ruckdeschel, R. A. and Farris, B. E. (1982), 'Science: critical faith or dogmatic ritual?', *Social Casework*, vol. 63, no. 5, pp. 272-5.

Saleebey, D. (1993), 'Notes on interpreting the human condition: a "constructed" HBSE curriculum', *Journal of Teaching in Social Work*, vol. 8, no. 1/2, pp. 197-217.

Saleebey, D. (1992), *The Strengths Perspective in Social Work Practice*, Longman, New York.

Samson, C. and South, N. (1996), 'Introduction: Social policy isn't what it used to be - The social construction of social policy in the 1980s and 1990s', in C. Samson and N. South (eds), *The Social Construction of Social Policy: Methodologies, Racism, Citizenship and the Environment*, Macmillan, London, pp. 1-13.

Schutz, A. (1962), *Collected Papers I: The Problem of Social Reality*, Martinus Nijhoff, The Hague.

Sibeon, R. (1981), 'The nature of social work - a social constructionist approach', *Issues in Social Work Education*, vol. 1, no. 1, pp. 45-64.

Sipilä, J. (1989), 'Cultural understanding and social welfare', in The National Board of Social Welfare in Finland *Clients or Co-producers? The Changing Role of Citizens in the Social Sector*, National Board of Social Welfare in Finland, Helsinki, pp. 19-37.

Smaje, C. (1997), 'Not just a social construct: theorising race and ethnicity', *Sociology*, vol. 31, no. 2, pp. 307-27.

Smith, C. R. (1975), 'Bereavement: the contribution of phenomenological and existential analysis to a greater understanding of the problem', *British Journal of Social Work*, vol. 5, no. 1, pp. 75-94.

Smith, C. R. (1982), *Social Work with the Dying and Bereaved*, Macmillan, London.

Soder, M. (1989), 'Disability as a social construct: the labelling approach revisited', *European Journal of Special Needs Education*, vol. 4, no. 2, pp. 117-29.

Spector, M. and Kitsuse, J. I. (1977), *Constructing Social Problems*, Cummings, Menlo Park, CA.

Stenson, K. (1993), 'Social work discourse and the social work interview', *Economy and Society*, vol. 22, no. 1, pp. 42-76.

Stenson, K. (1994), 'The social work interview as government, the dialectic between orality and literacy', Hänninen, S. (ed), *Silence, Discourse and Deprivation*, STAKES: National research and Development Centre for Welfare and Health, Helsinki, pp. 28-49.

Szacs, T. (1971), *The Manufacture of Madness*, Routledge and Kegan Paul, London.

Taylor-Gooby, P. (1994), 'Post-modernism and social policy: a great leap backwards?' *Journal of Social Policy*, vol. 23, no. 3, pp. 385-404.

Taylor-Gooby, P. (1995), 'In defence of second-best theory: state, class and capital in social policy', *Journal of Social Policy*, vol. 26, no. 2, pp. 171-92.

Thyer, B. A. (1994), 'Empiricists versus social constructionists: more fuel on the flames', *Families in Society*, vol. 75, no. 5, pp. 308-12.

Vance, C. S. (1989), 'Social construction theory: problems in the history of sexuality', van Kooten Niekirk, A. and van ter Meer, T. (eds), *Homosexuality, Which Homosexuality?*, GMP, London, pp. 18-24.

Wakefield, J. C. (1995), 'When an irresistible epistemology meets an immovable ontology', *Social Work Research*, vol. 19, no. 1, pp. 9-17.

Watters, C. (1996), 'Representations of Asians' mental health in British psychiatry', in C. Samson and N. South (eds), *The Social Construction of Social Policy: Methodologies, Racism, Citizenship and the Environment*, London, Macmillan, pp. 88-105.

Weeks, J. (1992), 'The body and sexuality', in B. Bocock and K. Thompson (eds), *Social and Cultural Forms of Modernity*, Polity, Cambridge.

Weick, A. (1993), 'Reconstructing social work education', *Journal of Teaching in Social Work*, vol. 8, no. 1/2, pp. 11-30.

Wetherell, M. and Maybin, J. (1996), 'The distributed self: a social constructionist perspective', in R. Stevens (ed), *Understanding the Self*, Sage, London, pp. 219-79.

White, M. and Epston, D. (1990), *Narrative Means to Therapeutic Ends*, Norton, New York.

White, V. (1995), 'Commonality and diversity in feminist social work', *British Journal of Social Work*, vol. 25, no. 2, pp. 143-56.

Witkin, S. (1991b), 'The implications of social constructionism for social work education', *Journal of Teaching in Social Work*, vol. 4, no. 1, pp. 37-48.

Witkin, S. L. (1991a), 'Empirical clinical practice: a critical analysis', *Social Work*, vol. 36, no. 2, pp. 158-63.

PART II:
PRACTICES OF ENCOUNTER

3 Using Narratives in Social Work Interaction

ELISABET CEDERSUND

I hope you enjoy this narrative, even though it is not a story. For sometimes reality is more unbelievable than any story. And perhaps reality is the greatest story of all (Erlingsson, 1996, p. 7).

This chapter deals with narratives that, at times, are more unbelievable than any story. For these narratives are taken from reality – which the Icelandic writer Fridrik Erlingsson describes as the greatest story of all. The people involved in these narratives are all participants in various types of encounters with social workers: clients speaking with social workers, social workers in encounters with their colleagues, or social work teachers instructing their students by using the narrative form. First, however, comes my own narrative about how I came to realize the great importance of narratives and narrative structures in the dialogue of social work.

Narrative as Form in the 'Public Encounter'

From 1987 to 1989 I gathered data for a research project that was to examine people's contacts with the authorities (Säljö and Cedersund, 1987). One of the situations I studied was contact between individual people seeking financial assistance and the officials who deal with this type of application. Around twenty-five applicants were followed from their first contact with social services until a decision on financial assistance was made. Conversations between social workers and clients were audiotaped and included as material in the study, along with written documents and interviews. It was not difficult to devise theories and methods to describe the process that deals with cases in a bureaucratic organization of this kind, and how people's problems are converted into cases by officials (Cedersund and Säljö, 1994). Political science theories on street-level bureaucracies (Lipsky, 1980) were used in combination with various types of discourse analytical methods for conversations and texts (e.g., Agar, 1985; Erickson and Shultz, 1982). However, the project had a more ambitious purpose than simply describing contacts between citizens and authorities: the individual's perspective on and interest in the 'public encounter' (Goodsell, 1981) was also examined. What methods were available for describing and understanding the individual applicant's part in the meeting? I looked for models and theoretical angles of approach to this aspect of the project. As usual in research on talk and texts, this question was directed toward the empirical material found in the project.

An intensive and thorough analysis of the conversations between clients and social workers began. In considering the material we posed such questions as: What were the individual clients' contributions to the conversations with the social workers, and what typified the clients' utterances? There were various possible approaches to answering these questions. Client utterances in the conversations could be described as 'stories' (Gülich and Quasthoff, 1986), 'narratives' (see, for example, Labov, 1972), or 'accounts' (Scott and Lyman, 1968), or they could be seen in the light of 'conversations on problems' (cf. Jefferson, 1988). Thus methods and theories were eventually found that could later be tested in the analytical work. The problem in this phase, therefore, was not a lack of suggestions but rather the number of ideas for possible analyses.

What, then, was the result of the analyses of individuals' meetings with authorities? In most conversations the *narrative* form was best suited as an analytical tool. When people contact authorities – in the case studied here, the social workers who handle applications for financial assistance – short or long narratives were often used. This may be illustrated by the following quote from one of the conversations:

Example 1

> *Social Worker*:[1] All right, let's take a look at this first. I got a call from Louise, something, at EO-housing ((name of landlord)) (C: Yeah) uhm, about the rent you owe, (C: Uh-huh) I found a certain document too (C: Yeah) and I see you have had trouble paying the rent in the past. (C: Yeah) Hmm. How is it that you get behind in your rent?
>
> *Client*:[2] Well, it's stuff that happened before, I was working at the Service Company ((name of company)) and made a lot of money back then (S: Mm-hmm) then when I had to quit working there I (S: Mm-hmm) owed some taxes (S: Mm-hmm) that happened because my tax statement was rejected and I owed over, uh, almost fifty thousand kronor in back taxes (S: Mm-hmm) and that has really dragged on, I reached a settlement with the enforcement officer where for several years they (S: Uh-huh) but it was a terrible hardship and it really knocked us for a loop at the time, (S: Mm-

hmm) I took out loans and everything like that and it is because of the loans, uh, that there is not enough money.

Social Worker: Well, but the important thing is to pay the rent you know. (C: Yeah) If you don't pay the rent then you don't have any place to live. (C: Right) Right. I read somewhere too that your wife is handicapped.

In the example above the social worker asks a rather penetrating question: 'How is it that you get behind in your rent?' The client, an elderly man, answers with a narrative in which he presents:

1) An *orientation* on his situation in the past:
   'Well, it's stuff that happened before, I was working at the Service Company and made a lot of money back then.'
2) A *summary of the 'complicating actions'* when his financial problems arose:
   'Then when I had to quit working there I owed some taxes (...) that happened because my tax statement was rejected and I owed over, uh almost fifty thousand kronor in back taxes'
3) A *solution*, and an *evaluation*:
   'I reached a settlement with the enforcement officer where for several years they (...) but it was a terrible hardship and it really knocked us for a loop at the time (...) I took out loans and everything like that'
4) The *result* of the reconstructed actions, and events:
   'and it is because of the loans, uh, that there is not enough money'.

The narrative form presents a strong way of relating events that individual clients could use to make themselves believed, even though certain details of their particular situation may not have been to their advantage when it came to the possibility of receiving financial assistance. This discursive form offered the client in the cited conversation a way to describe his problematic situation with the unpaid taxes and his unsuccessful attempt to find a good solution to his financial problems. Events in this client's past were put into a context, and a summary of what had happened could be conveyed to the social worker listening to the narrative. The picture of the social welfare interview that emerges in the introductory example clearly illustrates how the client contributes to the construction of his own 'case' during the interview (cf. Jönsson, Linell and Säljö, 1991). The narrative delivered by the client in example 1, however, was not a lengthy story. It was regarded as a first and preliminary version of a description of this 'case'. It included a careful selection of the 'appropriate' details in the client's past life, and its details seem to have been selected and put together in order to give the listener a sense of how 'things went wrong'. Events in the client's past related to the financial problems were assembled in the client's utterance. The client's utterance could thus be interpreted as an attempt to appear as a worthy human being, despite his own shortcomings.

In addition, the narrative forms found in conversations between clients and social workers were often constructed in such a way that the social worker (i.e., the party who listens to the narratives about problems and woes) was expected to present solutions to the problems with which the client had not managed to cope, despite his or her previous efforts. The client's narrative paints a picture in which he or she was the victim of unfortunate circumstances, rather than one where what had gone wrong was his or her own fault, or because resources had not been wisely used.

My analyses of the conversations included in the study showed that the clients' narratives played a key role in the interaction between the parties. The clients' talk about their financial difficulties and about the events that preceded their need for financial assistance were analysed in detail, and this analysis served as a basis for a typology of the clients' talk about themselves and their past and present financial situation. The discursive dimensions in the typology were mainly related to the following concepts: monologues vs. dialogues; extensive vs. minimal contributions; narratives vs. non-narratives. The typology contained the following basic discursive formats: 1) monological narratives, 2) dialogical talk, and 3) minimal contributions from the client; all of which had been identified as a result of the analysis of the conversations included in the study.

Monological Narratives

The most common discursive form used by the clients in the study consisted, as mentioned earlier, of 'monological narratives', and 17 of the 25 instances analysed were considered as belonging to this type. This form of narrative, which was called '*the client's narrative*', was similar to the spontaneous story tellings investigated in a number of studies in various settings (Labov, 1972; Gülich and Quasthoff, 1986). This was thus the most frequent form, and it consisted of monological utterances from the client, generally initiated by questions or statements from the social worker.

In order to illustrate the first type of account, I will, in the presentation below, give one more example from the data, which shows how the narratives were told in the context of the welfare encounters. Whereas in example 1 the client, in his telling, reports that he had reached a settlement with a representative at a public institution – the enforcement officer – we will, in the following example, see that the connection to the institutional structure and public life is even more prominent when this client is talking about some of her difficulties.

The client in the excerpt below was a young woman who visited the social welfare office in order to apply for financial assistance for the first time. She brought her unpaid rent bill as well as an application form for financial assistance, which she had completed before her arrival at the office. She immediately handed over the application form and the social worker began to read what she had filled in. While reading the completed form the social worker asked for further information concerning some of the details in the application. After the social worker's introductory questions – which were followed by short answers – the client started to talk about the reasons for her financial difficulties.

Example 2

> *Social worker*: [3] (...) And according to Lotta ((another social worker)) who I talked to (on the telephone) what you're primarily applying for is rent money and then food money?
>
> *Client*: [4] Yea, because I uhh handed in my notice at work (S: Yes, I see) and I uhh was barred from the union for four weeks (S: Mm) and then there was a one week qualifying period and then I handed in my employer's certificate (Sw.: arbetsgivarintyg) to uhh Dennis, which is the name of the man at the restaurant where I was working before, but I haven't got it I got it last Thursday and I handed it in at the beginning of September ((almost two months ago)) (S: Mm) I handed in my notice because I wasn't feeling well, mentally speaking, so I didn't get it until last Thursday so I was able to send it off last Friday and I don't know how long that sort of thing takes.
>
> *Social worker*: Well, haven't you phoned the union and talked to them yourself?

The client's talk in example 2 about her financial problem was related to her own experiences and difficulties, but the form of her utterance is nevertheless similar in several ways to the narrative told by the man quoted in example 1. The client's telling comes *early* in the social welfare encounter and gives are *construction* of the events that preceded the financial problems. Furthermore, the sequential analysis showed the same three-part structure: the social worker's *initiation*, the client's *delivery* of the narrative, and the social worker's *closing*.

Within this narrative format, the client's financial difficulties were construed as having been caused by a 'complicating event' over which the client has had little or no influence. The active agent in the situation is often a different institutional actor, over whose doings clients have had no influence and whose behaviour has been impossible to predict or comply with. This agent is quite often another institution – such as the employer, the labour union, the bailiff, or the housing company – that puts clients in an unfortunate position, which they cannot resolve on their own. These narratives had similarities with the 'sad stories' (Goffman, 1961) told by patients in mental hospitals in which responsibility was ascribed to forces outside the individual. In the social welfare interviews there was often, however, another ingredient that allowed for a potential 'success story' to be told: Provided the client was given assistance there were openings for the future (cf., also 'the dialogues', which are described below).

The study results clearly showed the importance of the narrative in processing social welfare claims. Whether or not the client was *allowed* to speak of his or her situation, however, was something that often seemed to be controlled by the official in the individual conversation (see p. 78: the social worker as co-creator of the client's narrative). For example, in one of the twenty-five conversations that were analysed the female client was interrupted when she first wanted to talk about her need for financial assistance. When the client in that conversation began her narrative about the help she needed and how this was related to the theft of her wallet, the social worker replied that first a financial assistance form had to be completed. Later during the conversation, however, the client was given an opportunity to say how she had come to be without money, when the social worker said 'So you say you lost your money?' (Cedersund, 1992a, p. 67). If the content of the client's narrative was not 'acceptable' as a reason for processing an application for assistance – a client who states at a social welfare office that his or her wallet has been stolen is probably seldom believed – then the client's narration did not seem to be of particularly great interest to the social worker.

Thus, the social worker's control over the individual and his or her ability to present narratives during a conversation at the social welfare office appeared to be a means of exercising the authority's power over the individual citizen. Being allowed to describe the circumstances surrounding the need for help is to be regarded as an important way for the client to be seen as a reliable person.

As in the two examples above, most of the clients used a monological narrative form, describing in this way their situation and why they needed financial assistance. In some of the conversations the narratives were, however, more in the form of dialogues between the two parties participating in the conversation and, thus, were more like what has in previous research been called troubles-telling (Jefferson and Lee, 1981).

The 'Dialogues' and the 'Minimal Utterances' from the Client

This second form of talk about the client's financial difficulties, which was found in some of the interviews, was called *'dialogues'* in the typology, as it followed a dialogical structure where the client as well as the social worker contributed verbally to the account in exchanges with frequent turn-taking. When the clients' comments about his or her financial difficulties were made in the form of a 'dialogue' this topic was similar in terms of pace or tone of voice with the rest of the interview. Both interlocutors took an active part in the jointly created 'talk about troubles' and the conversation seemed to continue just as before. These instances, with dialogically produced talk about the client's problems, seemed to follow a less specific structure compared with the form that was used in the 'narratives'. The sequential structure was therefore more difficult to identify and describe in one single model.

Through this alternative dialogical form the client was not forced to tell a 'story' on his or her own, but the social worker assisted with suggestions that allowed the client to give a description of his or her 'case'. This second form of conversational style – the dialogues – seemed to function both as a way to 'make light of the troubles' (Jefferson, 1988) and at the same time as an opportunity to elicit some information about the applicant. The dialogical format allowed the client and the social worker to achieve a jointly construed account of the past. In contrast to the monological narratives, the dialogues often ended up in some solution to the problem.

However, three of the conversations that were studied contained neither monological narratives nor narratives in the form of dialogues, but simply *minimal utterances* from the client's side when the latter was asked to state the causes of his or her financial difficulties.

The applications for financial assistance from these three individuals appeared to be relatively simple to assess, which may have been why the social workers did not expressly request longer narratives or accounts from their clients during the course of their discussions (Cedersund and Säljö, 1994, pp. 251-253). It could be assumed that there was some form of pre-understanding between the social worker and the client, which allowed the former to come up with appropriate characterisations and solutions to problems that were mentioned in the interview. The clients' narratives seemed to be replaced by several verbal contributions from the social worker (e.g., in the form of statements and tentative descriptions), which were responded to by the client through fairly short confirmations or other types of agreements.

However, the most common discursive form used by the clients in my study consisted of the 'monological narratives', and this discursive form was of great importance in different ways for the processing of the applications for financial assistance.

Narration in Different Contexts

The narrative analysis carried out also included an examination of texts in the form of documents related to decisions produced by the social workers in conjunction with the cases we followed (Cedersund 1992a). In analysing these documents, I found that most of them contained a summarized version of the narratives presented by the clients during the course of the discussions held during their visits (Cedersund and Säljö, 1994, p. 260). Thus, the circumstances in the lives of clients seeking assistance had been combined to form a whole via more or less lengthy narratives, which were subsequently written down in the social workers' documents. Thus, narratives produced by clients comprised a base used by the social workers to describe the clients and their situations and, in many cases, they provided important and necessary motivations for why financial assistance should be granted.

During the years in which the project on citizens' contacts with the authorities was conducted, the British researchers Andrew Pithouse and Paul Atkinson published a text that deals with narratives in social work. Here the focus was not on the encounter between individual clients and social workers, but on the conversations on current 'cases' between the social worker and his/her supervisor. These formed a type of conversation that may be called a *narrative style of case-talk* (Pithouse and Atkinson, 1988). The analyses made in our ongoing project were greatly assisted by this text. Judging from the results of our project, however, there was clearly a shortcoming in the text by Pithouse and Atkinson. According to our results, the social worker's narratives were not the first step in processing cases. In most cases, it was rather the client or his/her representatives, in the form of relatives or other affected parties, who presented the first narrative, which was then taken over by the social worker. This was followed by a gradual reshaping of the 'story' of the client's situation, his or her presumed troubles, and need for assistance. Generations of narratives were created here, as in other types of institutional conversations. Thus, terms such as *story-generation, tellings,* and *retellings* are fitting terms used to describe this phenomenon (cf., Jönsson and Linell, 1991).

In the first part of this chapter I have tried to let the reader follow my own story of how narratives have come to be considered important in social welfare-related talk. The method I have used to convince the reader can also be considered a narrative format. I have presented a chronological description of a course of events, a story that leads to a certain point. I have indicated a problem – how the individual's perspective and interests can be investigated – and then presented a solution to the problem – the narrative method of analysing conversations. Thus, we researchers, too, rely on narratives to produce texts that present research results.

Similarly, individuals who contact caseworkers in social service agencies attempt to use narratives to demonstrate relevant and important aspects of their situation. Each individual's story is then transformed into a *case-presentation* by the social worker. Using narratives as an organizing principle in conversations and texts is a basic linguistic pattern for conveying experience between people – both between researchers and between the various actors involved in social work.

Narrative Analysis as a Method in Social Work

Have thoughts on the importance of narratives in conversations at social welfare offices had any effect on what has been written on social work in recent years? A search of the literature showed that during the 1990s studies on narratives have been conducted by an increasing number of researchers in social work and other related disciplines. However, the articles I found consisted not only of research on narratives in social welfare interviews when social workers meet clients face-to-face (cf., Cedersund and Säljö, 1994) or during meetings between social workers (cf., Pithouse and Atkinson, 1988). They also dealt with events that took place in a variety of environments: waiting rooms, clients' homes, lecture halls at the schools of social work, or at on-the-job training where students in social work undergo part of their professional development. The authors of these texts are researchers and teachers who are working to develop theories, methods, and the practice of social work. The texts referred to below were chosen for the purpose of documenting and evaluating how narrative methods are used in different activities, as well as the potential strength of these methods as resources in today's society, where people's living conditions are more and more varied.

The literature review indicates that the use of narratives in social work has several different significations and sometimes serves different functions. Despite their considerable numbers, the texts found in my search of the literature deal with variations on a similar theme: the importance of social workers' listening to and helping to construct stories from individuals and groups in our society. It is also emphasized here that telling stories and creating narratives is not something that should be reserved for professionals – whether they are officials or other professional 'storytellers'. Instead, individual people and citizens who may not have spoken up before should be encouraged to create their own narratives.

Identification, Creation, and Co-creation of Narratives

The creation and co-creation of alternative narratives on 'reality' is an important aspect of supporting people so they may exercise control and influence over the development of their own lives and gain an understanding of how their lives have turned out (cf., Öberg, 1997). Thus, it seems that being a good listener to other people's stories is just as important as lending a helping hand to those who have lost their way in unfamiliar territory. For those who are active in social work there are still many stories to be told or, as one of the researchers in question put it:

> When empowerment is the phenomenon of interest there are many individual and collective stories waiting to be told. (Rappaport, 1995, p. 799).

When people's own alternative stories of important events in their lives are to be received, heard, and requested, it is also a matter of putting some important pieces in what can be likened to an 'emancipatory puzzle', which is intended to give people power over their own lives and over how various types of problems are described (cf., Rappaport, 1995, p. 805).

Individuals' stories of successes and setbacks in their lives, the significance and meaning of experiences in their past, or the possibilities and desires for their future lives appear to be important tools for those working in various socially oriented activities. People create an image of their story and if others hear this story it is confirmed and seen as 'real' (cf., the concept of validation below, and Sands, 1996, p. 182).

The basis of the studies that have been conducted on narratives in social work is usually described as a combination of critical literary studies and social science theories of social constructivism (see, e.g., Holland and Kilpatrick, 1993; Sands, 1996). Narratives as a phenomenon in various types of 'human-care' professions should thus be seen as more of an *interdisciplinary* field of research and knowledge. Social work is only one of the disciplines in which narrative methods are studied in various types of treatment-related work.

Collective and Individual Narratives

In the analyses discussed at the beginning of this chapter (cf., examples 1 and 2) people's narratives in conversations were presented as forms of utterances produced by individuals during encounters with one or more persons. A few of the texts I have found on narratives as a method in social work practice state that the individually produced narratives are only one of the narrative types that exist and that it is important to examine so-called community narratives, as well (Rappaport, 1995).

> A *community narrative* is a story that is common among a group of people. It may be shared by a group through social interaction, texts (although these are not necessary), and other forms of communication including pictures, performances, and rituals. A group of people with a shared narrative may constitute a community. Settings often have a story that is preserved and transmitted independent of any particular individual. (...) These narratives tell the members something about themselves, their heroes, their history, and their future (ibid., p. 803).

Thus, these *collectively* produced narratives express the common story of a group. The group may be constituted precisely in that the narrative is created and handed from person to person. Here narratives are seen as being linked to a certain environment and to the people who are part of that environment. This type of collective narrative has been described within various types of organizations whose goal it is to provide people with better living conditions, for example, volunteer organizations, helping-hand or religious associations, co-operatively operated social support activities, and various types of educational activities (ibid., p. 799).

The physical space that organizations of this kind have created for their activities make possible various types of narrative. Alcoholics Anonymous meetings within the AA movement can serve as an example of how discursive actions shape and reshape people's identity (cf., Arminen, 1996, p. 121, with an analysis of AA members' orientation both to communal mutuality and to individuality of personal experiences). The *individual* story of one's own life is influenced by the group's collectively produced narratives. In order for the individuals to discover alternative narratives of their lives and to create new ways of looking at themselves, they must have access to environments where such activities are permitted and encouraged (Rappaport, 1995, p. 796).

Parallel to these two levels of narrative, the individual and the collective, there is also a third level: the culturally formed narrative (ibid., p. 803). This third type of narrative may be seen via stereotypical narratives that often give simplified pictures of people and their personal qualities. We all recognize the culturally formed narratives of people who are called 'welfare cases' or 'bums', for example. Those stereotyped stories may deal with people who are presented as having character flaws, being lazy, or having other properties that are considered negative. Such stereotyped images have often been conveyed via narratives repeated in the media, but are also transmitted by gossip and so-called travelling myths, in which simplified versions of people's lives are presented (cf., narratives in what has been called the racist discourse, see e.g., van Dijk, 1987).

Frequently, however, collective and individual narratives that offer alternatives to the culturally formed stereotypical narratives have a difficult time being fully heard when they compete with the culturally shaped narratives of extremely tenacious prejudices.

Alternative Identities in Narratives

Social work studies that have been conducted from a feminist perspective have depicted narratives as an important tool for studying the reproduction of gender, the empowerment process, and the creation of new identities. While the text cited above, which dealt with community narratives (Rappaport, 1995), discussed the *content* of the narratives at length, feminist studies have devoted more space to analysing the *form* of the narratives.

Detailed analysis of conversations in which women participate can help identify new, underlying voices in conversations. For example, by listening to what are called false starts and repairs in conversations, it is possible to trace what is not said but could have been said (Sands, 1996). Such analytical methods were devised for certain gender-related aspects of narratives, but they have also proven suitable for use in many other types of analysis of language and social structure. The structures that are frequently mentioned in this context include in addition to gender, ethnic background, age, and social class (ibid., p. 178).

Studies of this kind have focused on narrative identity and its stability, but also on its possibilities for change. One example that is given in one of the cited texts involves a woman who was given the fictitious name 'Mary' and who participated in a project that examined mental health and illness in single women with pre-school children (ibid.). A long excerpt from the interview with Mary was presented and analyses showed her various identities. Others had previously described Mary's mental problems as a 'nervous breakdown', but during the conversation the interviewer was, together with Mary, able to produce numerous interpretations of the same events. These included an image of a Mary who was an insecure adult, a victim of previous injustices, and a despised person, as well as Mary as a born-again Christian, and as a person who was becoming more sure of herself.

None of the new alternative identities that emerged in the interview with Mary were totally in accord with what is usually called the dominant psychological discourse (ibid., p. 182). This example shows how, during a conversation with a clinically oriented social worker (who in this case was also the interviewer in a research project), a person can undergo a change through construction and reconstruction of his or her identity as formed in the narrative (ibid., p. 183). During the conversation little activity was required on the part of the interviewer to support Mary in her narrative; only a certain confirmation or 'validation' of what had been said at times when Mary hesitated to continue her narrative. Validation by her counterpart granted Mary the right to speak with her own 'voice' in the conversation. In this way, she was able to present her own versions of what happened to her on those occasions when others thought she had suffered a nervous breakdown.

In other conversations, the interviewer's role may become more active than in the interview with Mary described above. However, even in cases where the social worker must be a more active co-creator of narratives dealing with the client's past there are what may be seen as multiple identities that are not stable constructions and can vary over time.

Thus, a deeper analysis of the narrative in conversations has shown ways of finding alternative discursive patterns and alternative stories about people's reality. Narratives produced in the encounters between social workers and clients can contain features of dominant discursive patterns – 'collapse' is a nervous breakdown – or traces of alternative patterns or various voices that describe the same phenomenon in a new way. These provide new interpretations of the course of events and its consequences for the future. Thus, seeking 'silenced voices' is a special challenge described in some of the texts on conversations in social work (see, for example, Hall, Sarangi, and Slembrouck, 1997).

Opening up to Variation and Multiplicity through the Use of Narratives

A relatively widespread method that makes use of narratives and stories goes under the name 'reminiscence work' (Holland and Kilpatrick, 1993, p. 302). This method is frequently aimed at older individuals. Discussions of this method often point to the universally human aspect of one person telling another about his or her own experiences and reflections on life.

Stories constitute the basic structures all persons use to make sense in their lives. Hence, understanding narratives is fundamental to the practice of social work (...) Stories invite teachers, practitioners and students to consider how persons, in any culture, come to understand themselves as they do, how such understanding influences behavior and relationship, and how change inself-understanding occurs. One of the most promising approaches to studying these issues is the discipline of narrative analysis (Holland and Kilpatrick, 1993, p. 302).

Narrative as a method in clinical social work is described in detail in several of the articles produced in the literature search (see, for example, Holland and Kilpatrick, 1993; Kelley, 1995). These articles describe discussions with clients as an opportunity for the social worker to respond to the clients' stories and to bring out new details in these accounts.

As an example Kelley (1995) mentioned a series of contacts with a rural 'multiproblem' family. This was a family that from the outside was considered to function poorly. The mother supported the six children – two pre-schoolers and four at school – alone. The abusing father was in and out of employment and the home. One of the children had demonstrated violent behaviour against his classmates in school, and there was also sometimes violence between the older children at home. However, a closer examination of the family members' various stories–the deconstructions and reconstructions of their stories – revealed many positive aspects, as well, which the family members themselves had not noticed, as they had been focusing on the 'dominant story' about the family as problem family (ibid., pp. 355-356). Many stories of the family's success and strength had previously been ignored. For example, how the mother had found a job that allowed her to earn an income but also to care for her children, how the older children had cared for the pre-schoolers, how the father had been good to the children when he had been at home. These strengths could be drawn upon in both the family and individual sessions that followed. When this family began to reconstruct not only what was bad but also what could appear good it was possible for changes in behaviour to take place. For example, the violent behaviour that had previously been exhibited by the children could be changed.

Another way to view new patterns in the narratives that arise in the encounter between social workers and clients is to use a technique of 'reflection' by a group of social workers, which follows the work with individual clients or families by means of observations. It is also possible for the social workers themselves to relate stories to clients. The social worker can then use stories that demonstrate new ways of acting, new ways of relating, or alternative ways of viewing the issues that are focused on in contacts with a certain client or family (Holland and Kilpatrick, 1993, p. 306).

Epilogue on People's Contacts with the Authorities and on Narratives in Social Services Encounters

Telling stories and listening to the stories of others is one way of being a person (cf., Singer, 1976 in Engel, 1993, see quote below). In my own studies (Cedersund, 1992b; Cedersund and Säljö, 1994) I have shown numerous examples that illustrate how clients use the narrative form to describe their situation in conversations with social workers. The narrative invites the listener to show sympathy with one who is in a problematic situation. It can provide possible explanations, justifications, or arguments, as well as reasons for interpreting problematic statements in the light of certain circumstances in the individual's life (cf., Pithouse and Atkinson, 1988, p. 185).

In my literature search I also found that people active in social work as a discipline have begun to use a narrative approach as the basis for a systematic method in social work. This method allows room for individuals' *own* perspectives, which is achieved by way of an understanding of the context of their lives. What is true for all of us is also true for people who are in contact with authorities:

> If stories weren't told or books weren't written,
> man would live like a beast, only for the day...
> Today we live, but tomorrow today will be a story.
> The whole world, all human life, is one long story.
> (Singer, 1976, in Engel, 1993, p. 789)

If the telling of stories is regarded as one way of being a person, even in social services encounters, then there are several important and critical questions that ought to be asked. The principal one of which is: Who in our society has the right to tell another person's story? If narratives are recognized as a resource for power and influence, then we also need to study who controls them. If we can show *who* determines what value a certain narrative about an individual has or *how* a narrative gains a certain status, then we can also gain information on what mechanisms create oppression or freedom (Rappaport, 1995, p. 805).

Research is thus needed on who has the right to say what, and in what situations various people are believed. From this perspective, much effort in social work should be devoted to creating situations and environments in which people and narratives of their lives can be heard and respected and where individual citizens are equal and interacting parties in a continual dialogue (ibid., p. 796). Identifying who has been *deprived* of the right to tell his/her own story or the story of his or her group – whether this is due to their class background, ethnic origin, or gender – requires additional studies that focus on narratives and their importance in various social contexts.

Transcriptions

The social welfare interviews were transcribed according to a simplified modification of the transcription system developed by Gail Jefferson (cf., Schenkein, 1978). All audible words were transcribed including, for example, repetitions and restarts. The following conventions were used:

.	a period indicates a concluding fall in tone;
,	a comma indicates a continuing intonation;
?	a question mark indicates a rising inflection;
-	a dash indicates an abrupt cut-off;
=	equal signs are used when one turn is followed immediately by another i.e., the turns are latched;
va (S: Ja)	underlining is used to show simultaneous speech;
italics	emphasis is indicated by italics;
( )	parentheses are used to indicate back channelling (feedback) from the current listener; parentheses are also used for (almost) inaudible words;
((pause))	indicates a marked (untimed) pause;
(1 s.)	pause timed in seconds;
(.........)	indicates omitted words;
(( ))	double parentheses are used to enclose a description of what the participants are doing during the conversation, e.g., if someone is writing; double parentheses are also used for translations and miscellaneous comments;
/ /	slashes are used to mark laughter.

The following abbreviations were used: S= social worker, C= client. All names, addresses, and other identifying information have been changed in order to protect the participants' anonymity.

Sequences from the social welfare interviews quoted in the paper have been translated from Swedish to English. This translation has been kept as literal as possible, with minor modifications in order to preserve conversational style.

Notes

1 See appendix for transcription rules. In this example the social worker is a 25-year-old woman.
2 The client is a 60-year-old man.
3 The social worker in example 2 is a 25-year-old woman.
4 The client is a 21-year-old woman.

Bibliography

Agar, M. (1985), 'Institutional Discourse', *Text*, vol. 5, pp. 147-168.
Arminen, I. (1996), 'The Construction of Topic in the Turns of Talk at the Meetings of Alkoholics Anonymous', *International Journal of Sociology and Social Policy*, vol. 16, pp. 88-130.
Cedersund, E. (1992a), *Från personligt problem till administrativt beslut. Att ansöka om ekonomiskt bistånd*, [From Personal Problems to Administrative Decisions. To Claim Financial Assistance], SIC (Studies in Communication) 33, Department of Communication Studies, Linköping University.
Cedersund, E. (1992b), 'Client Narration about Financial Problems in Social Welfare Interviews', in *Talk, Text and Institutional Order. A Study of Communication in Social Welfare Bureaucracies*, Linköping Studies in Arts and Science, 78 (Diss.).
Cedersund, E. and Säljö, R. (1994), 'Running a Bit Low on Money. Reconstructing Financial Problems in the Social Welfare Interview', in Walter M. Sprondel (ed) *Die Objektivität der Ordnungen und ihre Kommunikative Konstruktion. Für Thomas Luckmann*, Suhrkamp Verlag, pp. 226-260.
van Dijk, T. A. (1987), *Communicating Racism. Ethnic Prejudice in Thought and Talk*, Sage, London.
Engel, D. M. (1993), 'Narratives of Authority, Resistance, Disability, and Law', *Law & Society Review*, vol. 27, pp. 785-826.
Erickson, F. and Shultz, J. (1982), *The Counselor as Gatekeeper. Social Interaction in Interviews*, Academic Press, New York.
Erlingsson, F. (1996), *Benjamin Duva Riddareav Ršda Draken* [Benjamin Duva, Knight of the Red Dragon] (original Icelandic title: Benjam'n Dœfa), Bonnier Carlsen.
Goffman, E. (1961), *Asylums. Essays on the Social Situation of Mental Patients and Other Inmates*, Garden City, New York.
Goodsell, C. T. (1981), *The Public Encounter. Where State and Citizen Meet*, Indiana University Press, Bloomington.

Gülich, E. and Quasthoff, U. M. (1986), 'Story-telling in Conversations. Cognitive and Interactive Aspects', *Poetics*, vol. 15, pp. 217-241.
Hall, C., Sarangi, S. and Slembrouck, S. (1997), 'Silent and Silenced Voices: Interactional Construction of Audience in Social Work Talk', in A. Jaworski (ed) *Silence: Interdisciplinary Perspectives*, Mouton de Gruyter, Berlin - New York, pp. 181-211.
Holland, T. P. and Kilpatrick, A. C. (1993), 'Using Narrative Techniques to Enhance Multicultural Practice', *Journal of Social Work Education*, vol. 29, pp. 302-308.
Jefferson, G. (1988), 'On the Sequential Organization of Troubles-talk in Ordinary Conversations', *Social Problems*, vol. 35, 418-441.
Jefferson, G. and Lee, J. (1981), 'The Rejection of Advice: Managing the Problematic Convergence of a "Troubles-telling" and a "Service-encounter"', *Journal of Pragmatics*, vol. 5, pp. 399-422.
Jönsson, L. and Linell, P. (1991), 'Story Generations: from Dialogical Interviews to Written Reports in Police Interrogations', *Text*, vol. 11, pp. 419-440.
Jönsson, L., Linell, P. and Säljö, R.(1991), 'Formulating the Past. Remembering in the Police Interrogation', *Multidisciplinary Newsletter for Activity Theory*, 9/10.
Kelley, P. (1995), 'Integrating Narrative Approaches into Clinical Diversity Through Understanding', *Journal of Social Work Education*, vol. 31, pp. 347-357.
Labov, W. (1972), *Language in the Inner City. Studies in Black English Vernacular*, University of Pennsylvania Press, Philadelphia.
Lipsky, M. (1980), *Street-level Bureaucracy. Dilemmas of the Individual in Public Services*, Russell Sage Foundation, New York.
Öberg, P. (1997), *Livet som enberättelse. Om biografi och åldrande* [Life as Narrative. On Biography and Aging], Acta Universitatis Upsaliensis (Diss.), Department of Sociology, Uppsala university.
Pithouse, A. and Atkinson, P. (1988), 'Telling the Case: Occupational Narrative in a Social Work Office', in Nikolas Coupland (ed), *Styles of Discourse*, 183-200, Croom Helm Ltd, Beckenham.
Rappaport, J. (1995), 'Empowerment Meets Narrative: Listening to Stories and Creating Settings', *American Journal of Community Psychology*, vol. 23, pp. 795-807.
Sands, R. G. (1996), 'The Elusiveness of Identity in Social Work Practice with Women: A Postmodern Feminist Perspective', *Clinical Social Work Journal*, vol. 24, pp.167-186.
Schenkein, J. (ed) (1978), *Studies in the Organization of Conversational Interaction*, New York: Academic Press.
Scott, M. B. and Lyman, S. M. (1968), 'Accounts', *American Sociological Review*, vol. 33, pp. 46-62.
Säljö R. and Cedersund, E. (1987), *Myndighetskontakt i medborgarperspektiv* [Contact with Authorities from the Citizen's Perspective], Plan for a research project at the Department of Communication Studies, Linköping University.

4 Examining the Artfulness of 'Risk Talk'

SUSAN WHITE

Introduction

Similar observations about shifts in child welfare policy and practice in the United Kingdom have been made by a variety of commentators (e.g. Howe, 1992; 1994a, 1994b; Otway, 1996; Parton, 1991; Thorpe, 1994; Department of Health, 1995). There is a general consensus that social work with children and families has become more focused and specialized, so that it is now concerned, not with child welfare generally, but with 'child protection' specifically. It is argued that a pre-occupation with the identification of risk and dangerousness has led to a focus on the forensic and evidential features of cases, and that this *modus operandi* has contributed to the withering away of the more preventive and supportive aspects of social work.

Several different analytic frameworks have been used to account for this shift. For example, some commentators have focused on developments in policy, and on the direct impact of a number of high-profile inquiries into child abuse scandals of various kinds, whilst others have adopted a Foucauldian perspective, focusing on the ascending discourses of risk and dangerousness and on the normalizing 'gaze' of welfare professionals and its role in the regulation and construction of parenthood and childhood. However, despite their differences, all these frameworks neglect the ways in which notions of risk, dangerousness, deviance and normality are reproduced and instantiated in the cut and thrust of everyday talk amongst social workers. They thus tend either to reify 'discourses', or to cast the social work profession as a kind of docile executive which simply implements policy directives.

By examining transcripts of naturally occurring conversation, this paper seeks to remedy this general neglect of talk but, in adopting this analytic focus, I do not intend to imply that social workers are entirely 'free' to choose how they work. Clearly, many of their strategies for sense-making bear traces of 'discourses', explanatory frameworks and legislation which are *imported*.[1] However, social workers (as agents) do have room for 'invention within limits' (Bourdieu, 1977), and their risk-talk should properly be seen as 'ethnopoetics' (Pithouse and Atkinson, 1988) – as skilful oratory, with certain ritualized and routinized features.

Moreover, I shall argue that these ritual narrations have a pivotal role in the maintenance and display of a child-care social work 'identity'. Recent years have seen a shift in the position taken by the Department of Health (e.g. Department of Health, 1995) on child protection and child welfare. Social services departments are being urged to take a softer approach to investigation of suspected abuse, and to shift resources into preventive services. The data presented in this paper suggest that this is likely to be a somewhat slow process. Not only because there has been no promise of increased resources, but also because a display of child centredness and the performance of doubting in relation to parental accounts have become so central to the social work *habitus*.

Here I am drawing on a particular reading (and there are many) of Bourdieu's concept of *habitus*, taken here to mean a 'strategy-generating principle enabling agents to cope with unforeseen and ever-changing situations' (1977, p. 72). This is Bourdieu's remedy for the existential 'free' self, characteristic of ethnomethodology and phenomenology. The habitus provides the *sens pratique,* the practical reasoning through which the individual negotiates everyday encounters. Yet the habitus is also the embodiment of *experience* and thus brings with it an inescapable historicity. The actors within each field will each have an individual habitus, through which their experience is embodied and transported to the present, but this individual habitus will also have elements appropriate to the particular field in which they are situated. It is through the acquisition of this habitus (or inclination, predisposition, habitual state, Bourdieu, 1977, p. 214) that competency within a field is achieved. Thus, the term habitus refers here to a set of presuppositions held by social workers as an occupational group, an embodiment of ways of doing and being based on ways of having done and been before. The historicity of the *habitus* means that ways of doing 'business as usual' are rendered relatively durable across time.

This paper begins with a brief methodological discussion, which seeks to explain the nature of the study and to justify my rather eclectic approach to the data analysis. The concepts of 'narrative', occupational identity and other tools I shall use in the data analysis are explained.

Extracts from transcripts of talk in a weekly 'allocation meeting' are then analyzed, with attention to their narrative features and how they rhetorically 'do' risk. The paper concludes with a further consideration of the importance of ritual and display in the maintenance of an occupational identity, and the implications of these observations for the contemporary 'child protection vs. family support' debate.[2]

Methodological Notes

The data presented here are taken from a more detailed ethnographic study which was conducted in a metropolitan social services department between 1993 and 1995 (White, 1997). The analytic focus of the study is upon the routines and linguistic practices used by child-care social workers. Particular attention is paid to social workers' collegial discourse which is revealed as a vehicle for the accomplishment and reproduction of occupational identity. Using transcripts of naturally occurring conversation, interview data, and documentary analyses, the work shows how referrals received from other professionals and the public are coded and categorized, and how social workers artfully accomplish 'caseness', by referencing danger, risk and deviance in their talk.

Although I draw on other conceptual material in the data analysis, my *methodological* orientation is more or less captured in Miller's (1994) recipe for 'ethnographies of institutional discourse'. Miller describes and justifies such an approach as follows:

> Ethnographies of institutional discourse combine ethnographers' interest in in-depth observations of diverse settings in everyday life, conversation analysts' construction and analysis of transcripts of naturally occurring talk within settings, and the Foucauldian focus on the formulation, dispersion and uses of knowledge within and across social settings. Whereas ethnomethodologically informed ethnographers, conversation analysts, and Foucauldian discourse analysts disagree on many issues, they agree that social realities involve more than looking and seeing. Social realities are produced (or accomplished) by seeing and communicating from standpoints (or gazes) that are simultaneously ways of understanding and being in social worlds (ibid., pp. 281-2).

On a similar note, Walker (1988) distinguishes between Discourse, as a body of knowledge, and discourse, as talk (for further arguments in favour of paradigmatic synthesis see, Atkinson, 1988, 1995a; Bourdieu, 1989 – citation, Bourdieu and Wacquant, 1992, p. 29; Law, 1994; Silverman, 1985; 1993; 1997). After Miller and Walker, I contend that Discourse (as a body of knowledge) must be reproduced within discourse (talk) at 'the point of its articulation' (ibid., p.55). Thus, although the focus of this paper is on discourse as talk, it will become clear that much of this discourse can be traced to particular artefacts (e.g. the law) and ultimately to specific forms of knowledge (Discourses). Thus, I reiterate that I have no intention of implying that social workers have an unlimited repertoire of 'competent' accounts or that all 'order' is produced *within* their encounters (as Sharrock and Button, 1991, contend). It is for this reason that I have eschewed the rampant situationalism of some conversation analytic studies (for example, by using the concept of *habitus*). However, I have also jettisoned the reified 'discourse as prison' orientation of many Foucauldian studies, since this marginalizes or ignores the artful activity of agents.

Narrative and 'Truth'

I refer to social workers' accounts of their cases as 'stories', which perhaps carries unintended connotations, possibly suggesting that I believe they are, in some way, a contrast to factual reporting – that they are works of fiction. However, I am not intending to pass judgement on the ontological status of social workers' accounts. My concern is not with whether their stories about cases are true or false, but with understanding and describing practitioners' ways of doing 'business as usual', of doing 'risk' through their talk.

At this point it is worth saying a little more about narrative and rhetoric. Mishler (1986) defines narrative as a particular kind of 'recapitulation', which preserves 'the temporal ordering of events' (cf. Labov, 1972). Others (e.g. Reissman, 1993, p. 17) have argued that narratives may not proceed in this linear manner, but may be organized 'episodically' or thematically. Useful though such definitions are, there are some dangers in using classifications of this kind to analyze narratives. As Edwards (1997) asserts:

The temptation for analysts using [Labov's] scheme is to start with the categories and see how the things people say can be fitted into them, and, having coded everything as one category or another, to call that the analysis, and then compare it to other findings. In that role, as a coding scheme, these kinds of structural categories impose rather than reveal, obscuring the particularity of specific details, and how that particularity is crucial for the occasioned, action-performative workings of discourse (Edwards, 1997, p. 276).

It is with these rhetorical, or action-performative features of social workers' narratives that I am concerned in this paper. I have treated narratives as the products of contingent (but not unlimited) choices (cf. Atkinson, 1995), and will go on to show how (not necessarily self-conscious, but partly habitual) decisions about 'where to start a story [are] major and rhetorically potent [ways] of managing causality and accountability' (Edwards, 1997, p. 277). This analytic focus builds upon the general agreement that narratives, by definition, embody some sort of chronology, with certain events being presented as the antecedents of others. So that:

....narrative confers a meaning on the event which, when it actually occurred, no doubt had several meanings or perhaps none. This postulating of a meaning dictates the choice of facts to be retained and of the details to bring out or dismiss according to the demands of the preconceived intelligibility (Gusdorf, 1980, p. 42, citation, Freeman, 1993, p. 31).

When social workers order their accounts of cases, they are dealing with a reality already *re*presented at the point of referral. They are rarely physically present when abuse takes place for example. In turn, *re*presented information is *re*ordered in the social work account 'according to the demands of the preconceived intelligibility' of the occupational group. For example, I shall go on to show that for a case to be claimed as 'ours' – as a social work case – some attribution of risk or dangerousness is usually necessary.[3] This attribution is accomplished in the case narrative.

Embedded in this definition of narrative is a rejection of the easy distinction often drawn between facts and rhetoric. Rather than 'facts' being a contrast to rhetoric, the artful ordering of facts within a narrative account becomes the very source of its rhetorical potency (cf. Billig et al., 1988). This does not mean that social workers could, if they tried, present cases in some more authentic way, which does not involve the narrative *re*presentation of events, since, after McIntyre (1981) and Freeman (1993),

I suggest that 'in order to carry out the most basic task of identifying and trying to understand what someone (including ourself) is doing any given moment in time, there is the need to place the action in a narrative context' (Freeman, 1993, p. 110). This act of trying to render information meaningful through the construction of a narrative account involves, as I stated earlier, *contingent* choices about where to start a story and what are its salient features. The story so produced clearly bears more than an arbitrary relation to the events it describes, but it is not a neutral report.

Narrative and Occupational Identity: Speaking the Social Work Habitus

The idea that culture 'speaks itself' (Reissman, 1993, p. 5) is now well established. For example, in their work on the peace and justice movement in the USA, Hunt and Benford (1994) describe how collective identity is literally talked into being through a variety of associative and disassociative claims (cf. also Travers, 1994, on 'radical' lawyers; Rawlings, 1981, on a therapeutic community). I shall argue below that through case narratives social workers, too, learn how to 'do being' social workers, how to do the social *work* in social work. The legitimacy of the work is endorsed and occupational identity reaccomplished and reinforced. This takes place through the telling of stories and also through the *responses* to these stories (co-narrations), which affirm that certain situations are 'very worrying' or 'concerning' and are hence a legitimate focus for social work activity. In these stories, injuries to a child (the damaged material body – e.g. bruises, burns) have a pivotal symbolic significance.

In representing aspects of the social work *habitus* thus, I do not wish to ascribe an artificial homogeneity upon social workers as individuals. I have made it clear elsewhere (White, 1997) that no such 'hideous purity' (Law, 1994) exists. Rather my point is that certain ways of thinking, become positions which must be argued away from, trangressions become accountable. The habitus is displayed at its purest in ritualized encounters and I shall argue below that alongside its manifest function of allocating work to social workers, the allocation meeting has a ritual significance as an arena for identity talk.

Doing Risk Talk

In his recent ethnographic work amongst a group of haematologists in the United States, Atkinson (1995) notes that,

> ....medical students and practitioners make frequent appeals to matters of opinion, or judgement that cannot be validated unambiguously by scientific knowledge. But personal knowledge and experience are not normally treated by practitioners as reflections of uncertainty, but as warrants for certainty.... Distinctions between theory and practice, or between science and experience are not drawn in order to contrast feelings of certainty and uncertainty, or to justify alternative ways of problem-solving. *Both* are ways of warranting knowledge for practitioners' practical purposes (ibid, pp. 114-5, original emphasis).

Atkinson urges analysts to pay attention to the ways in which certainty and uncertainty are marked during talk. These markers are available to social actors in their situated encounters, the important analytic task is to examine how they are *mobilized* in talk.

The analysis below will seek to illustrate some of the routine ordering frameworks in use by social workers, attending to how deviance, risk, certainty and uncertainty are marked in the talk and to the nature and artfulness of causal attributions.

The following data extract is taken from a transcript of an allocation meeting[4] which is a weekly forum, in which the team manager attempts to allocate to an individual social worker those referrals which require further action. I have used a selection of conversation analytic conventions. However, the data have inevitably have been 'cleaned' and speech 'normalized' (West, 1996). So, whilst I have indicated emphases, interruptions, repetitions, significant pauses, and 'non lexical vocalizations' (Mishler, 1984, p. 21), I have generally given words conventional spelling, hence effectively 'deleting' regional accent. This decision was taken quite consciously, because my opinion is that the inclusion of such detail would not have helped this particular analysis, and the cost in terms of researcher's time and 'readability' of the transcripts would be too high. The extract is chosen for its typicality and not for any unusual features.

Risk, Danger, Certainty and Uncertainty: Claiming the Case

AL3/T1 Extract 1

TL   Can I just discuss the one that came in yesterday. Somebody's going to have to pick it up in confidence I think. I'm conscious not everybody's here, erm (0.3). Joseph is fourteen months old mother moved over the last few months to Cromer Street, [town], erm (0.1) Rebecca's mum. No previous history, basically Joseph, we had a call night duty had a call rather from erm ( ) on Monday night. Joseph had been admitted earlier that day with a condition called ( ) which is where the foreskin appears to have been pulled back and gets stuck and it becomes very swollen and sore. When the referral came through, we were told it was impossible for the child to have done this to himself, or to happen spontaneously. I have subsequently had a number of *other* medical opinions which has been one of the difficulties. The original referral said there were other bruises that Joseph had on his cheek on his frenulum and which is clearly torn, she *said* a pinch mark although it was quite old. His mum is she's quite upset at the mention of NAI but she's co-operative. She has a boyfriend but he doesn't live there. She says she's always present when he's with Joseph. They'll be keeping him in for observation. She's very very woolly about the story, there seems to be lack of clarity about whether it's accidental or non accidental. I've spent most of the day trying to pin down senior medics. It was getting to the point where I was getting put through to theatre to find people who were doing all sorts of dramatic things. The surgical registrar was saying it's not impossible but it is unusual and children of that age can pull back their foreskin, but it seems unusual. I spoke to the consultant who was more concerned in a way about the bruises and the mark on the thigh. It was also the history of being seen in the clinic in [town] in July and having a small bruise on the ear then ( ) last night the grandmother was quite angry and threatened to discharge Joseph and Anne [consultant paediatrician] did a good job of persuading, but we did have to contact the police who were *very* helpful, the child protection police in [city] were actually going to take a police protection and we felt we would be very negligent to let him out last night. There've been further *very* detailed conversations this morning and the consultant was perfectly happy for us to get a second opinion and Dr Jones who's a consultant at [regional children's hospital] ....Anne went up today and saw the .. and she's saying that there are clear concerns, but the gran's said that the child falling out of the water bed he slept in could have caused this injury, so we'll have to look at this waterbed. SHE [consultant paediatrician] feels the condition of the penis would be very difficult for the child to have done himself at his age, but it is not totally impossible. So what she's saying is there are some very suspicious things, but the three she's most worried about are the penis swelling, the mark to the thigh and the mark on the ear. She thinks the bruising on the cheek which is right in front of the eye *could* have been caused by falling on a table which is what grandma and mum said. He's falling a lot he is very active and all the consultants seem to agree that those things may or may not be. The frenulum could have been torn in a fall, cos apparently children of that age do get those sorts of injuries from falling and probably are not aware. Mum says she thinks he did it again when he was on his bed, which of course is not impossible. We need to go and look at that. The long and the short of it is Joseph has gone home we're going to follow it up with the police, do more visits make more checks erm because it isn't *totally* and *absolutely* clear this must have happened this way it is actually quite difficult for us to remove the child and it has made it harder him not being at [local general hospital] where we have our own social work department. So Paul and Sally are going to pick it up and work with it and we hope to conference next Wednesday, but it obviously then has to come to the [name] team and it's a difficult one. They will do what they can but I suspect we're into a comprehensive assessment looking at everybody in this child's family. If Jane is back in time I think she would be happy to pick that one out but if not I *may* be having to look at other people and a holding operation and unless someone is going to offer which looks unlikely. It's to alert you. Cos I don't want it to be conferenced and then we have a great gap with nobody seeing the family.

SW. So you think a comprehensive assessment?
TL. I would expect that, I would expect it. In which case we would need to find somebody to do it anyway, it may be Jane and another to try and do some *sort* of comprehensive assessment really.....
SW1. =When did the injury happen?
TL. I don't know we'll have to do some more checks........
SW2. What's he called?
TL. Joseph Potter. There have been one or two different names but he's *become* Joseph
SW2. Why?
TL. I don't know, I don't know
SW2. So he's got injuries under another name (laughs)
TL. I don't know any more. I know we have other worries but I don't know
SW2. Right OK
TL I'm very grateful thanks, thank you that is super (0.8). Right, I'm really quite concerned and the difficult bit is getting a concrete medical opinion ( ).

96 *Constructing Social Work Practices*

The extract above begins with statements of fact. The team leader reports the events, which are temporally marked as occurring on 'Monday night'. However, with her assertion,

> When the referral came through, we were told it was impossible for the child to have done this to himself, or to happen spontaneously.

the speaker begins to mark the 'hearsay' nature of the evidence and hence a lower degree of reliability ('we were told'), whilst also constructing the case as the proper concern of a child-care social work team. Social services are, to borrow Callon's (1986) term, an 'obligatory passage point' for other professionals dealing with non-accidentally injured children, and thus, with the statement 'it was impossible for him to have done this to himself' the case is claimed as 'ours'.

After the speaker has described the damage to child's body (injuries), first factually (in relation to the penis) and then with a degree of uncertainty (in relation to the bruises), the mother's story is retold with the insertion of phrases such as 'she says', 'she was very very woolly', which mark scepticism.

Throughout the account, a social worker co-narrates (Eder, 1988) concern and worry. Eder (1988) has pointed to the role of co-narration in the construction and reinforcement of collective identity. There are frequent interjections as the social worker asks questions which convey her concern, but also display her own professional competence. For example,

> SW. So you think a comprehensive assessment?.....

(This refers to an assessment carried out according to guidelines issued by the Department of Health, 1988.)

In the following section, humour is used to display a certain professional 'savvy', a seasoned scepticism and suspicion,

> TL. Joseph Potter. There have been one or two different names but he's *become* Joseph
> SW2. Why?
> TL. I don't know, I don't know
> SW2. So he's got injuries under another name (laughs)

The impossibility of the team leader's task is referenced throughout her slightly comic narrative account of her attempts to contact doctors and to grapple with and reconcile competing explanations.

> I've spent most of the day trying to pin down senior medics. It was getting to the point where I was getting put through to theatre to find people who were doing all sorts of dramatic things. The surgical registrar was saying it's not impossible but it is unusual and children of that age can pull back their foreskin, but it seems unusual. I spoke to the consultant who was more concerned in a way about the bruises and the mark on the thigh. It was also the history of being seen in the clinic in [town] in July and having a small bruise on the ear

The story then takes a dramatic turn,

> last night the grandmother was quite angry and threatened to discharge Joseph, and Anne [consultant paediatrician] did a good job of persuading, but we did have to contact the police who were *very* helpful, the child protection police in [city] were actually going to take a police protection and we felt we would be very negligent to let him out last night

This serves to reinforce the professional mandate and to amplify the risky nature of the referral. The social workers become detectives *and* lawyers, with accounts of the opinions of both medics and family laden with linguistic codes which mark the speaker's scepticism about such 'hearsay' evidence, and which convey 'degrees of (un)reliability' (cf. Chafe, 1986; Atkinson, 1995b). For example,

> SHE [consultant paediatrician] *feels* the condition of the penis would be very difficult for the child to have done himself at his age, but it is *not totally impossible* (emphasis added)

In using the adverb 'totally' in the phrase 'it is not totally impossible', the speaker, in fact, signals that she believes it is *probably* impossible for the child to have injured himself. Thus, a referral characterized by equivocation amongst medical personnel is artfully presented as a risky child protection case.

> The long and short of it is Joseph has gone home, we're going to follow it up with the police, do more home visits, make more checks erm because it isn't

totally and *absolutely* clear this must have happened this way it is actually quite difficult for us to remove the child

Here the emphases, within what superficially appears to be a 'hedge', – 'it isn't *totally* and *absolutely* clear'– serve to amplify the rhetorical force of the team leader's construction of 'dangerousness', rather than to mark its uncertainty. Thus, subtle and carefully hedged attributions of causation are woven into the account, and reluctance to accept 'accidental' explanations is powerfully conveyed, with doubt, and a certain canny 'pull the other one' scepticism displayed.

Conclusion

In the introduction to this paper, I argued that many commentaries on current practice have failed to examine the rich detail of the everyday. They have paid little attention to 'thinking as usual' (Atkinson, 1995). Thus, their work has tended to imply that dominant forms of practice have, in some way, been imposed, either directly by Government, or the judiciary, or are a consequence of the forms of knowledge and regulation associated with late modernity. In short, in failing to examine the hurly-burly of institutional discourse, they have tended to edit out the productive and reproductive capacity of agents.

This paper has shown how transcripts of naturally occurring conversation can be rich sources of data about the artful constructions which comprise risk-talk. Paradoxically, this observation does not lead to a view of social workers as 'free' agents, defining their own world. Rather, the liturgical nature of many of the exchanges ensures a durability to their displays of 'concern' and 'worry'. However, despite the focus in my research upon rhetoric and artfulness, it is important to note that it remains a powerful *material* fact that children's bodies are sometimes damaged by adults, and it is social workers and other child care professionals who are charged with the task of dealing with these situations. It is an occupation which often deals with life *in extremis,* and this is reflected in the forms of thought, in particular the quest for certainty in assessment. Risk is not entirely a rhetorical creation, it is often a material fact. However, like the social workers, we as analysts of their story have no algorithmic means of determining whether the injuries to Joseph were inflicted or accidental (but, unlike the social workers, we shall not be held personally culpable for any retrospectively obvious 'error').

So, practitioners clearly *must* continue to make practical judgements about cases, because that is their job. However, these data demonstrate that social work is a profoundly *moral* enterprise for which few rational-technical tools exist. They make choices about whom to believe often based on the moral adequacy of the account offered (cf. Cuff, 1993). This morality is founded on a discourse of child-centredness, which, for the most part, it is not treated as 'position taking' at all, simply as the only right and proper way to think. Transgressions are thus cast as acts of individual deviance, or at best, misguidedness. They are almost unthinkable. Stories about cases are artfully crafted so that some explanations appear more plausible than others – they are products of contingent, though not necessarily fully conscious, choice.

These data provide a snapshot of action at a particular time and in a particular space. The debates about the pros and cons of a 'softer' approach to social work with children and families continue. However, the place of ritual as a force as social stasis has largely been ignored. I contend that, because of its high level of integration, the discourse of child centredness with its concomitant notions of parental dangerousness is by far the most significant aspect of an 'ordering' social work *habitus*, and, in the medium term, is likely to render practitioners resistant to major policy change, because:

> Each agent, wittingly or unwittingly, willy nilly, is a producer and reproducer of objective meaning. Because his actions and works are the product of a *modus operandi* of which he is not the producer and has no conscious mastery, they contain an "objective intention"..... the virtuoso finds in the *opus operandum* new triggers and new supports for the *modus operandi* from which they arise, so that his discourse continually feeds itself like a train bringing along its own rails....It is because subjects do not, strictly speaking, know what they are doing that what they do has more meaning than they know (Bourdieu, 1977, p. 79).

Transcription Symbols

[ ]	overlapping talk
( )	inaudible, and hence untranscribed, passage
(0.8)	pauses timed in tenths of second
(.)	audible short pause
talk	italics indicate emphasis
TALK	upper case indicates loudness in comparison to surrounding talk
tal-	abrupt end to utterance
<slow>	noticeable slowing of tempo of talk
=	latching of utterances

Notes

1 In making this statement, I am drawing implicitly upon actor-network theory (see, *inter alia*, Callon and Latour, 1981; Callon, 1986a and b). It is not necessary or appropriate to expand upon this here - see White, 1997, for a more detailed discussion about freedom and determinacy.
2 *Acknowledgements* I should like to thank the social workers and managers who allowed me access to their meetings, Rob Flynn for helpful comments throughout the research, and the ESRC for the award of a studentship.
3 There are some exceptions to this tendency, but I am not able to deal with these 'disconfirming' cases in this paper. See White, 1997, Chapter 7.
4 Meetings were taped over a four week period in two separate teams.

Bibliography

Atkinson, P. (1988), 'Ethnomethodology: a Critical Review', *Annual Review of Sociology*, vol. 14, pp. 441-65.
Atkinson, P. (1995a), 'Some Perils of Paradigms', *Qualitative Health Research*, vol. 5, pp. 117-24.
Atkinson, P. (1995b), *Medical Talk and Medical Work*, Sage, London.
Billig, M., Condor, S., Edwards, D., Grane, M., Middleton, D. and Radley A. 1988, *Ideological Dilemmas: A Social Psychology of Everyday Thinking*, Sage, London.
Bourdieu, P. (1977), *Outline of a Theory of Practice*, Cambridge University Press, Cambridge.
Bourdieu, P. (1989), *La noblesse d'Etat. Grandes corps et Grandes ecoles*, Editions de Minuit, Paris.

Bourdieu, P. and Wacquant, L. (1992), *An Invitation to Reflexive Sociology*, Polity, Cambridge.

Callon, M. and Latour, B. (1981), 'Unscrewing the big Leviathan: how actors macro-structure reality and how sociologists help them to do so' in K. Knorr-Cetina and A. V. Cicourel (eds), *Advances in Social Theory and Methodology: Towards an Integration of Micro- and Macro- Sociology*, Routledge, London.

Callon, M. (1986), 'Some elements of a sociology of translation: domestication of the scallops and the fishermen of St Brieuc Bay', in J. Law (ed) *Power, Action and Belief: A New Sociology of Knowledge? Sociological Review Monograph 32*, Routledge, London.

Chafe, W. (1986), 'Evidentiality in English conversation and academic writing' in W. Chafe and J. Nichols (eds) *Evidentiality: The Linguistic Coding of Epistemology*, Ablex, Norwood, New Jersey.

Cuff, E. C. (1993), *Problems of Versions in Everyday Situations*, University Press of America, London.

Department of Health (1988), *Protecting Children: A Guide for Social Workers Undertaking a Comprehensive Assessment*, HMSO, London.

Department of Health (1995), *Child Protection: Messages from Research*, HMSO, London.

Eder, D. (1988), 'Building cohesion through collaborative narration', *Social Psychology Quarterly*, vol. 5, no. 3, pp. 225-235.

Edwards, D. (1997), *Discourse and Cognition*, Sage, London.

Freeman, M. (1993), *Rewriting the Self: History, Memory, Narrative*, Routledge, London.

Gusdorf, G. (1980), 'Conditions and limits of autobiography', in J. Olney (ed) *Autobiography: Essays Theoretical and Critical*, Princeton University Press, Princeton, New Jersey.

Howe, D. (1992), 'Child abuse and the bureaucratisation of social work', *The Sociological Review*, vol. 40, no. 3, pp. 491-518.

Howe, D. (1994a), 'Modernity, postmodernity and social work', *British Journal of Social Work*, vol. 24, pp. 513-532.

Howe, D. (1994b), 'Knowledge, power and the shape of social work practice' in M. Davies (ed) *The Sociology of Social Work*, Routledge, London.

Hunt, S. A. and Benford, R. D. (1994), 'Identity talk in the peace and justice movement', *Journal of Contemporary Ethnography*, vol. 22, no. 4, pp. 488-517.

Labov, W. (1972), 'The transformation of experience in narrative syntax' in W. Labov, *Language in the Inner City*, University of Pennsylvania Press, Philadelphia, pp. 532-96.

Law, J. (1994), *Organizing Modernity*, Blackwell, Oxford.

Miller, G. (1994), 'Toward ethnographies of institutional discourse: proposal and suggestions', *Journal of Contemporary Ethnography*, vol. 23, no. 3, pp. 280-306.

Mishler, E. G. (1984), *The Discourse of Medicine: Dialectics of Medical Interviews*, Ablex, Norwood, New Jersey.

Otway, O. (1996), 'Social work with children and families: from child welfare to child protection' in N. Parton (ed), *Social Theory, Social change and Social Welfare*, Routledge, London.

Parton, N. (1991), *Governing the Family: Child Care, Child Protection and the State*, Macmillan, Basingstoke.

Pithouse, A. and Atkinson, P. (1988), 'Telling the Case: Occupational Narrative in a Social Work Office', in N. Coupland (ed) *Styles of Discourse*, Beckenham.

Rawlings, B. (1981), 'The production of facts in a therapeutic community' in P. Atkinson and C. Heath (eds), *Medical Work: Realities and Routines*, Gower, Farnborough, pp. 1-18.

Reissman, C. K. (1993), *Narrative Analysis*, Sage, Newbury Park, California.

Sharrock, W. and Button, G. (1991), 'The social actor: social action in real time', in G. Button (ed), *Ethnomethodology and the Human Sciences*, Cambridge University Press, Cambridge.

Silverman, D. (1985), *Qualitative Methodology and Sociology*, Gower, Aldershot.

Silverman, D. (1993), *Interpreting Qualitative Data: Methods for Analysing Talk, Text and Interaction*, Sage, London.

Silverman, D. (1997), *Discourses of Counselling: HIV Counselling as Social Interaction*, Sage, London.

Smith D. (1978), 'K is mentally ill: the anatomy of a factual account', *Sociology*, vol. 12, pp. 23-53.

Thorpe, D. (1994), *Evaluating Child Protection*, Open University Press, Buckingham.

Travers, M. (1994), 'The Phenomenon of the Radical Lawyer', *Sociology*, vol. 28, no. 1, pp. 245-258.

Walker, T. 'Whose Discourse?' (1988), in S. Woolgar, *New Frontiers in the Sociology of Knowledge*, Sage, London, pp. 55-79

West, C. (1996), 'Ethnography and orthography: a modest methodological proposal', *Journal of Contemporary Ethnography*, vol. 25, no. 3, pp. 327-352.

White, S. (1997), *Performing Social Work: An Ethnographic Study of Talk and Text in a Metropolitan Social Services Department*, Unpublished PhD Thesis, University of Salford.

5 Doing 'Delicacy' in Institutions of Helping: A Case of Probation Office Interaction

EERO SUONINEN

The interaction between the professional help worker (such as a social worker or a therapist) and his/her client does not consist of simply transmitting and receiving messages. Rather, this interaction is a complex search for a shared understanding. In this article, I will focus on the subtlety of those means that help work professionals and their clients have at their disposal when creating shared understanding. This I will do by introducing some of the findings of my discourse analytical work on interaction in probation office. I will follow some of the representatives of the social constructionist tradition, such as John Shotter (1993) and Kenneth Gergen (1994), in viewing shared understanding as not self evident, but as something that must be created and re-created over and over again, in and through ongoing negotiations by the participants of interaction. My research forms part of a larger research project, called 'Institutions of Helping and their Activities as Everyday Practices'.[1] By institutions of helping, our project refers to different organisations in the field of social work and therapy.

When we talk to each other, we choose the words and concepts we think will convey our meaning in the best possible way. But words do not usually carry just single, unambiguous meanings – instead, they are bearers of a meaning potential with multiple interpretations. For example, one potential interpretation may be culturally 'face threatening' but another interpretation 'positive' or understandable. One of the ways that we as language users have at our disposal to address the problem of multiple interpretations is the 'marking' (or indexing) of words that carry ambiguous meaning potential. This marking can take the form of different tones; or of 'adding' something extra during the course of the conversation. I have come to suspect that in conversation, there is a lot more sensitivity to potentially 'embarrassing' matters than what we normally assume as mundane actors or even researchers. In my article, I will look at markings where one of the participants in the conversation is doing something 'extra' in order to accentuate that a topic is somehow sensitive or difficult to handle. This sort of sensitivity may be an essential part of help work encounters, because institutions of helping are specifically designed to handle issues that are somehow difficult. Following David Silverman (1997) I will use the term 'delicate' of such sensitive (or vexed) issues, which we often also interpret as emotional. As a starting point, I am employing a very flexible strategy in observing the data: all those instances of speech that in some way depart from plain simple talk may be markers of delicacy in a way that is essential for the creation of shared understanding.

My basic assumption is that there are no universal, clear-cut rules laying out what is delicate. Negotiating what is a delicate matter and what is a routine issue is always a local process (Silverman ibid., pp. 77-78; Heath, 1988; Bergman, 1992; see also Garfinkel, 1967). Accordingly, in analysing the data, I am trying – as much as possible – to distance myself from my own pre-understanding about the things that are usually considered delicate in our culture. What I want to do instead is to consult the data: what kind of matters are regularly marked as delicate, and in what way are they marked? My data consist of 10 encounters between probation officers (these, as a rule, are social workers), and their clients. These encounters have been audio-taped and transcribed in detail.

The aim of this particular professional encounter is to provide the social worker with such information about the client that is needed for writing a suitability assessment report about the client, whose suitability for community service is judged. The statement is important since it is one of the crucial documents on which the jury will base its verdict. Community service is a 'soft' alternative to prison sentence: instead of being imprisoned, the sentenced person can lead a normal life as long as he or she performs some (usually four) hours of community service a week, according to an agreed timetable, and under supervision. The interactional sequence in these assessment interviews normally goes as follows: first the social worker informs the client, as much as is needed, about the community service alternative; then he or she asks questions about the items listed on the assessment form, one by one. The specified items include training and work experience; financial situation; social relations; housing; health; substance abuse; and the client's potential need for additional support services. In addition, most of the employees also give advice to the client, or offer their assessment about the client's overall situation. This happens normally towards the end of the interview. However, there is plenty of flexibility within this overall scheme (informing, asking questions, and giving advice), as each case is different, and so are the personalities involved.

The article is divided into three parts. I will first discuss an extract of my data, in order to give an idea about the different ways of marking delicacy. I will then make a suggestion about the kind of things that seem to be marked delicate. Thirdly, I will try to outline the functions of delicacy marking in the institution of professional social work. The basic purpose of this article is to illustrate what is possible in probation office interaction, not to offer a statistical analysis or sweeping generalisations about the frequency of those possibilities.

How Delicacy is Marked

My starting point, thus, was the idea that whatever constitutes a departure from the plain simple (or straightforward) course of conversation can possibly be a sign of delicacy (of one sort or another). These departures may include:[2]

- perturbations or hesitations: pauses, word repetitions and additional fillers
- hedging or softening words: 'softer' alternatives in the choice of words
- humour or playfulness
- hedging or softening explanations or accounts; either before or after the delicate item

The following extract serves to illustrate departures from plain simple communication in a way that may indicate delicacy. It looks like the social worker is saying something like 'It is important that you won't lie to me'. It is noticeable that the social worker does not say this explicitly; instead, she seems to talk in a much more complicated way.[3]

Extract 1 Different ways of marking delicacy

1   SW: In the assessment one does not n- does not need to

```
2            worry about crimes or anythi[ng
3     C:                              [Yea
4     SW:  Whereas in the background information[4], on the other
5          hand, (.) it is permitted to (2) like for
6          example like if you look at this (.) summary then
7          there, (.) [it,
8     C:              [Yea
9     SW:  You were judged guilty there in any case. (1)
10         Afterwards I was wondering whether you were
11         fooling us here or ( ) was the last heh an attempt
12         like to avoid (already) this matter ((after "fooling
13         us" there is laughter up until now)) since it after all
14         stood in such a contradiction [to the record where
15    C:                                 [my-hy
16    SW:  you had confessed .hh But that is an old story it
17         does not matter any more.
```

There are many kinds of departures in the extract:

PERTURBATIONS:
- Repetition ('does not n- does not') on line 1.
- Extra pauses; twice 'like', once 'in any case' on lines 5-9.
- Complicated search for main point on lines 6,7 and 9.
- The 'extra' 'after all' on line 13.

WORDS:
- Instead of talking about 'lying'; the social worker says 'fooling us' (line 11).
- Instead of 'you were obviously fooling us' she says 'I was wondering whether you were fooling us' (line 10).
- A careful expression 'it is permitted' is used, and not something like 'one must consider...' (line 5).

HUMOUR:
- Laughter and speaking with laughter in one's voice, lines 10 to 11.

EXPLANATIONS:
- On the last line, 'But that is an old story it does not matter any more'.
- Also the alternative attempt at an account for 'fooling': 'or was it last ...' (lines 11-12).

What is marked as a delicate issue is 'fooling us' on line 11. This is done by (1) the many perturbations before the potentially hot issue, (2) softening the words used for the issue (3) laughter starting from the first mention of the issue and (4) explanations after the issue. In the extract where the social worker does not ask questions but delivers information, the minimal responses of the client are enough to indicate that the speech of the social worker does make sense to him. After this brief illustration, let us turn to the second question mentioned in the beginning: what kinds of things are usually marked as delicate?

What Kinds of Things are Marked as Delicate?

I assume that what is marked as delicate is neither known beforehand nor a coincidence but an essential part of the sense making process. The appropriate strategy for studying delicacy, then, consists of trying to interpret the local particularity of each delicacy marking.

Delicacy marking is often an *indication of the special character of an issue in the moral sense*. For example, stealing cars may be a much more delicate issue in most conversational environments than, say, fishing (as a harmless hobby). Thus, it would be 'natural' for a social worker to ask her/his client a simple question like 'By the way, have you been out fishing lately?', but it would be unlikely for her/him to ask (unless it is explicitly marked as a humorous question) 'By the way, have you been stealing any cars lately?'. This is the case even in probation office conversations, where crime ultimately is the subject matter of the encounter. In this sense, it seems that there is a pedagogical aspect involved: the client is guided towards recognising and acknowledging some of the values that can be thought to be the most essential ones from the point of view of probation work. It is thus not surprising that the social worker marks often as delicate such issues as the expected discipline in the community service, the descriptions of the crimes the client has committed, the client's ability to control his drinking[5], and the ability to manage his life in general. Still they are delicate during the course of the encounter only to the extent that they are marked delicate. Extract 1, presented above, gives an illustration of this kind of moral work.

These issues are also potentially face-threatening to the client, since they include elements that can be interpreted as guilt-invoking. In communication, hedging may prove to be an excellent way of *saving the client's face.* Face-saving activities may lessen the risk that each party digs in deeper in their opposite positions. The client, too, can mark issues as delicate in his turns, and it is possible that there is a 'set of codes' of delicacy which gets its exact form in the course of the professional encounter: if one of the parties in conversation marks an issue as delicate, the other party is likely to 'tune in' and join in this marking in the ensuing conversation.

There are also instances where the social worker marks as delicate such issues that involve her/his own work. These instances occur at such points in conversation where *his/her own face* may be threatened. These instances are indicative of the kind of impression that the social worker wants to construct about herself. The following extract is an example a self-reflecting comment that was uttered in order to close off a questioning sequence where the social worker tried to find out what was the postal address of a homeless client.

Extract 2 Humorous self-reflection on the part of the social worker

1   SW: Okay. (1.5) I'm questioning like a policeman.

With this additional humorous comment (some kind of 'explanation') ('I'm questioning like a policeman'), the social worker is actually distancing herself from a policeman's authoritarian image and comes out very different from an interrogating police.

In my data, usually the image the social workers try to convey and maintain about themselves includes such characteristics as being client-centred and understanding (though not easily fooled); not wanting to control overtly; not wanting to give superficial advice or be a mere bureaucrat. This kind of image-building may have a similar interactional function as the activities attuned to save the client's face: to contribute to the *smoothness and flexibility of the shared sense-making.*

The examples I mentioned above are from such sequences in professional encounters that may threaten either the client's or the social worker's face. Delicacy markers are to be found, however, in some of the social worker's turns of talk which do not belong to this category. The following extract serves us as an example:

Extract 3 The fragile nature of professional-client relations

1   SW: If you are sentenced to community service then

```
2         what happens is that (.) that that (.) I will then
3         carry out the practicalities that is .hhh (.) that is
4         that is we will go on working together.
```

Starting from line 2, the extract includes markers of delicacy: the use of seemingly futile words ('that that'; 'that is' repeatedly), gaps and an audible in-breath. This sensitivity is produced in such places towards the end of the conversation where the *personal relation between the client and the professional* is described. What the social worker is here constructing is obviously some kind of close relationship with her client – rather like friendship – where emotional aspects in tone of speech are included; aspects that would not be reflected in plain simple matter-of-fact talk.

Choices of Strategy

It is important to observe that all potentially delicate issues are not always and automatically marked as delicate in the same way. Firstly, some social workers (two out of ten in my data) seem to prefer the strategy of straight, man-to-man talk, where there are very few clear markers of delicacy in situations which normally would display a sense of delicacy. This is illustrated in the following two extracts:

Extract 4 Enquiry about alcohol consumption, without clear markers of delicacy

Case 1:

```
1    SW:   You're healthy (reference to the previous issue)
2          (1)
3    SW:   .hhh Well what about substance abuse.
```

Case 2:

```
1    SW:   .hhh But now then this substance abuse
2          (5)
3    SW:   .hhh Every week?
4    C:    Yea
5    SW:   Daily?
6    C:    Let's say once or twice a week now these days
```

In these openings, there are no more markers of delicacy than in other openings. This does not necessarily imply, however, that the client's heavy drinking would not be marked as delicate in the ensuing discussion. In Case 2, the discussion continues with focus on just such delicacy.

Extract 5 The emerge of delicacy after the subject has been discussed for some time

(Case 2 continues)

```
1    SW:  How much
2         (5)
3    C:   As much as I can handle.
4         (1)
5    SW:  .hhh That's quite a lot hhh. (5) As much as you can handle. What should
6         I write down That is, properly pissed (.) as much as you've got money
7         or booze.
8    C:   Yea.
9    SW   Don't you ever stop until you're completely paralysed?
```

Delicacy is marked in the social worker's talk by a delay (one second pause on line 4) before responding to the client, more audible breathing than usually (line 5), an additional filler 'quite' (line 5) and extra talking to himself 'What should I write down' (lines 5 - 6). The client's long delay before answering (line 2) may also be a mark of delicacy. It is interesting that the social worker picks up the straight talk strategy on line 9.

Another example of shifts in delicacy marking represents, in a way, an opposite strategy. Sometimes the first production of an issue may be clearly marked as delicate by the social worker, but during the course of the conversation, an issue that has previously been delicate is gradually turned into an item of shared understanding. Let us now focus on such a sequence. In this extract, there are three instances where a potentially delicate issue, work discipline, is discussed. These instances appear here in their original order of presentation.

Extract 6 The construction of 'work discipline': from delicacy to a matter-of-fact issue

Phase 1: (the first instance where need of discipline is discussed)

Doing 'Delicacy' in Institutions of Helping 111

```
1   SW:    And then when the timetable has been agreed and
2          also the plan for the service has been written down,
3          (.) that is where this service will take place and, (.)
4          these, (.) such basic things what tasks there are or
5   →      whe- where they then are and what one does
6   →      there. (.) .hhhh Then, (.) one has to stick to ithhhh,
7   →      (.) like a slave and and ((these two words are
8   →      uttered with laughter)) like with discipline
```

The social worker then moves on and spends a couple of minutes giving examples of the kind of work discipline that is expected.

Phase 2:

```
1   SW:    That is, (.) this is the, (.) discipline that one has to
2          stick to the timetable
```

Again, a couple of minutes are spent in telling the client about the kinds of medical reasons that can be accepted as reasons for absenting.

Phase 3:

```
1   SW:    And this is the discipline we are controlling...
```

In Phase 1, the social worker clearly marks as delicate the metaphor 'like a slave' and the word 'discipline' (lines 5 and 8) using (1) pre-delicate markers (such as repeating pauses, in-breaths and the lengthening of the sound) (2) laughing (3) and the use of the extra word ('like'). In the second phase, the social worker uses the expression 'the (.) discipline' in a more straightforward way, still marking 'discipline' with a meaningful pause. In the third phase, the social worker moves on to a very straightforward expression 'the discipline' without gaps or any other hesitations. It is possible that during the three phases 'discipline' has been (in a way) institutionalised as a shared local meaning ('The discipline'). Although only incidental example and not commented on by the client (because the social worker is not asking anything, but only delivering information), this strategy of 'doing away with delicacy' seems very interesting.

The Functions of Delicacy in Professional Encounters

The presence of the kinds of extra features of speech discussed above (features which could even be called 'disturbances'— perturbations or hesitations, looking for the 'softest' possible words, humour and softening explanations) may look like lack of professional routine in handling difficult matters. I would like to suggest, however, that they may constitute an essential part of the communicative act itself and an essential quality of professional skills.

I will attempt here a tentative synthesis of the issues outlined above. It would seem that the production of delicacy might have several meaningful functions for the professional encounter:

1. *The 'pedagogical' maintenance of morally special issues:*
  - When an issue is marked as delicate, it becomes distinctive from less important matters.

2. *Saving client's face:*
  - Prevents 'turn-off' reactions in issues that may be felt to be threatening (psychological level).
  - Maintains continuity and smoothness in conversation (interactional level).

3. *The production of the social worker as an understanding person:*
  - Creates a positive atmosphere for example for giving personal advice and hints.

4. *The construction of a 'local culture' between the social worker and the client* (This might even be called an overall function?).
  - Meanings that are thought to be central can be turned into self-evident (shared) items.
  - Helps to build a long-term professional-client relationship including also emotional aspect.

Delicacy marking, then, is a way of foregrounding issues without threatening the client's face even when these issues are potentially sensitive. The encounters are more easily managed and their future will be smoother, while even the pedagogical functions of social work are fulfilled.

It seems to me that sensitivity and delicacy in conversation are signs of the probation officers' willingness to do more than just strictly follow (in the narrow sense) their job description and assess their clients' suitability for community service. In many different ways, they lend their support to their clients so that as many as possible of those clients that are selected for community service would also succeed in it – and also in their lives in the long run.

Some Problems and Possible Solutions

I hope to have illustrated how a potentially delicate issues may be uttered by means of different kinds of styles or strategies. By the concept 'potentially delicate' I refer to the notion that there are some kinds of cultural regularities (some issues are regularly interpreted as delicate), but these regularities are not deterministic in their nature. The actors (in probation office encounters) may call up the potential delicacy of some issues or not. These kinds of choices are essential from the point of view of the mutual sense making process, because they invite the other party to accept certain ways of seeing and discussing things. The point – that is a great challenge to the research – is thus that social workers are much more than mere 'cultural dopes', automatically following simple routines or institutional obligations. This, then, makes for the rationale of studying in a detailed way the variety of different styles or strategies that are possible in dealing with difficult issues in help work interaction, and of studying how they work in practice.

If the starting point is to study the subtleties of how actors construct a mutual understanding in interactional processes the very essence of which is their ever-changing nature, it is no good to analyse e.g. questionnaires or interviews made after the professional-client conversations. Sensitive details cannot be recalled afterwards. They may mostly have gone unnoticed from the actors even in the interactional situation. It is necessary to analyse the original conversation between a social worker and her/his client and make a very thorough transcription of the data. In recognising and interpreting the details of the data, I have found the transcription methods used in conversation analysis especially useful (e.g. Drew and Heritage, 1992; Silverman, 1997). If we also try to find out what special meanings are being constructed by the details of the actors' language use, we will find useful methods from such discourse analytical approaches where variation in the meaning constructions is analysed (e.g. Potter and Wetherell, 1987; Billig et al., 1988; Silverman, 1993, pp. 120-124; Suoninen, 1997). These two research traditions, conversation analysis and discourse analysis, differ to some extent. Conversation analysis deals mostly with the 'formal' structure of interaction, while discourse analysis is also interested in meaning structures appealed to in the course of interaction. However, since their theoretical orientation is similarly focused on joint sense making they can be accommodated in one interpretative framework. In this sense, the tools of discourse analysis and conversation analysis may combine into an efficient approach.

One concrete difficulty in this particular mode of analysis that seeks markers of delicacy is the fact that a 'departure' from the plain simple communication may mean different things which are not always obvious from the surface. A departure may be a sign of delicacy, but it may as well be something else. One explanation might be based on the influence of personal style in people's talk: some people speak with less hesitations and more certain manners than others. In this sense, it is necessary to compare not just different people's styles, but the different departures within one person's talk. An additional difficulty is brought about by the fact that not all perturbations arise from perceived delicacy: they may also be caused by the person in question just searching through his memory, or more concretely taking notes. Unfortunately, note taking does not show in the audio-tape and is thus impossible to ascertain in the transcript. On the other hand, these problems are made less grievous by the fact that, in the end, what is most essential in the construction of interaction is not what the speaker meant with the changes in the tone or style she/he used, but how the other party in conversation interpreted those changes. These interpretations (which are only partially in scope of the present paper) are worth studying from the contributions of the parties in conversation, though this is a challenging task.

Notes

1 The research project is funded by Finnish Academy.
2 There are also some other related terms used to mean some kind of departures from the plain simple course of conversation, e.g. 'caution' (Maynard 1991), 'expressive caution', 'litotes' and 'discretion' (Bergman 1992). I have tried to avoid overlapping of terms as much as possible.
3 Symbols used in the extracts:

SW: refers to social worker in probation office
C: refers to client
(.) (2) parentheses are used for pause (numbers in parentheses indicate elapsed time in silence in seconds; a dot indicates a gap of less than a second)
[left (square) brackets indicate the point at which a current speaker's talk is overlapped by another's talk.
.hh indicates an audible inbreath.
4 Background information is routinely filed when the client is under 18 years old.
5 According to the social workers, drinking is the most common reason for calling an end to community service.

Bibliography

Bergmann, J. (1992), 'Veiled Morality: Notes on Discretion in Psychiatry', in Drew, P. and Heritage, J. (eds) *Talk at Work*, Cambridge University Press, pp. 137-62.
Billig, Michael, Susan Condor, Derek Edwards, Mike Gane, David Middleton and Alan Radley (1988), *Ideological Dilemmas*, Sage, London.
Drew, P. and Heritage, J. (eds) (1992), *Talk at Work*, Cambridge University Press, Cambridge.
Gergen, Kenneth (1994), *Realities and Relationships – Soundings in Social Construction*, Harvard University Press, Cambridge.
Garfinkel, Harold (1967), *Studies in Ethnomethodology*, Englewood Cliffs, Prentice-Hall, NJ.
Maynard, D. W. (1991), 'Interaction and Asymmetries in Clinical Discourse', *American Journal of Sociology*, vol. 97, no. 2, pp. 448-95.
Potter, Jonathan and Margaret Wetherell (1987), *Discourse and Social Psychology*, Sage, London.
Shotter, John (1993), *Conversational Realities – Constructing Life through Language*, Sage, London.
Silverman, David (1993), *Interpreting Qualitative Data – Methods for Analysing Talk, Text and Interaction*, Sage, London.
Silverman, David (1997), *Discourses of Counselling – HIV Counselling as Social Interaction*, Sage, London.
Suoninen, Eero (1997), *Miten tutkia moniäänistä ihmistä? Diskurssianalyyttisen tutkimusotteen kehittelyä*, Acta Universitatis Tamperensis 580, Tampereen yliopisto, Tampere.

6 Speaking of Emotions in Child Protection Practices

HANNELE FORSBERG

Introduction

In this study I will be examining the ways in which child protection workers conceptualise and speak about their clients' emotions. I am interested in what kind of emotional rules frame the encounters between clients and experts of child protection and particularly in how and what kind of emotions are produced and presented in these encounters. What are the functions and implications of expressed emotions?

Using the child protection work done in social welfare offices and in family support centres as case examples, I will describe child protection work as emotion work. Rather than approaching emotions as subjective, individual and untouched phenomena, I will look at the contribution to our understanding of emotions and helping work provided by the idea of emotions as socially constructed phenomena.

I will begin with a brief discussion of the rather limited literature focusing on child protection as emotion work. I will then clarify my approach to emotions in this particular study. Next, I will discuss the setting and data of my study and then move on to examine the child protection workers' ways of verbalising emotions in social welfare offices and in family support centres. The study concludes with a discussion of my findings and their implications for social work practices.

Child Protection as the Domain of Emotions

Child protection has been described as the domain of forbidden and hidden emotions (Peltonen, 1996). Anger, bitterness, fear and the sense of being rejected are perceived as self-evident and natural emotions in child protection; nevertheless, we know very little about child protection in terms of emotions.

Emotions have rarely been thematised as the subject of empirical study within child protection research, or social work research in general. Has the belief that the worker is always neutral and objective made emotions a taboo? On the other hand, emotions are usually regarded as belonging within the realm of psychology, and their role in social work is generally ambiguous. Within social work, emotions are more typically perceived as something undefined, individual, often wordless, as something inside one's head or body, in other words, as something difficult to study.

However, this basis has started to totter; emotions are no longer regarded solely as something disturbing and vague, as something that we cannot study. Emotions have begun to be perceived as an integral part of individual helping work. Particularly in women's studies, the emotional dimension of helping work is beginning to be observed (e.g. Wise, 1990; Eräsaari, 1990). The concept of rationality of responsibility (see Simonen, 1990, pp. 25-26), developed within women's studies, combines in an exiting manner the dimension of emotional commitment to work with the dimension describing the rational aspect of work. More typical in Western thought has been the polarisation of rationality and feeling (Crawford et al., 1992, p. 17). Emphasis has been given to the way social workers use their intuitive emotional knowledge within child protection (Forsberg, 1996; Heino, 1997; for other initiatives which approach social work as emotion work, see England, 1986; Rostila, 1990; Tuomi, 1992; Lee Treweek, 1996; Ruane, 1996). A new kind of interest towards emotions is on the rise in many disciplines, comprising philosophers (Niiniluoto and Räikkä, 1996), psychologists (Crawford et al., 1992; Harré and Stearns, 1995) and social scientists (Gubrium, 1992; Gergen, 1994; James and Gabe, 1996), who also offer interpretative resources on the reflection of child protection as emotional work.

Besides being a characteristic of the client relationship, emotions can provide one source of knowledge for the experts of child protection. Another example of how the domain of emotions is present in child protection encounters is the way in which the client's emotions are made topical and treated. The latter is the dimension I will concentrate on in this study.

Towards a Constructionist Approach

What kind of interpretative resources are there, then, in scientific discourse with which to approach emotions? The possible approaches could roughly be divided into three loose camps. First, one commonly held approach seems to be *to avoid discussing emotions*. Emotions are either considered unimportant and not part of the rational realm of science, or emotions are considered to be a subject matter which academic processes are seen to manipulate and distort. Methodology for studying emotions has not received much attention. It is thought that emotions should be allowed to remain aside and unaltered in science (James and Gabe, 1996, p. 2).

Secondly, in cases when previous research has considered emotions, it has, for the most part, approached emotions from a realistic or *naturalistic point of view*. This has been done either by using a phenomenological viewpoint and treating emotions as experiences, or by measuring and observing different (physical) expressions of emotions. These approaches are based on the idea that emotions such as love, fear, hate etc. exist naturally and self-evidently and that we can 'read' these emotions from facial expressions, tone of voice and bodily movements. The approaches presuppose that emotions are individual, even though it is generally thought that they can have an impact on the interaction between people (Gergen, 1994, p. 220, 222).

The third camp of researchers of emotions base their study on the belief that our culture has social vocabularies for emotions. These researchers do not treat emotions as self-evident truths but as something that finds its form in people's actions and in social relations. From this *constructionist point of view*, emotions are sociocultural constructions. They find their form in social activity in a certain historical and cultural context with its own emotional norms (e.g. Harré, 1986; Stearns, 1995, pp. 41-44; Egerton, 1995; Gergen, 1994; Harré and Parrott, 1996). Constructionism is the great new theoretical paradigm of the late twentieth century in emotions research, unifying various disciplines. This approach has signified a move away from a perception of emotions as fixed and natural categories; emotions may vary depending on the context. According to this approach emotions can be recognised 'in and through communication, the hallmark of public life', as Gubrium (1992, p. 167) points out.

If we accept the fact that emotions are individual and natural, we cannot pose questions about the social aspects of emotions. However, emotions as social acts in child protection practices were the reason why I took notice of emotions. When gathering the data on which I will base my analysis in this study, I was struck by the social formation of emotion, and I realised that emotions are not independent of acts of emotion management. I needed an approach which does not deny emotions as a research topic or treat them as self-evident truths, and which allows me to see how emotions are named, sorted and categorised by institutions, such as child protection organisations. My interests led me to the constructionist camp. In this way, I came to approach emotions in the context of child protection as a process of putting them into words; without language emotions are unarticulated. This does not mean that I would in advance exclude the deeper-than-words level of experience or the bodily aspect of emotions from my study. Instead, it means that I will pay attention to these aspects as well in so far as they are made topical in the contexts examined.

Setting and Data

The evidence and the examples I will present to illustrate the construction of emotions in child protection practices are taken from my recent doctoral study of family definitions within child protection practices, where emotional issues have become topical. Thus, I have not intended emotions to be the main topic of my study. The material for the study was collected by ethnographic methods, mainly by observing, in three Finnish social welfare offices during 1990 and in three family support centre units during 1995. Both social welfare offices and family support centres are examples of institutions where the handling of other people's feelings (and those of the workers), in other words, emotional labour and management of emotions (Hochschild, 1983; Gubrium, 1992) are part of the everyday work.

In Finland, the implementation of micro-level child protection or child welfare is primarily in the hands of local authorities, i.e. municipalities. Put in simple terms, the Finnish child welfare system is obligated to take measures (according to the Child Welfare Act of 1983), if the health or the development of a child is seriously endangered by lack of care or other conditions at home, or if the child seriously endangers his or her health or development, the extreme case being that the child is taken into care or substitute care is provided. Social workers in social welfare offices often work according to what is known as the integrated social work model. This means that, besides the child protection work, a social worker is also responsible for such matters as the treatment of intoxicant abuse problems and assistance in financial problems. The official job description of the social workers whom I observed covered these tasks. For this study, I have analysed only client situations which dealt with child protection issues.

Family support centres[1] are part of the municipal child welfare system in Finland, but they are a fairly recent working method, established only in a very few municipalities simultaneously with the dismantling of the system of child welfare institutions. Family support centres attempt to solve the psycho-social problems of families with children. The work is motivated by the view that the family (especially the biological family) is of utmost importance to the development of a child, even in cases where the capability of the parents to take care of their children is considered inadequate. The expressed aim of the family support centres is to work in a solution-oriented and family-centred way, and the focus of helping is in the use of people's own resources. Most of the clients are referred to family support centres by the social workers of local social welfare offices.

The idea of comparing these two practices arose from the fact that social welfare offices and family support centres operate from the same legislative basis and deal with similar child protection problems. However, important differences exist between them, too. Social workers in social welfare offices (who have an academic education) are higher in the professional hierarchy of the child protection system than the staff members[2] of family support centres. Because of their professional position, social workers in social welfare offices have more legal responsibilities, but more legal power as well, in child protection cases than do staff members of family support centres. They also have heavier case loads than child protection workers in the family support centres. But, what is important, after being established the family support centres constructed themselves as something different, as an alternative to the child protection work traditionally done by social workers in social welfare offices. In a way, this was a challenge to this comparative setting.

The material analysed for this study consists, for the most part, of 37 child protection encounters in social welfare offices and 30 client meetings in family support centres. To a lesser extent, I have analysed discussions among child protection workers outside client meetings.

Contrasting Feeling Rules

Social welfare offices and family support centres have both similar and differing ways for dealing with emotions and for making emotions topical in client encounters. Their ways are similar in the sense that in about half of the client encounters people hardly touch the topic of emotions in either setting. The encounters focus on dealing with and taking care of different practical matters, such as talking about money matters and trying to find solutions to a son's or a daughter's problems at school. It is in the cases where emotions are taken up and talked about with greater intensity that the two settings differ from each other; their predominant ways of doing this are, for the most part, different. This study focuses on this last, selected part of my data, because I am interested in the differences between the two settings in dealing with emotions. However, highlighting the differences of focus in dealing with emotions does not mean that all the activities in the child protection units would fall under either of these opposing categories. I will underline differences at the expense of similarities, interfaces and overlappings. I will pick out such select extracts from the actual data where contrasts are most striking. This kind of construction is potentially valuable in that it can provide a sense of confrontation and contrast, as well as bring alternative interpretations to our notice (Coffey and Atkinson, 1996, p. 125).

On the basis of my analysis of the data, it seems possible to speak about ruling local cultures (Gubrium, 1989) or 'emotionologies'[3] (Stearns and Stearns, 1988; ref. Harré and Gillett, 1994, p. 148) of social welfare offices, on the one hand, and of family support centres, on the other, in assigning meanings to clients' emotions. The first one is connected with the problem-centred tradition of helping applied in encountering and treating child protection problems, while the second draws from the solution- and resource-oriented disciplines of helping. The two seem to have different ruling feeling rules when dealing with clients' problems. Feeling rules guide emotion work and set limits to the interpretative resources available to the workers. It is possible to recognise feeling rules by examining how the experts assess their clients' feelings and set limits to the emotional choices of clients. Feeling rules are statements about clients' supposed feelings (Hochshild, 1983, pp. 49-57).

Revealing and Naming Feelings

In social welfare offices, emotions are discussed more often and with a greater emphasis in client encounters where the need for child protection is interpreted as evident. In these situations, the social workers have also openly taken up their worries concerning child protection in the discussions with the clients. The clients have been aware of the fact that child protection authorities are worried about their or their families' situation. It may, in fact, come to pass that in social welfare offices, where the aim is integrated social work, clients can be categorised as clients of child protection without them knowing about it. A social worker can, for example, become concerned about the ability of a mother to care for her children because of her constant financial worries and start to monitor the situation, but the worker's concern does not come up in the conversations with the client. In client meetings where social workers were somehow worried about the child's situation in the family but did not have any serious evidence against the parents, it was the rule to be quite polite and not to pose serious questions about the client's emotions. Considerate and discreet actions of this kind can be interpreted to aim at creating a confidential relationship with the client. They have been described in many studies related to child protection practices (e.g. Dingwall et al., 1995; Kuronen, 1994).

The borderline of politeness and caution is crossed in child protection situations which social workers regard as serious. Very often such appraisal is based on a long mutual relationship. In these situations, emotions are also more explicitly present. They are talked about, but one can also feel their presence in the atmosphere, in facial expressions, and in tones of voice.

In the next extract taken from a discussion in a social welfare office, a client, the mother of two children (M), is visiting her social worker (S). The children have been placed in a children's home some time ago. The social worker keeps contact with the mother because she is still considered to be important to her children in an emotional sense, and it is this relationship that the social worker is trying to support by meeting the mother.

> S: How has your life been this past six months?
> M: I don't know.
> S: Have you been contented?
> M: Maybe, I don't know.

S: Have you had other difficulties except for those with money?
M: No.
S: You were dating this Pekka Suomalainen, but it didn't work out, did it?
M: No.
S: How do you feel about this past six months? Are you happy?
M: Well, quite happy, I guess.
S: So, Susanna and Sami have now been in the children's home for exactly six months. Do you feel guilty?
M: I don't know, maybe.
(On the social worker's initiative, the talk moves on to the mother's drinking and housing situation; the social worker also leads the conversation back to the mother's emotions.)
S: How did you feel when you were packing (refers to the fact that the mother moved away from her flat), after having lived there all through Susanna's and Sami's childhood?
M: I don't know.
S: What about Susanna's and Sami's clothes, have you kept them?
M: I threw them away with the rubbish.
(Conversation continues with talk about the children's visiting their mother.)

Several questions concerning emotions are posed to the mother. With her questions, the social worker is trying to get the mother *to name her feelings* in the situation when she gave up her children. But she only gets the scanty 'I don't know' or 'maybe' as the answer. It is worth paying attention to the social worker's questions. As a rule, they offer answering alternatives with an implicitly negative charge, like 'Are you feeling guilty?' Guilt and suffering are suggested as the mother's hidden or unknown emotions. The mother is expected to feel guilt, sorrow and pain, because she crossed the limit of being a good parent. The social worker seems to be most interested in past family events and the mother's emotions about them. The striking tone in dealing with the client's emotions is very negative.

On the basis of the data collected in social welfare offices, we may present the interpretation that the function of the negatively charged emotion talk is not so much to point at clients' failures as to make them acknowledge their failures and weaknesses. The experts offer hypotheses to the clients about their emotions, and by doing so, they invite their clients to open up. The idea is that, through this kind of acknowledgement, they could embark on a collaborative relationship, the past and present 'emotional lumps' – as the social workers call them – could be discarded and the client would be ready for something new. But this idea does not necessarily come true in practice, if the client does not respond to the social worker's invitation, as was the case in the previous example.

The backstage, or the discussions among the social workers themselves, is the other context where emotions often become topical in social welfare offices. In the next extract, social workers discuss amongst themselves the mother we saw in the previous example visiting a social welfare office:

> S: One has to admit that such poor expression of emotions is typical of that family. The mother can't express her feelings. For example, she can only express her devotion to her children by crying in difficult situations and moaning that she doesn't want to lose them. But in everyday situations she just can't say to her children that please, come and let me hold you. I love you. It would be so unlike her in a cultural sense to behave like that.

The negative tone concerning emotions is evident here as well. The mother is portrayed as very poor, even dumb, in her emotional expression towards her children. Beyond this negative frame, we can discern a norm for the feelings and the expressions of feelings of a good mother. To be a loving and caring mother means recognising and showing it through words and through physical contact with one's children.

Many authors have pointed out the close relationship between moral order and emotions. Morality is present in both of the previous examples as well. The expressed emotions are a confirmation of societal values: the mother is expected to feel guilty because of doing wrong. A number of emotion words belong to the specific language of moral criticism, to the system of judgement, both moral and legal (Crawford et al, 1992, pp. 122-126). Is the client mother challenging the moral order, resisting the authority of the social worker or just reflecting her conflicting emotions in a situation when she is not expressing her guilt clearly in the client encounter? In any case, it is clear that the context of child protection frames the ways in which the client mother is expressing or not expressing her emotions. The clients identify their emotions according to their knowledge of the social context at hand.

When made a topic, emotions were generally described in social welfare offices as cold, bitter, distant, full of guilt etc.; in other words, as something very negative. In a way this is easy to understand because the setting is a context where problems are dealt with. In anthropological research, it has been noticed that it is more common to express emotions when dealing with problems (Jokinen, 1996, p. 26). In the social welfare offices, the social workers believed that recognising, naming and verbalising the (hidden) negative emotions is a way for the clients to solve their problems. The interest of the experts lay more in the past. They believed that working off past emotional burdens would help take a new view of the future. Janet Landman (1996, p. 105), for example, has pointed out that we tend to think of negative emotions as particularly paralysing, but in principle, they have much motivational potential. Acknowledging and working through the negative emotions has the potential to free one from the thrall of the past and to entertain a better future.

Reinterpreting Negative Feelings

In the family support centres, the role of emotions seemed to be different from that in the social welfare offices, especially in practices which were framed quite solidly by the solution-oriented method[4], as the following example taken from a family support centre suggests. There are two staff members (S1, S2), a mother (M) and a father (F, who is not visible in this extract) present in the meeting. The issues discussed are similar to the example from a social welfare office, because the child of the parent has been removed from his home to substitute care some time ago.

> S1: How have you been doing this past five months that Niilo (the child) has been away? Is there anything that's different now?
> M: It's lonelier now. There are only two of us left. I've started to think of something to do. I've begun to bake bread just to have something to do. It's a way to save money too.
> ( )
> S1: Is there anything else you used to like to do, which you could think of doing now?
> M: I don't know. I've started to bake bread and I like that very much.

In this extract, emotions become topical after the staff member's question 'How have you been doing?'. The mother answers the question by describing her feelings. She is feeling lonely, because her child is not at home any more. The experts, however, are not interested in her feeling of loneliness, but pass over the mother's statement. When the mother says that she has started to bake to have something to do, one of the experts interprets it as something that feels good and wants to know if there are other things which give a good feeling to the mother. In her answer the mother agrees that baking feels good, but she does not seem to find anything else that would feel good, for now.

At the end of the meeting the experts give positive feedback to the parents, where they try to further strengthen the parents' positive feeling:

> What we feel very good about is that you've been able to control your drinking. The fact that Niilo (the child) exists must be very important to you. Although he's not at home any more it was good to hear that you (the father) have been able to stay away from your old friends and you (the mother) have found the baking, which feels good. You could try to find more of these things that feel good.

In the same way as in the social welfare offices, parenthood is constructed to be important in an emotional sense in a situation where the child has been removed from his home. But, instead of focusing on the negative feelings of the parents, the staff members try to concentrate on things that make the parents (especially the mother) feel good now and in the near future.

Emotions have an interesting role here. With their questions and with their feedback, the experts attempt to bring out the clients' positive emotions, such as joy and success. Moreover, their statements contain assumptions about the clients' feelings. It is not useful for family members to think negative thoughts and have negative feelings about each other. Every situation has some good aspects, and they are the ones that are important in family support centres. Emotional rules seem to be quite opposite to the ruling rules found in the social welfare offices, in a different culture of helping.

Are the child protection workers of the family support centres challenging the common-sense societal values and the moral order when trying to make the mother feel good in a situation where her child is taken away from home because of her incapability to take care of him? Maybe they are just trying to challenge the traditional way of helping. It is in other words worth noticing that happiness, an emotion which the staff members of the family support centres try to evoke in client meetings, also has a moral aspect. Happiness is connected with freedom and autonomy, on the one hand, and with security and love, on the other (Crawford et all, 1992, p. 124). The idea of the experts seems to be to support such positive resources of the mother, and in this way, to encourage her to look into the future in a new way.

The next extract illustrating the positive feedback from the experts shows even better than the previous one how emotions are typically constructed in family support centres. A client family has come to the meeting because of the problems their eldest son has at school.

> S: Timo, it was nice that you came along. You're such a nice and cheerful fellow. We can see that you care about your brother, your sister and your mom and that they care about you.
> Siiri, your calmness and harmony made an impression on us. You have the courage to say what you think about things. You are an open-minded person. You take it easy.
> Toni, you're such an honest and open person. You've been thinking about your school issues and you seem to know what you have to do to do well in school. You're a young man who can express his feelings and that is a good quality, especially in a man.
> Anni, you are clearly the head of this family. You have the power and the will to get things going. You can also negotiate. The way you talk about your kids tells us that your children are very important to you, also the "black angel" Toni.

With his very positive words, the staff member is framing the emotional climate of the client family as loving, caring and open, in a word, great. There is some in-built irony in this, since one cannot help asking how on earth people like this could end up as child protection clients. It is, however, a question of the professional manner of speaking used in the practices of family support centres, and this particular manner of speaking tries to motivate to clienthood and to solving problems. The data extracts presented by the American researcher Gale Miller (1987, pp. 254-256), who has studied family therapy practices, are thrillingly similar, with respect to their stereotypical character – so similar is the manner in which client families are surrounded with feelings of love and mutual caring. Their stereotypical character reveals that there is a professional manner of speaking behind them.

In the family support centres the ruling way of interpreting emotions[5] was different from that in the social welfare offices. First, the child welfare experts in the family support centres were not interested in their clients' past emotions, their interest lay more in the future. Secondly, they tried to put their clients' emotions in a very positive light. The emotions between the members of client families in this child welfare setting were described as loving, caring, warm and happy. Thirdly, the staff members of the family support centres seemed to believe that emotions are linguistic constructions and capable of being changed linguistically. Most of the workers were not interested in the kinds of emotions that are believed to be somewhere beyond words (unknown or hidden). Also, there was a rule which forbade the posing of questions about clients' emotions when they were not present. The experts of the family support centres seemed to believe that the problems of the clients were solved by reinterpreting the negative feelings positively, using positive words instead of negative. In this way, emotions were rational speech acts, like choosing one's style.

Discussion

Many theorists have pointed out the growing significance of psycho-social experts in consulting people's emotions (e.g. Beck and Beck-Gersheim, 1991). Some see the role of psycho-social experts as so remarkable that they are seen to guide the way we are likely to feel, even without us having any contact with them (Rose, 1990; Kivivuori, 1992). In my paper I have offered one example of the ways in which child protection experts manage their clients' emotions.

The widely held ideas in many approaches where emotions are seen as individual, authentic and natural are rendered doubtful by the contrasting images of the two treatment settings I have explored here. It can be argued that emotions exist very much within the treatment philosophies and frameworks used in the local cultures of social welfare offices and family support centres. In the local culture of social welfare offices, the experts seem to believe that there are real emotions hidden somewhere outside the client meeting and that it is helpful for the clients to reveal them in the interaction with experts. In the local culture of family support centres, emotions are more often believed to be speech acts and part of the interactive system with the experts. These two different ways of approaching clients' feelings lead to very different ways of communicating with the clients. The fundamental question from the point of view of social work is, of course, to what extent one succeeds in causing the desired change by these different approaches.

Ultimately, different professional versions for approaching emotions take shape in the encounters between clients and experts. By, for example, going along or by refusing to do so, the clients have an impact on the content and form of emotion discussions, as well as on the success of emotion work in helping them in a problematic situation.

However, on the basis of my data it can be argued that the emotions expressed in child protection practices are, to a great extent, professionally agreed codes of communication and social vocabularies for emotions rather than emotions in their traditional (subjective and natural) meaning. According to Beck and Beck-Gernsheim (1995) the nature of emotions is thus changing; emotions have become empty categories which people themselves must fill in. My analysis of the emotion work of child protection experts is one example of this filling-in work.

Notes

1. From an international point of view, Finnish family support centres are not a unique phenomenon. Similar activities have been organised lately in several Western European countries, for example, in Sweden under the title of 'hemma-hos-arbete' (Hessle, 1997, p. 247), in Britain as part of the varied 'family centre' activities (e.g. Stones, 1994), in Holland (van den Bogaart 1995), and in the United States at least under the name 'family-preservation' (Whittaker, 1990).
2. The staff members of family support centres often have a lower degree educational background than do social workers in social welfare offices, although this is not always the case. Besides their basic professional education, all of the staff members of family support centres have been in training for a couple of years to learn the methods of solution-oriented family work. They do not call themselves social workers, but family workers or child protection workers.
3. Stearns and Stearns (1988, ref. Harre and Gillett, 1994, p. 148) use the word 'emotionology' to refer to the ways in which the people in a particular local culture identify, classify and recognise emotions. Discovering an emotionology means discovering the rules of use of the local vocabulary of emotion words.
4. The solution-focused therapy perspective is well-known and originally developed by Steve de Shazer and Insoo Kim Berg together with their team at the Brief Family Therapy Center in Milwaukee (see e.g. de Shazer, 1985). Solution-orientation is a frame accepted by all the staff members of family support centers in principle, but in practice, they use it differently. Most of the staff members use it as a positive attitude towards clients, some of them as a strict frame for organising the questions they ask the clients, as a way they talk to them and as a way they organise the structure of the whole meeting with the clients. Among the staff members of the family support centres that I have studied, there is a small group of female staff members whose emotion work at times differs from the solution-oriented practices of the main-stream. In

their work, clients' emotions can be localised in their bodies – as pain in the back, as fatigue in legs, as dizziness in the head – and are treated as such. The treatment is nonverbal and physical, massage and relaxing the body, for example. These bodily treated feelings constitute only part of the identity of client mothers.
5   It is really a matter of reinterpretation by the experts. When clients are telling about their problems, the tone of speaking about emotions is as negative as it is in the social welfare offices, but the experts of the family support centres try to reinterpret them in a positive light.

Bibliography

Beck, U. and Beck-Gernsheim, E. (1995), *The Normal Chaos of Love*, Polity Press, Cambridge.
Coffey, A. and Atkinson, P. (1996), *Making Sense of Qualitative Data*, Complementary Research Strategies, Sage, Thousand Oaks and London and New Delhi.
Crawford, J. and Kippax, S. and Onyx, J. and Gault, U. and Benton, P. (1992), *Emotion and Gender*, Sage, London and Newbury Park and New Delhi.
De Shazer, S. (1995), *Keys to Solution in Brief Therapy*, Norton, New York.
Dingwall, R. and Eekelaar, J. and Murray, T. (1995), *The Protection of Children*, Avebury, Aldershot.
Egerton, M. (1995), Emotions and Discoursive Norms, in R. Harré and P. Stearns (eds), *Discursive Psychology in Practice*, Sage, London.
England, H. (1986), *Social Work as Art*, Making Sense for Good Practice, Allen and Unwin, London.
Eräsaari, L. (1990), *Nilkin naamio*, Gummerus, Jyväskylä.
Forsberg, H. (1996), Mikä on tietoa lastensuojelussa? Nonverbaalisen tunnetiedon verbalisointiharjoitus, *Janus*, vol. 4, no. 4, pp. 381-394.
Gergen, K. J. (1994), *Realities and Relationships*, Soundings in Social Construction, Harvard Univ. Press, Cambridge.
Gubrium, J. F. (1989), Local Culture and Service Policy, in J. F. Gubrium, and D. Silverman (eds), *The Politics of Field Research*, Sociology Beyond Enlightments, Sage, London and Newbury Park and New Delhi.
Gubrium, J. F. (1992), *Out of Control, Family Therapy and Domestic Disorder*, Sage, Newbury Park and London and New Delhi.
Harré, R. (ed) (1986), *The Social Construction of Emotions*, Blackwell, Oxford and New York.
Harré, R. and Gillett, G. (1994), *The Discursive Mind*, Sage, Thousand Oaks and London and New Delhi.
Harré, R. and Stearns, P. (eds) (1995), *Discursive Psychology in Practice*, Sage, London.

Harré, R. and Parrott, G. W. (eds) (1996), *The Emotions, Social, Cultural and Biological Dimensions*, Sage, London.
Hessle, S. (1997), Den sociala barnavården inför 2000-talet – några lärdomar från 1900-talet, *Janus*, vol. 5, no. 3, pp. 243-260.
Heino, T. (1997), *Asiakkuuden hämäryys lastensuojelussa*, Stakes, Tutkimuksia 77, Gummerus, Jyväskylä.
Hochschild, A. R. (1983), *The Managed Heart*, Commercialization of Human Feeling, University of California Press, Berkeley and Los Angeles and London.
James, V. and Gabe, J. (1996), Introduction: Connecting Emotions and Health? in V. James and J. Gabe (eds) (1996), *Health and the Sociology of Emotions*, Blackwell, Oxford.
Jokinen, E. (1996), *Väsynyt äiti*, Äitiyden omaelämänkerrallisia esityksiä, Gaudeamus, Tampere.
Kivivuori, J. (1992), *Psykokulttuuri*, Sosiologinen näkökulma arjen psykologisoitumisen prosessiin, Hanki ja Jää, Helsinki.
Kuronen, M. (1994), Normaalit ongelmat ja ongelma-asiakkaat, Etnografinen tarkastelu asiakkaiden ongelmien määrittelykäytännöistä äitiys- ja lastenneuvolatyössä, *Janus*, vol. 2, no. 4, pp. 341-351.
Landman, J. (1996), Social Control of 'Negative' Emotions: The Case of Regret, in Harré, R. and Parrott, G. W. (eds) (1996), *The Emotions*, Social, Cultural and Biological Dimensions, Sage, London.
Lee, T. (1996), Emotion Work in Care Assistant Work, in V. James, and J. Gabe, (eds), *Health and the Sociology of Emotions*, Blackwell, Oxford.
Miller, G. (1987), Producing Family Problems: Organization and Uses of the Family Perspective and Rhetoric in Family Therapy, *Symbolic Interaction*, vol. 10, no. 2, pp. 245-265.
Niiniluoto, I. and Räikkä, J. (toim.) (1996), *Tunteet*, Yliopistopaino, Helsinki.
Peltonen, I. (1996), Lastensuojelun vuoristoradassa ja kummitusjunassa, *Sosiaalityöntekijä* 4, pp. 31-32.
Rose, N. (1990), *Governing the Soul*, The Shaping of the Private Self, Routledge, London and New York.
Rostila, I. (1990), Tunnetyöstä sosiaalitoimistoissa, *Sosiologia*, vol. 27, no. 4, pp. 257-266.
Ruane, S. (1996), Maternal-baby Unbonding: Rituals for Undoing Nature, in V. James and J. Gabe (eds) (1996), *Health and the Sociology of Emotions*, Blackwell, Oxford.
Simonen, L. (1990), *Contradictions of the Welfare State, Women and Caring*, Acta Universitatis Tamperensis ser A, vol. 295, University of Tampere, Vammala.
Stearns, P. (1995), Emotion, in Harré, R. and Stearns, P. (eds) (1995), *Discoursive Psychology in Practice*, Sage, London.
Stones, C. (1994), *Focus on Families*, Family Centres in Action, Practical Social Work, Macmillan, Basingstoke and London.

Tuomi, A. (1992), *Sosiaalityöntekijä – tunnetyöntekijä*, Ajatuksia sosiaalityöstä tunnetyönä, Sosiaalipolitiikan laitos, Tutkimuksia, Sarja B, no. 13, Tampereen yliopisto, Tampere.

Van den Bogaart, P. H. M. (1995), 'The Application of Intensive Family Support Programs, Evaluation and its Impact on Practice', Presentation in *the IVth EUSARF European Congress: 'There is no Place Like Home*, Supporting Children in Need and Their Families', 6-9 Sept 1995, Leuven, Belgium.

Whittaker J. K. (1990), *Reaching High-risk Families: Intensive Family Preservation in Human Services*, Aldine de Gruyter, New York.

Wise, S. (1990), Becoming a Feminist Social Worker, in Stanley (ed), *Feminist Praxis, Research, Theory and Epistemology in Feminist Sociology*, Routledge, London and New York.

7 Masculinity Discourse in Work with Offenders

SALLY HOLLAND AND JONATHAN B. SCOURFIELD

> I have seen plenty of examples on estates like yours where it's the women, the mums, who've had enough and are setting up homework classes and so on. Trying to get men more involved in community action is important. In so many cases of young men who get into serious trouble there is a problem with their dad or their father figure (Jack Straw in Turner, 1998).

Jack Straw, the UK Home Secretary, who has responsibility for crime and family policy, is being interviewed here in *The Guardian* newspaper by a young man with a history of offending. The excerpt is interesting in many different respects; the important ones in the context of this chapter being that it raises two substantial concerns about men and masculinity that have come to the fore in the UK in recent years and have featured to differing degrees in the discursive fields of academia, politics and the media. The two concerns are dangerous young men and dangerous fathers (Hearn, 1998; Williams, 1998). These concerns have been strongly linked with the crime debate that absorbed the British public in the mid 1990s. Although, as Hearn (1998) points out, there is some continuity in the discourse about young men and crime with older preoccupations with a 'dangerous underclass', there is also emerging a new focus on how the ways in which we bring up boys as 'masculine' can result in their damaging behaviour as adult men.

The academic process of deconstructing masculinities has become fairly mainstream in the humanities and social sciences in recent years. The field of literary criticism has shown an interest in the study of textual representations of men for some time and a critical approach to men is also gaining ground in historical work, such as that of Roper and Tosh (1991). In the last decade or so, the study of men and masculinities in the sociology and social policy field has mushroomed. There have been, amongst others, studies of crime and criminal justice (Newburn and Stanko, 1994), sport (Messner and Sabo, 1990), schooling (Mac an Ghaill, 1994) the factory shopfloor (Cockburn, 1991), managers (Collinson and Hearn, 1994), fathers (Lupton and Barclay, 1997) and the law (Collier, 1995).

There has been a variety of different intellectual approaches; psychological, psychoanalytical, anthropological and sociological, which have been ably summarised by Edley and Wetherell (1995) and Connell (1995). Some of the different political positions have been described by Clatterbaugh (1990) as liberal pro-feminist, radical pro-feminist, men's rights and socialist. Bob Connell (1995) is considered by many to be the most important theorist in the sociological field. He insists on a post-structuralist emphasis on the diversity of masculinities and a variety of 'configurations of practice' which can be seen to form into a hierarchy. He uses the terms hegemonic, marginalised and subordinated masculinity.

In the social work literature there has been some recent attention to the intersection of masculinities with a range of social welfare provision (Cavanagh and Cree, 1996; Christie, forthcoming; Pringle, 1995). In social welfare practice, there have been interesting practice developments in youth work ('boyswork'), work with a range of male offenders including perpetrators of physical and sexual violence, and work with fathers. Apart from an increasing awareness of the connection between masculinity and mental health, there has been less work in the adult community care field that has focused on the social construction of masculinity. This chapter aims to build on existing work by exploring discourse about working with men in the occupational culture of the UK probation service. It does so through discussion of qualitative data, set in the context of the knowledge base of the organisation and the contemporary crime debate in the UK.[1]

Work with Offenders

Most front-line criminal justice personnel spend most of their time working with marginalised men, and this is particularly true of probation officers. Fielding's research in the early 1980s (Fielding, 1984) found officers to be on the whole fairly comfortable that their role was one of both promoting offenders' welfare and of social control. May's research a decade later (May, 1991) found considerably more disquiet about lack of autonomy, and since then, central government has increased its determination that front-line practice should exercise more control over offenders. Despite these trends, we maintain that there remains a determination on the part of probation officers to combine the unavoidable tasks of social control with an orientation towards helping offenders.

Some criminologists are currently researching and theorising the link between constructions of masculinities and a range of crimes (e.g. Jefferson, 1996; Newburn and Stanko, 1994). Alongside this activity, there has been a call for probation officers to make masculinity explicit in their work (McCaughey, 1992; Buckley, 1996). Such authors write of 'challenging', 'confronting' or 'deconstructing' masculinity. Some of these authors might argue that young men end up on probation because their communities are more policed and also because their behaviour is conspicuous, often deliberately so, and is amplified by reputation. They are stigmatised by the state and their communities, and they are also genuinely a threat to the safety of people living in those communities. In this literature, their gender is seen to be central to their criminal behaviour. Messerschmidt (1993) writes that crime is a resource for doing gender. Connell's framework for gender relations uses the term 'marginalised masculinity' (Connell, 1995). It is men who indulge in what he calls a 'spectacular display' of 'masculine protest' that probation officers most commonly encounter. These are men who have restricted access to the power that a traditional working class man's job, such as manual labour, can give them. They usually cannot construct their masculinity through work, education, ownership of property or lasting consumer items. We see discussions of gender in the probation service as important because we see the central task of the organisation as one of managing marginalised masculinities.

In the light of this new emphasis on the social origins of crime by *men*, the research reported below sets out to explore the constructions of masculinity within the Probation Service. The research studied how probation officers, who have an important role in the sentencing of some offenders and in their management in the community, understand men's crime and their work with men. The research is already reported elsewhere (Scourfield, 1998). What follows is a very different discussion that illustrates how social work practice is constructed within gender discourses in occupational culture, which draw heavily on discourse from the popular media, 'experts' and local knowledge. The contention of the chapter is that there are conflicting discourses of masculinity current in the probation service with potentially very different implications for work with men who offend.

Researching Probation Culture

One of the authors, Jonathan Scourfield, conducted semi-structured interviews with fourteen probation officers (six women and eight men) in South Wales during 1996. He also read 50 client files and 30 pre-sentence reports, chosen from districts other than those where the interviewed officers worked, so as not to hold up any individual officers to particular scrutiny. He was, at the time, a probation officer colleague of both those interviewed and those whose files and reports were studied.

The position of practitioner researcher is both privileged and problematic. Familiarity with the setting presents a challenge to the researcher who is seeking an open questioning perspective (McCracken, 1988). The researcher may be seen as belonging to a particular sub-group within the organisation, creating expectations in the participants of what the researcher may wish to hear. Conversely, the practitioner researcher may be able to gain in-depth information more quickly and participants may be more willing to be frank with a colleague than with an outside 'expert' (Hammersley and Atkinson, 1995).

The interviewer's sex and gender identity will also inevitably affect the research process (McKeganey and Bloor 1991). It is possible that in this study the researcher might have been identified as a man with an interest in masculinity. If so, assumptions about his particular perspective might vary widely. In fact, he was little known to these particular respondents. Assumptions were probably made by interview respondents about required rhetoric on masculinity within the organisation. This is interesting in itself since it reveals something about an influential discourse of masculinity.

The probation offices studied are all in the South Wales valleys. This is an area of major industrial decline. Employment opportunities for men in traditional men's jobs have declined considerably and levels of women's economic inactivity are some of the highest in the United Kingdom. A disproportionate number of probation clients live in particularly stigmatised hilltop council estates which are often remote from most services and from the next nearest community.

Although the prime focus of the study was constructions of masculinity, it was important to consider accounts of working with women as well, since masculinities are inherently relational, that is, they are constructed and produced in relation to femininities and other masculinities. The study was conducted on a relatively small scale, but did examine an element of probation culture in some detail. The themes discussed below, relating to how probation officers' understand men offenders and communicate with them, may reflect something of the wider occupational culture of the service outside of a few South Wales offices.

The interview and file recording data reveal some valuable insights into probation officers' accounts, for different audiences, of men and of work with men. Pre-sentence reports give background information about offence and offender to sentencers, and conclude with a sentencing proposal. Although their contents are confidential to the author, defendant, sentencer and lawyers, these reports can be seen as public accounts of masculinities. This data is discussed elsewhere with an emphasis on the difference between the constructions of masculinity in the interviews and in the documentary evidence (Scourfield, 1998). The discussion below focuses on spoken and written accounts together, to argue that three distinctly different and often conflicting discourses of masculinity can be found.

Discourses of Masculinity

The concept of discourse is particularly useful for discussion of occupational culture. It conveys the idea of a body of concepts, values and beliefs within which people operate, which become accepted as knowledge. Within a probation office, everyday talk about practice goes on within the discursive fields of the law, social work knowledge (itself a hybrid of the discursive fields of sociology and psychology) and the media, and in the context of locally popular beliefs about crime and men. Weedon (1997, p. 34) writes that 'discursive fields consist of competing ways of giving meaning to the world and of organizing social institutions and processes' and that 'within a discursive field... not all discourses carry equal weight or power'.

Middleton (1992, p. 142) writes that 'to speak legitimately of a discourse of masculinity it would be necessary to show that a particular set of usages was located structurally within a clearly defined institution with its own methods, objects and practices'. It can be argued that probation officers do have to negotiate discourses of masculinity according to Middleton's definition. Knowledge about men is located in institutional practices such as the writing of reports and records, court decisions, and reference to the medical and social sciences. We do not propose that our characterisation of different trends and approaches as separate discourses implies these are unassailable categories. To borrow the term Connell (1995) uses in relation to hierarchies of masculinities, these are 'configurations of practice' rather than tightly bounded approaches.

There are many dimensions of gender construction in occupational culture that could be explored. It would be interesting to analyse how men working with offenders negotiate their masculinity. This is the focus of Christie's (1998) work on men as social workers. There is also considerable scope for detailed ethnomethodological study, in the tradition of several contributions to this volume, of talk about men or by men, and for detailed analysis of how accounts of clients are constructed for particular audiences. In this chapter we have chosen to present an overview of male and female probation officers' expressed opinions about men in research interviews, pre-sentence reports and case records. We have distilled these opinions into three broad discourses. These discourses are characterised as traditional (boys will be boys), new (explicitly challenging masculinity) and mainstream (implicitly challenging masculinity). We found that most probation officers in this study appeared to be negotiating more than one of these discourses in their professional lives.

Traditional Discourse – Boys will be Boys

Some of those interviewed found it difficult to talk about men as men. Qualitative interviews are often demanding for respondents, but this particular difficulty reflects the fact that the process of looking critically at masculinities is a new one. One probation officer said:

> I suppose the culture over the last few years has been... gender awareness has been more female awareness as opposed to male awareness (interview nine, male officer).

Traditionally probation officers have not named men as men and have not had a critical perspective on masculinity. We describe four approaches which we characterise as reflecting a traditional masculinity discourse: ostensibly non-gendered causal explanations for crime; accepting explanations at face value; a men-centred approach; and an approach to sentencing that constitutes almost blanket mitigation. In relation to the concept of marginalised masculinity, it could be argued that this discourse emphasises the marginalisation of men who offend rather than their masculinity; their powerlessness rather than their use of power.

The study found evidence of the persistence of common sense explanations for men's crimes in probation culture. A traditional probation discourse on men makes a simple causal link between men's behaviour and causal factors other than his gender identity, deflecting responsibility for his actions away from the man himself. So, for example, with a client on probation for constant harassment of a woman, including regular threats to kill her, the officer discussed alcohol, family relations and social skills, but not apparently anything about his views about this woman, or women in general (file 46). The pre-sentence reports studied were almost always framed within this traditional discourse. Alcohol and drugs were commonly used as single explanatory factors, in a rather deterministic way. So, for example, a report will describe a young man as stealing a car because he has taken some temazepam, and will conclude that if he takes the advice of a drug counsellor and reduces or stops his drug use he will not steal so many cars. A pre-sentence report author wrote that the client had changed from drinking cider to drinking beer 'because he recognised the adverse effect cider was having upon him and his relationship with his partner' (in file 14). Young men's behaviour is explained not with reference to the culture of the male peer groups in which context most offending takes place, and not in terms of the young men's claim to identity or power through their chosen behaviour, but rather in terms of simple causation by an external factor. Violence against women partners is, almost without exception, described with euphemisms such as 'volatile relationship', 'stress in the family' and 'domestic problems'. Again, intoxication is used as a simple causal connection to the damaging behaviour. Such causal accounts do not consider the man's agency in the violence.

Behind this simple connection may be an assumption that the disinhibiting effects of alcohol or drugs allow the natural aggressive social character of men to come out. Boys will be boys, when the mask slips. One interview respondent stated this belief overtly when he explained sexual violence by saying that 'men have a greater libidinal drive than women'. He concluded that when working with men who commit acts of violence (his own broad term), 'the best we can reasonably hope for [is to] make some effort to control it' (interview four, male officer).

The traditional discourse of masculinity is offender-centred in the sense that offenders' explanatory accounts of their offences are usually accepted on face value. This is in keeping with the influential 'non-treatment paradigm' outlined by Bottoms and McWilliams (1979), with its emphasis on a negotiated helping relationship rather than an agenda imposed by the officer. An exception to this acceptance of offenders' explanations on face value is the use of a psychodynamic model in a significant minority of cases. We see this too as rooted in a traditional masculinity discourse, insofar as it again suggests a link between men's behaviour and causal factors other than his gender identity, and deflects responsibility for a man's actions away from any sense of his own agency. Psychodynamic models held sway in social casework in the 1970s (Mayer and Timms, 1970) and, though they have since been subject to some criticism, they are still, in our experience as practitioners, influential across mainstream social work practice.

> Mr. Jones's childhood insecurities manifesting themselves in his obsessive relationship with his ex-wife that culminated in the conviction of Arson being reckless as to whether life is endangered (pre-sentence report in file 13).

> (the client has been influenced by)... adverse influences of inconsistent relationships he experienced with his parents in former years, and he still clearly suffers from the alternating effects of rejections and reconciliations (report 9).

We also include within the traditional discourse a men-centred or masculinist approach. There are some officers, albeit a small minority of those interviewed, who are more comfortable working with men than women. They probably represent the historical tendency of the probation service to only cater in practice for men whilst not being aware that this is the case. One respondent explained how he saw the differences between men and women clients:

> The women are more, I would say, manipulative, perhaps more difficult to work with in specific areas... to a great extent I would say that women tend to be less receptive to wanting to work closely, or even to have a working relationship at all... they use the fact of their feminism, I think, they use that to some extent to try and get out of the situation... (male) clients tell you they don't want to co-operate and there's no pretence about it... that's the difference (interview one, male officer).

New Discourse – Explicitly Challenging Masculinity

Most of those interviewed showed some familiarity with the recent attention given in feminist-inspired academic and practitioner literature to the masculinity-crime connection and its implications for probation work. It was evident that discussion of these issues had a certain profile in the organisation. Most officers referred to the influences in men's upbringing, including family, peers, community and media, that encouraged a desire to dominate and to be seen to perform appropriately aggressive, independent masculinity. They commonly offered the examples of violence, both physical and sexual, and car crime, when talking about the distinctive features of men's crime. They talked about using these insights into the making of men in their work, sometimes explicitly, in the sense of announcing to clients that that was what they were doing.

> If a man's offences involve women – either against them or a knock on effect – I will make a point of raising it... I will attempt to challenge, confront or just discuss those things (interview two, male officer).

> I adapted some exercises – 'women/men are...', 'women/men should be...'. Their responses would then be discussed, trying to find out where their attitudes come from, what they're all about (interview seven, female officer).

> I'm linking with the bits of masculine behaviour that I personally find unacceptable... that will bring him into conflict with the law (interview twelve, female officer).

Only a relatively small amount of case recording described this explicit addressing of masculinity. One officer showed a particular interest in working with violent men, whether or not they were on probation for violence, from the perspective of overtly discussing their views on being a man. Several other officers seemed occasionally to focus directly on their clients' masculinities, where the relevance of these was particularly stark. An innovative example of this was the spontaneous group discussion with a client and his friends, who had spoken of their intention of going out that day for a revenge attack on a group of young men from a neighbouring district. The discussion focused on their need to uphold the honour of their home area by using violence.

Distinctive general features of this new discourse on men include the influence of feminist critiques of male power, attention to the experiences of victims and a different approach to male cultures of crime. Several interview respondents talked about men's social power and the subordination of women. Examples include the following:

> Arran is a highly immature and volatile young man who is seeking to adopt the mantle of being 'hard' (file 11).

> Used Duluth power and control wheels to try and get at Lee's use of his partner as a servant (file 5).

This discourse has a rather different view of men's agency from the traditional discourse. Men are seen as responsible for their actions in the sense that part of socially constructed masculinity is a desire to control, to get their own way. However, some of the respondents' talk of damaging models of masculinity tends to see men as imprisoned by upbringing, and therefore not free to choose.

> He talked of feeling "out of control" at times. Linked to family background – beaten by dad as was mother (file 30).

The new discourse pays more attention to the experience of victims than does the traditional one. The importance of a victim perspective, for example in the writing of court reports, has been stressed in government guidance on probation work in recent years, and left realist criminology (for example, Young and Matthews, 1992) has prioritised the experience of victimisation in the study of crime. Several interview respondents quickly moved on to the topic of victimisation of women and children when discussing the distinctiveness of men's crime. The new discourse requires a fresh look at the cultures of crime. It questions and challenges the explanations that men offenders themselves give for their behaviour, not accepting common sense notions, but instead looking at the masculinities of individuals, peer groups and communities. There is an interest in how manhood is proven through conspicuous displays and in the controlling of women and children.

Many of the probation officers identified the specific geographical setting of their workplace as having an influence on local masculinities. Unemployment and traditional close-knit communities with specific local cultures were amongst the factors identified as influencing local men, whether clients, friends or themselves.

> I suppose it's an area where it's difficult for men to break out of the stereotypes and what's expected of them. Small valley communities with quite entrenched views of what men should do and what women should do, perhaps more so than other areas I've worked in (interview eleven, female officer).

> I see people now who I drink with, whose views about men and women frighten me and I see a lot of myself in the past in them. I think to myself 'fuck me, I used to be like that'. The language they use about women, about themselves, it's quite frightening (interview two, male officer).

Some of the comments about 'valleys men' suggested the connection between lack of economic status and assumptions of power and authority over others that is conveyed by Connell's (1995) concept of marginalised masculinity.

> I don't what the strains are like on men trying to grow up in a situation where 25 per cent of the valley are unemployed and yet there's still a culture of thinking that men go out to work and women don't (interview ten, female officer).

However, the new discourse can be seen to be more about masculinity than marginalisation; more about gender than class. It emphasises men's social power rather than their powerlessness.

Mainstream Discourse – Implicitly Challenging Masculinity

The renewed rehabilitative optimism of the 1990s, stimulated by effectiveness research such as that in McGuire's collection (1995) has arguably led to a change in emphasis in mainstream probation culture. The preoccupation has become 'what works'. It has been stated that the client-worker relationship has to be reformulated in the light of what is known about effectiveness (Raynor and Vanstone, 1994). Offence-focused cognitive-behavioural work has become an orthodoxy in many areas. The dominance of cognitive-behavioural approaches is reflected in many of the accounts of working with men in this study. A significant amount of the accounts of practice in both files and interviews could be seen as implicitly challenging masculinities through practice that can broadly be labelled cognitive-behavioural. This label is very broad. As Saunders (1989) has written:

There is no monolithic theory or integrated set of procedures that can be called 'cognitive-behavioural'. Rather the term covers a collection of principles and procedures that many practitioners have not attempted to link theoretically' (p. 77).

Most cognitive-behavioural therapy could be described as helping people see how their thoughts or beliefs trigger emotions which in turn trigger actions, and helping them break these connections and therefore change their behaviour. Much of the practice described in probation officers' accounts draws on these ideas in some way, particularly in linking clients' beliefs with their actions, challenging the logic of those beliefs, and tracing the consequences of particular ways of thinking. File recording often refers to analysing clients' 'self-talk'. This refers to the cognitive-behavioural technique that focuses on the messages people give to themselves that predict particular behaviours are likely to result, as a response to the message.

This practice is ostensibly gender neutral in the sense that the therapeutic methods are intended for men and women alike. However, the data reveal that there are often-mentioned examples of methods, linked to cognitive-behavioural therapy, which perhaps do address masculinities, without necessarily naming them as such. Examples of these are:

- helping clients to see the consequences of their actions;
- discussion of the values on which their behaviour was based and alternatives to these values;
- helping them see the effects of what they had done on other people, particularly women and children;
- comparing their offending with pro-social aspects of their behaviour;
- encouraging them to talk about emotions instead of acting on them in a destructive manner;
- discussion of responsibilities.

Perhaps these techniques can be seen as addressing a masculinity which involves rigid thinking and internalised beliefs in the right to dominate others. These are some examples of how officers expressed this approach:

> Trying to get them often to locate what I consider to be their more female side, to look at their values, to look at why they are behaving in particular

ways, why they think that's important and to consider whether those values are really being pushed on them by other people or whether they are what they really believe in... I mean things like acknowledging feelings, thinking about... how their families experience what they're doing (interview eight, female officer).

Getting them to talk about their feelings, getting them to express what their beliefs are about themselves and about women (interview eleven, female officer).

Working on him increasing self-control, understanding the effect he has on others, thinking about his reactions, taking slow steps (interview twelve, female officer).

There was some considerable overlap between the respondents who described using these approaches with men and those whose explanations of men's behaviour were also informed by feminism. We have characterised the mainstream approach as a separate discourse so as to emphasise the important difference between an explicit and an implicit challenging of masculinity. The discourse of 'what works' in probation does not specifically address men. The methods given prominence are intended to be gender neutral. Our data show, however, that they may have the unintended effect of challenging masculinity.

Obviously these characterisations of discourses of masculinity are not an attempt to create unassailable categories. They merely represent trends from the data which we hope have some theoretical coherence. Probation officers negotiate these conflicting discourses from day to day and many practise within all three. Accounts of practice in the interviews were most often within the new and mainstream discourses. File recording revealed both traditional and mainstream discourses and very little of the new discourse. The pre-sentence reports were written primarily within the traditional discourse of masculinity, with some evidence of the mainstream discourse but none of the new. Both file recording and report writing are an essential part of probation practice, whereas research interviews are not. This may suggest that there is relatively little explicit challenging of masculinities going on in practice, at least in the geographical area studied (Scourfield, 1998). However, many probation officers appear to be in the process of at least thinking about and discussing the possible implications of their understanding of masculinities for their practice, and some mainstream practice methods may have the unintended effect of challenging male clients' values and beliefs as men.

The dominance of the traditional discourse in pre-sentence reports may reflect the discursive limits of the court setting. Emerson and Pacey (1992) write that

> Decision-makers... do not see and treat cases as self-contained, isolated entities, but rather as practical decision tasks embedded in known and foreseeable courses of institutional action (p. 234).

For probation officers these 'known and foreseeable courses' will include the various sentencing options available to the court and the limited possibility of bringing about a positive outcome from a largely punitive criminal justice system. Probation officers will also be influenced by an established and largely traditional discourse on offending within the court setting. That rhetoric on masculinity in the interviews draws heavily on both new and mainstream discourses on men may suggest that these discourses currently have the status of dominant forms of knowledge in the organisation.

Discussion and Conclusions

This study did not set out to evaluate practice. We do not intend, therefore, to make prescriptive judgements on the basis of the data. There are, however, some interesting issues that might need discussion within the probation service. Perhaps probation officers need to consider the conflicting discourses of masculinity and how they impact on their own personal practice. Several respondents spoke of a general lack of honest debate about gender, in part because there are such divergent views around in the organisation. Honesty is certainly needed, if the service is to grapple with the complexities of gender, crime and social work.

Each of the discourses on men can be seen to have strengths and weaknesses. Of course, the traditional discourse is open to criticism from feminists for failing to deconstruct masculinities, thus reinforcing traditional justifications for abusive behaviour. Conversely, there is a risk that the new discourse of explicitly challenging masculinity may not recognise that probation officers are in the business of working specifically with marginalised men, not men in general. The marginalised status of the clientele should perhaps have implications for methods of intervention.

The traditional discourse does take account of the very real welfare needs of men who offend. Whereas an extreme adoption of the traditional discourse would mean only helping men with these welfare needs, thus helping change marginalised masculinities into hegemonic ones, a caricature of the new discourse might involve treating all men clients as uniformly powerful, as if they make completely free choices, unaffected by other social factors, to abuse and dominate women, children and other men.

The care-control debate that has at various times raged in the probation service needs to be revisited in the light of feminist work on men's crimes. There are two new perspectives to enter the debate: a reclamation of men's agency in understanding masculinity and a pressure for criminalising abusive behaviour that has historically been excused by the criminal justice system. Both perhaps challenge a simplistic stance that 'punishment' is always wrong and that probation officers should always avoid a controlling role. It might be argued that the new discourse on men and probation presents a credible alternative to what is popularly perceived to be the overly liberal approach of traditional probation and the macho punitive approach that has become the mainstream rhetoric of party politics. There are risks, however, that the rhetoric of 'challenging' and 'confronting' masculinity could itself become a macho response (Sheath, 1990).

Perhaps tensions between discourses of masculinity are in fact strongly linked to care-control tensions inherent in the probation officer role; tensions which remain despite governmental action to emphasise the control function. In some respects, what we have labelled the traditional discourse on masculinity represents a traditional welfare approach, with an emphasis on mitigating the worst effects of a punitive system on socially marginalised clients. The new discourse, with its emphasis on male offenders' responsibility, and challenging or confronting them, has some common ground with the socially authoritarian consensus that the current government represents. The new discourse also brings back the idea of the probation officer defining the client's problem. This aspect of 1970s psychodynamic casework was criticised on the basis of the power imbalance involved (see Bottoms and McWilliams, 1979). An officer deciding that, despite a male offender's own explanations of his behaviour, s/he knows that it can *really* be explained by the social construction of masculinity, is returning to the tradition of probation officer knows best. This basis for the probation relationship may well be entirely appropriate, but feminist-inspired officers perhaps need to acknowledge that this is the basis on which they work.

The mainstream discourse, influenced by cognitive-behavioural work, is an interesting development in changing men. The very influential social work discourses of 'what works' and anti-oppressive practice are usually considered separately. Where they have converged, debates have focused on whether programmes that have been found to reduce reconviction rates are oppressive or liberating (Neary, 1992; Raynor and Vanstone, 1994). It is possible that, in fact, practice which is found to be effective in reducing reoffending is effective because it is helping to change masculinities, and is therefore anti-oppressive, without making this explicit (personal communication with Richard Thurston, April 1996). Probation officers need to consider whether the next stage should be to make it explicit, or whether the work is more effective because challenging masculinities is implicit and avoids making men defensive by addressing them as men.

There has been considerable discussion in probation services in recent years about the historical marginalisation of women from mainstream provision for offenders, although it is not clear whether services for women have improved because of this discussion. To echo Hearn's (1996) warning about the concept of masculinity/masculinities in academia, there is perhaps a danger that the new interest in masculinity and probation practice might have the effect of diverting attention away from women and making them invisible once more.

Note

1   *Acknowledgements*   We should like to thank Jonathan Scourfield's former employers for allowing time and access for the research referred to above and, in particular, those colleagues who agreed to be interviewed or to give access to their files and reports. We are also grateful for the support of a Cropwood Fellowship at the Cambridge Institute of Criminology and to Betsy Stanko and Richard Thurston for their valuable advice.

Bibliography

Bottoms, A. and McWilliams (1979), 'A non-treatment paradigm for probation practice', *British Journal of Social Work*, vol. 9, no. 2, pp. 159-202.

Buckley, K. (1996), 'Masculinity, the probation service and the causes of offendingbehaviour' in T. May, and A. A. Vass (eds), *Working with Offenders*, Sage, London.

Cavanagh, K. and Cree, V. (eds) (1996), *Working with Men: Feminism and Social Work*, Routledge, London.

Christie, A. (1998), 'Is social work a "non-traditional" occupation for men?' *British Journal of Social Work*, vol. 28, pp. 491-510.

Christie, A. (ed) (forthcoming), *Men and Social Work: Theories and Practices*, Macmillan, Basingstoke.

Clatterbaugh, K. (1990), *Contemporary Perspectives on Masculinity*, Westview Press, Colorado.

Cockburn, C. (1991), *Brothers: Male Dominance and Technological Change*, Pluto Press, London.

Collier, R. (1995), *Masculinity, Law and the Family*, Routledge, London.

Collinson, D. L. and Hearn, J. (1994), 'Naming men as men: implications for work, organisations and management', *Gender, Work and Organisation*, vol. 1, no. 1, pp. 2-22.

Connell, R. W. (1995), *Masculinities*, Polity, Cambridge.

Edley, N. and Wetherell, M. (1995), *Men in Perspective: Practice, Power and Identity*, Prentice Hall/Harvester Wheatsheaf, London.

Emerson, R. M. and Pacey, B. (1992), 'Organizational horizons and complaint-filing', in K. Hawkins (ed), *The Uses of Discretion*, Clarendon Press, Oxford.

Fielding, N. (1984), *Probation Practice: Client Support Under Social Control*, Gower, Aldershot.

Hammersley, M. and Atkinson, P. (1995), *Ethnography: Principles in Practice*, 2nd edition, Routledge, London.

Hearn, J. (1996), 'Is masculinity dead? A critique of the concept of masculinity/masculinities' in M. Mac an Ghaill, (ed) *Understanding Masculinities*, Open University Press, Buckingham.

Hearn, J. (1998), 'Troubled masculinities in social policy discourses: young men.' in *Men, Gender Divisions and Welfare*, edited by J. Popay, J. Hearn and J. Edwards, Routledge, London.

Jefferson, T. (ed) (1996), *Masculinities, social relations and crime*, special edition of *British Journal of Criminology*, vol. 26, no. 3.

Lupton, D. and Barclay, L. (1997), *Constructing Fatherhood. Discourses and Experiences*, Sage, London.

Mac an Ghaill, M. (1994), *The Making of Men. Masculinities, Sexualities and Schooling*, Open University Press, Buckingham.

May, T. (1991), *Probation: Politics, Policy and Practice*, Open University Press, Buckingham.

Mayer, J. and Timms, N. (1970), *The Client Speaks*, Routledge and Kegan Paul, London.

McCracken, G. (1988), *The Long Interview*, Sage Newbury Park, CA.

McCaughey (1992), 'Making masculinity explicit in work with male offenders' in Senior, P. and Woodhead, D. (eds) *Gender, Crime and Probation Practice*, PAVIC, Sheffield.

McGuire, J. (ed) (1995), *What Works: Reducing Reoffending*, Wiley, Chichester.

McKeganey, N. and Bloor, M. (1991), 'Spotting the invisible man: the influence of male gender on fieldwork relations', *British Journal of Sociology*, vol. 42, no. 4, pp. 195-210.

Messerschmidt, J. (1993), *Masculinities and Crime: Critique and Reconceptualisation of Theory*, Md., Rowan and Littlefield, Lanham.

Messner, M. and Sabo, D. (eds) (1990), *Sport, Men and the Gender Order*, Human Kinetics Books, Champaign, Illinois.

Middleton, Peter (1992), *The Inward Gaze. Masculinity and Subjectivity in Modern Culture*, Routledge, London.

Neary, M. (1992), 'Some academic freedom', *Probation Journal*, vol. 39, no. 4, pp. 200-202.

Newburn, T. and Stanko, E. A. (eds) (1994), *Just Boys Doing Business? Men, Masculinities and Crime*, Routledge, London.

Pringle, K. (1995), *Men, Masculinities and Social Welfare*, UCL Press, London.

Raynor, P. and Vanstone, M. (1994), 'Probation practice, effectiveness and the non-treatment paradigm', *British Journal of Social Work*, vol. 24, pp. 387-404.

Roper, M. and Tosh, J. (1991), *Manful Assertions: Masculinities in Britain Since 1800*, Routledge, London.

Saunders, D. G. (1989), 'Cognitive and behavioural interventions with men who batter: application and outcome' in P. L. Caesar, and L. K. Hamberger (eds) *Treating Men Who Batter: Theory, Practice and Programmes*, Springer, New York.

Scourfield, J. B. (1998), 'Probation officers working with men', *British Journal of Social Work*, vol. 28, pp. 581-599.

Sheath, M. (1990), 'Confrontative' work with sex offenders: legitimised nonce-bashing?' *Probation Journal*, vol. 37, no. 4, pp. 159-162.

Turner, J. (1998), 'Talking shock tactics', *The Guardian*, section 2, pp. 6-7

Weedon, C. (1997), *Feminist Practice and Poststructuralist Theory*, second edition, Blackwell, Oxford.

Williams, F. (1998), 'Troubled masculinities in social policy discourses: fatherhood.' in *Men, Gender Divisions and Welfare*, edited by J. Popay, J. Hearn and J. Edwards, Routledge, London.

Young, J. and Matthews, R. (eds) (1992), *Rethinking Criminology: the Realist Debate*, Sage, London.

PART III:
DISCURSIVE STRUGGLES

8 The 'Social Construction of Child Maltreatment': Some Political, Research and Practice Implications

NIGEL PARTON

Introduction

The purpose of this paper is to reflect critically upon the recent 'official' adoption of social constructionism as a key perspective in opening up debates about the future direction, shape and balance of child welfare and child protection services in the United Kingdom. Such an analysis helps us to understand firstly that our increasing attraction to social constructionist approaches must be located in wider social transformations for it is not by chance that, increasingly, social constructionism is becoming acceptable, mainstream and even 'official'. Secondly, however, while we need to understand the space which is opening up in which social constructionism can flourish we also need to recognise there are myriad social constructionisms which perhaps constitute a somewhat fragile group of only loosely connected perspectives, some of which are not necessarily challenging, critical or destabilising. As my example illustrates, such approaches are quite amenable to be drawn upon for administrative uses and to prop up and repair problems within the normative social welfare discourses which has always been very capable of drawing on and using various bits of sundry theoretical and analytical perspectives to address and try and resolve the problems it is addressing. The overall purpose, therefore, is to inject a note of caution and a degree of reflexivity into the way we think about and use social constructionism in our analyses of social work.

The 'Re-focusing of Children's Services' Debate

I have been sensitised to these issues by my engagement in a number of developments which are taking place in the UK and which go under the umbrella of the 're-focusing of children's services' debate. Following the completion of twenty major research studies on child protection (primarily funded by the central government Department of Health) it is being argued that current child welfare practice is far too concerned with the investigation of alleged incidents of child abuse so that concerns about child protection have become all-pervasive to the point where overall child welfare policies and priorities have been fundamentally re-ordered and re-fashioned in its guise. In effect the central philosophy and principles of the Children Act 1989 in terms of its emphasis on prevention, family support and responding to 'children in need' has been introduced very partially while at the same time the child protection system has become overloaded and seen not to be coping with the increased demands made of it. It is felt that too many cases are being dragged into the child protection net and that as consequence the few who might require such formal interventions are in danger of being missed. Not only are children not being helped and parents and carers becoming angry and alienated, but scarce time and resources are seen as being wasted with little apparent benefit. The focus should be on identifying and assessing needs and producing flexible and non-stigmatising services. This is an important debate which is currently exercising policy makers, managers and practitioners in the UK and most parts of the English-speaking Western world (Parton, 1997) in terms of the future aims and shape of child welfare services.

What is of particular interest for my purpose here however is the way the problems and issues are conceptualised for the purposes of opening up the debate. The definition of child abuse, or child maltreatment as it is called in the research overview document produced by the Department of Health (1995) and called *Messages from Research*, is key. It is notable that, rather than rely on more traditional and positivistic approaches, it is argued that the phenomena is socially constructed. The overview document quotes one of the research studies (Gibbons, Conroy and Bell, 1995, p. 12) that 'child maltreatment is not the same sort of phenomenon as whooping cough: it cannot be diagnosed with scientific measuring instruments. It is more like pornography, *a socially constructed phenomenon* which reflects the values and opinions of particular times' (p. 15, my emphasis). It is important to note at the outset that *Messages from Research* differentiates between the natural and self-evident, in which whooping cough is located, and the socially constructed in which child maltreatment is located. It is easy to suggest that such an approach to social constructionism is ambivalent, partial and confusing – what Woolgar and Pawluch (1985) call 'ontological gerrymandering'. What it does, however, is open up a debate on the most appropriate relationship between state and family and the most appropriate forms of intervention in the private family when there are concerns about child maltreatment. In arguing that society continually constructs and re-constructs definitions of maltreatment that sanction official state intervention and that this varies historically (time) and culturally (place) it also argues that the *thresholds* for state intervention also vary and currently, by implication, need refocusing because these have got out of balance.

My interest in these developments for the purposes of this paper are two-fold. First to my knowledge this is the first time that *official* discourses on child welfare or social work more generally have explicitly laid claim to a social constructionist approach. Such a claim should be taken seriously and its significance and implications carefully thought through. On what basis and for what reason(s) is such a claim being made and how far does it point to important changes in the political and cultural climate in which it is felt appropriate to conceptualise a phenomenon of official concern, such as child abuse, in social constructionist terms? What does such a development signify about my current times and about contemporary social work itself?

This connects with my second interest for in some respects I can be seen to be heavily implicated in this apparent official sympathy for social constructionism. As I have already noted the definition of child maltreatment in social constructionist terms in the overview document (DoH 1995) quotes from the study by Gibbons, Conroy and Bell (1995) – who in turn reference Parton (1985) to support and legitimate such a position.

What has happened, however, is that any political analysis of the term child abuse – how this was constructed historically and is operationalised in practice – has been lost and any recognition of the essentially contested nature of the problem and what I do about it reduced to the administrative and technical and given to local agencies and front line practitioners to resolve. A central theme of this chapter is to re-locate the issues in the political and the moral and in conclusion outline a version of social constructionism which I feel is more productive for both understanding the nature of contemporary practice and ensuring that a more critical version of social constructionism is not lost in developments in policy, practice and research.

The analysis will be pursued along two trajectories. First I will consider some of the more immediate factors which informed the decision(s) to establish the research programme by the Department of Health and some of the issues it was anticipated such a programme could address. Secondly I will locate these more specific issues in a much wider analysis which considers some of the more significant and embedded disruptions and anxieties we are currently experiencing related to the changing role of the state and the increasing uncertainties about knowledge and authority – both political and scientific – in the Western world. The issue of child abuse and what to do about it can be seen as emblematic of a number of contemporary issues – socially, culturally and politically.

Contemporary Debates in Child Protection in the United Kingdom

The decision by the Department of Health to fund the research programme in the late 1980s was a direct consequence of the fall-out from the Cleveland Inquiry (Secretary of State, 1988). While there had been over 30 child abuse public inquiries in the UK between 1973 and 1987 they had all been concerned with cases where children had died from physical abuse and neglect at the hands of their parents or carers and where the welfare agencies had failed to intervene. In particular they were seen to have failed to use available research and knowledge to spot or identify cases of high risk when the children were under their care or supervision.

The situation in Cleveland was quite different. One hundred and twenty one children were removed from their parents on statutory orders on the basis of allegedly questionable medical diagnosis of sexual abuse (see Parton, 1991, chapter 4, for a more extensive analysis of the Cleveland affair). Not only did it seem to demonstrate the paucity of knowledge in the area of child abuse but it was seen to demonstrate the manifest confusions in the responses of the investigative agencies. The issue of child abuse was problematised in quite new ways. As I have argued elsewhere (Parton, Thorpe and Wattam, 1997), whereas until the mid/late 1980s the key metaphor for child abuse had been the medical 'battered baby syndrome' with detectable signs and symptoms (albeit through X-rays and medical diagnosis) via Cleveland the issue was riven through with a new metaphor of the unsigned child victim (or, quite consequentially, the verbally signed child) which brought quite new uncertainties. I would suggest there are three contributing factors as to why this should be the case and these have pervaded the whole area of child protection since such that they capture the essential tensions and ambiguities that are now embedded in policy and practice and which the Department of Health research and the subsequent debates on 'refocusing children's services' are attempting to address.

First, by the late 1980s the concerns were with both over – as well as under – intervention such that child protection is now focused not only on protecting children from significant harm and injury, but also on protecting the family from unwarrantable state interventions. More than ever practitioners have to walk a fine balance and the costs of getting that wrong can lead to considerable public, political and media opprobrium (Aldridge, 1994; Franklin and Parton, 1991).

Second, the whole area has become contested in quite new ways. Different perspectives and arguments have developed about not just the nature and causes of child abuse but, crucially, what can and should be done. More particularly, not only had traditional medical science, which proved so crucial in 'discovering' and framing 'the battered baby syndrome', been found wanting, but arguments developed between medical practitioners and experts themselves as to the significance of certain signs and symptoms and whether and how far they were indicative of child abuse. As a consequence not only have the *signs* of child abuse lost their previous significance but considerable doubt is cast on the (scientific) category of child abuse itself. It had the effect of undermining traditional medical authority and questioned both my knowledge about child abuse and what should be done and who should do it. Not only did it seem that knowledge was inadequate but that the knowledge was heavily implicated in *producing* the problems. It seemed that the system which had been set up to identify, regulate and prevent child abuse was itself culpable as well as the practitioners themselves. The *scientific* basis to the way we had attempted to tackle child abuse had as many negative consequences as it did positives.

Dennis Howitt has argued that *science* played an important role in what were seen as errors in child abuse work:

> the close interplay between the 'science' of child abuse and practice is important to understanding how some sorts of child abuse occur. It is the incorporation of key elements of positivist science into social policy. This mode of thinking, to the extent to which it occurs in the thinking of all

professionals in dealing with child abuse, is part of the genesis of errors (Howitt, 1992, p. 49).

Third, and perhaps most significantly, Cleveland was about sexual abuse, which touches a range of sensitivities which were rarely evident in earlier concerns about physical abuse and neglect: it reaches into the most intimate, hidden and private elements of family life and adult-child relations; it represents a major set of debates around patriarchy and male power and thereby opens up a range of political arguments never evident previously; and for the first time the issue threatened not just men but middle-class and professional households in ways which had never happened previously. No longer could child abuse be seen to be associated only with the marginalised, excluded and disreputable. It seemed to permeate 'normal' families.

As a consequence the issue of child abuse was problematised in quite new ways. The key policy and practice issue becomes: How can cases of child abuse be differentiated when in many respects the key signs and symptoms which have come to be associated with it are not only contestable but seem to characterise a wide range of 'normal' families and seem to typify adult-child relations? It is not just that the category of child abuse is contested but it is riven through with a level of uncertainty which casts doubt on the legitimacy of the category itself. As I have argued elsewhere (Parton, 1991; Parton, Thorpe and Wattam, 1997) there resulted an important shift in the discourse from the socio-medical to the socio-legal, where the legal gaze and forensic ways of thinking and acting became dominant. Whereas practitioners, in the socio-medical approach, could choose to work on a hypothesis and look for symptoms to confirm or disconfirm diagnosis (the orthodox scientific approach), in the socio-legal approach, they could have no hypothesis but were directed to identify child abuse according to forensic rules of evidence. While the foundational 'reality' of child abuse wasn't challenged i.e. child abuse exists, the methods of its diagnosis and identification were.

However we should not see these developments in relation to child abuse and child protection in isolation from more wide ranging and significant social transformations and reconfigurations. I will now consider these in more detail.

Wider Social Re-configurations

It is increasingly common for political and social theorists to identify the contemporary as a period of dramatic and significant social transformation particularly in terms of: the increasing *pace* of change; the growing significance of *difference*, *plurality* and various emergent political movements and strategies; and the pervasive awareness of *relativities*, the opening up of individual 'choice' and 'freedom'; and, which is central to my purposes here, the *increasing awareness of the socially constructed nature of reality*.

What I suggest is that these transformations should be likened in scope and form to those that took place in the late nineteenth century. This part of my analysis is heavily influenced by the recent work of Nikolas Rose (1993a; 1993b; 1996) and Peter Wagner (1992; 1994) in terms of characterising the contemporary in terms of 'advanced liberalism' or 'extended liberal modernity'.

Peter Wagner (1992; 1994) has argued that there is a central ambiguity or tension which lies at core of the modern condition as it emerged from the early seventeenth century onwards, namely that between the aspirations for individual liberty and self-creation and the need for social discipline. However the nature of this ambiguity and more particular the nature of the relationship and balance between the two varies in different historical periods and that important shifts can be identified in terms of two key crises of modernity – and it is the second crisis and its implications we are currently living through.

The post-enlightenment project of a liberal society focused on the idea that human autonomy was in principal universal and without boundaries. Freedom was in theory utopian but in reality was much more limited and restricted to an elite group, what Wagner terms *restricted liberal modernity*. However as these liberal freedoms were opened up together with the social transformations which they both represented and made possible, the socially dangerous nature of liberal modernity was increasingly recognised, and a number of critical commentators argued that the project – in its original form – was not feasible. From a variety of perspectives it was argued that nineteenth century liberalism had failed, and was powerless in the face of the forces of social transformation and individualisation of modern society evidenced by rates of suicide, crime and general social disaffection. Economic affairs and the impact of the laissez-faire market had profound social consequences; they damaged health, produced danger through the irregularities and vagaries of employment and encouraged the growth of militant labour and the 'mob'. All these elements fed into growing concerns about 'the social question' or as Wagner (1994) calls it – *the crisis of restricted liberal modernity*. In the last quarter of the nineteenth century, increasingly, the political debate centred around the question of how a criterion could be introduced into liberal reasoning that would allow for dealing with the social question without re-imposing a strong (sovereign) state on the wishes and activities of individuals. Though perhaps put differently the same question was being asked in a number of Western European countries at the same time.

In the liberal view the 'social question' should not have emerged in the first place. Automatic adaptation and individual preferences should have precluded widespread poverty and hardship. However the increased wealth of the nations was far too removed from the many who had experienced social, geographical and economic disruption so that pervasive uncertainty and insecurity prevailed. The major objective of the reform movements of the late nineteenth and early twentieth century was to re-establish a new form of solidity and security into the social fabric – the bourgeois elite to safeguard some order and the male working class to define and represent its own interests.

The attempts to resolve the crisis of restricted liberal modernity at this time laid the foundation for what Wagner calls *organised modernity* or what is more commonly referred to as the growth of welfarism and the establishment of the welfare state in the first half of the twentieth century. In organised modernity the setting of boundaries and the social production of certainties is generally privileged over and above the liberal assertion of unlimited autonomy of everyone to create and recreate themselves and their social contexts.

From the doubts and debates arising from the first crisis of modernity it became evident that no natural or automatic way of regulating social affairs would emerge under the auspices of modernity. Merely relinquishing earlier traditional restrictions and conventions lead to chaos and disorder. A socially constructed order had to be put in the place of the previously assumed natural order. To construct order socially meant introducing conventions about how to understand and constitute common social phenomena and about how to act in recurring problematic situations.

From the late nineteenth century, political economy gradually relinquished its earlier explicit interlinking of economic and moral laws, and formulated itself as a distinctively *economic* doctrine; at the same time, the domain of civil society became *socialised*. Statistical investigations gradually revealed the population as a domain with its own specificity and irreducibility. Statistical techniques and sociological investigations revealed the *nation* as a set of aggregated statistics with regular fluctuations, and as a knowable process with its own laws and cycles (Abrams, 1968). The towns became the target of a diversity of interventions – social hygiene, police – which gave rise to further detailed statistical mapping of urban space. As the social body became subjected to new government norms, eg registration of births, marriages, deaths, types and number of crimes, new realms of social visibility could become the objects of investigation by sociologists and social statisticians (Hacking, 1991). A 'social' domain came into being that could be both the object of science – *social* science – and the territory of a variety of policies – *social* policies – and interventions and practices, including *social* work. The basic means of social policy was as a technology to collectively deal with risk. The basic idea of the emerging social policy was the socialisation of risk particularly by the introduction of social insurance schemes (Ewald, 1992; Swaan, 1985).

The emergence of social work in the late nineteenth century is associated with the transformations that were taking place around a series of anxieties about the family. While the changes in the sphere of government were wide-ranging and complex and social work formed only a small element within it, nonetheless, it was to play a key part of the processes which drew individuals and families into other spheres of government. It provided a personalised strategy to enable 'government at a distance' and was to prove important if the liberal ideal of maintaining autonomous individuals who are at the same time governed was to be realised (Donzelot, 1979; Parton, 1998a).

The welfare state had little in common with the liberal state of the mid-nineteenth century which was little more than a 'night-watchman state'. What emerged with the welfare state was a set of authorities, practices and knowledges whose task was the calculated supervision and administration of all under the guise, ultimately, of the state and a series of experts. Such developments were programmatic in the sense that they were characterised by an optimism that society could be improved and that reality was in some sense identifiable and programmable.

Such an approach rested on a strong set of assumptions about the nature of the state and the social sciences as well as about the entire social formation in which both were embedded. The state was regarded as unitary, coherent and capable of action; social science was seen as methodologically and epistemologically secure and providing objective knowledge; and society was characterised as having an identifiable structure. It was assumed that a cognitive mastery of society could be pursued in the service of the welfare state so that the focus of social science was in analysing the laws and the predictable character of social reality in the same way as the natural sciences were concerned with identifying the underlying laws and realities of nature. The dominant forms of social science were positivistic and functionalist.

Wagner (1994) suggests that the configuration of organised modernity achieved something of a coherence or closure, during the 1960s – in terms of the various institutions, their specific embodiments of collective agency, their interlinkages and respective reaches into society. It appeared as a 'naturally interlocking order'. This social configuration did not halt the dynamics of modernity, but channelled them into apparently controllable avenues whereby the ambiguities related to liberty and discipline while not completely expunged seemed to be peripheral.

What, in retrospect, was largely neglected was a recognition that this social configuration had been constructed over a long period and through a series of intense struggles. By the 1950s and 1960s a series of conventions and assumptions had become so embedded and institutionalised that their socially constructed nature had been lost and had disappeared from consciousness. The classifications and processes which had been set up to increase intelligibility and manageability gave the appearance of representing some natural order of reality.

However since the late 1960s there has been a gradual demolishing of these arrangements, mostly without being replaced by any analogous arrangements that might be more adequate for the new problems and situations. Increasingly it seems that there is no alternative notion of collectivity offering itself in the same way as the nation-state did from the late nineteenth century, when the first steps were being taken towards organised modernity. From the late 1960s many of the social conventions that characterised organised modernity have increasingly broken down: the disappearance of the socio-economic regularities; the reconsideration of the contours of most post-war organisational forms; the bursting of representations and expectations and increasing uncertainties about the future and how to act. What Wagner calls the second crisis of modernity, the crisis of organised modernity, is characterised by a de-conventionalisation and pluralisation of practices, knowledge and authorities: the agreement to set the terms of industrial relations on the national level was broken; the Keynesian consensus to develop a national consumption based economy eroded; the organisational rules that fixed and secured position and task were reshaped; and technical innovations whose applications tended to break existing conventions were no longer upheld.

At the height of organised modernity the state was regarded as strong and coherent. In principle it was assumed it could acquire all the necessary knowledge about society and had the ability to intervene in a harmonious and consensual way. By the 1990s this image of the state has changed dramatically as has faith in developing any incontestable science of society to guide policies and practices.

From posing as the omniscient regulator and leader the state is now, at most, represented as partner or moderator. The clarity of the model of the all-pervasive interventionist state has disappeared and given way to a new diffuseness of the boundaries between the spheres of public and private regulation. This blurring of boundaries raises important issue of legitimacy and sovereignty.

The crisis of organised modernity was also evident in terms of its mode of representation, for its achievements were bought at the price of strict boundaries and conventions. Critiques of organised modernity were thus directed at the *constraining* effects of these boundaries and conventions. Intellectually, the recognition of the *social construction* of conventions and their alternatives becomes central to such critiques (Fuchs and Ward, 1994). Politically the right to be different is a claim which interrelates with such reasoning and which has been central to the growth of most political and social movements over the last twenty five years (Williams, 1996). This cultural revolution has introduced a strong, almost unlimited, attempt at de-conventionalising and the recreation of ambivalence in a social order that was regarded as over conventionalised and closed to any freedom of action beyond pre-established channels. This questioning of the order of practices quickly extended to a questioning of the order of representation to the point where the very possibility of representation has itself come under serious doubt.

It is in this intellectual and social context that debates about postmodernity emerge and which in its strong versions postulates the end of modernity, the subject, social science and much, much more. While it has often been argued that postmodernist claims are exaggerated, contradictory, and demonstrably wrong (for example Norris, 1990; O'Neill, 1995; Simons and Billig, 1994) its significance lies with the way it has contributed to re-opening questions which the social sciences of organised modernity had effectively closed off (Parton, 1998b). The discourse on postmodernity sees most social science as being founded on the assumptions, a priori, of the intelligibility of the social world, of the coherence of social practices, and of the rationality of action. Increasingly it is accepted that, whether one characterises the contemporary as postmodern or not, the notion of the *contingency* of all social phenomena is evident and needs to inform all social research and conceptions of both community and self-hood.

As Martin Hollis (1985) has argued one of the central traits of modernity is 'the idea that we construct our own social identity' (p. 230) and the existence of this idea is what modern societies have had in common over the last two to three hundred years The key element however is that there has been a widening in the scope of the constructibility of identities and this has proved an important distinguishing feature between the three broad types of modern configurations. There has generally been an historical weakening of the assumptions for constructing social identities; from ascriptive and natural (in restricted liberal modernity) to socially acquired and quasi-natural (in organised modernity), to chosen and socially negotiated (in extended liberal modernity).

One of the considerable achievements of organised modernity was to make practices appear fairly coherent and to make social arrangements appear quasi-natural. This naturalisation of the social order closed off discussion about foundational issues and precluded strong doubts about their viability or thoughts about alternatives. The more widely diffused awareness of the constructiveness and constructability of the social world has strengthened doubts about the possibility of valid, natural and incontestable knowledge. The current condition is marked by doubts about both intelligibility and shapeability for the increased awareness of the plurality and diversity of social practices makes it difficult to imagine a collective actor who can intervene in the name of any self-evident universalist ideas. As Wagner (1994, p. 33) has argued 'the increase in social constructiveness as well as the awareness of such constructedness, thus make the political issue of justification highly problematic'. Risk, uncertainty and reflexivity are increasingly seen as characterising contemporary times (Beck, 1992; Beck, Giddens and Lash, 1994; Lash, Szerszynski and Wynne, 1996). More and more social conflicts are characterised as having no unambiguous solutions. They are distinguished by a fundamental ambivalence which can usually be grasped by calculations of probability, but not removed by them.

So long as traditions and customs were widely sustained, experts were people who could be turned to in order to make key decisions and, in the public eye at least, science was, during organised modernity, imbued with some sense of monolithic and generic authority. In effect science and experts were invested with the authority of a final sovereign court of appeal. But increasingly shorn of formulaic truth, all claims to knowledge have become corrigible. We are now living in a world of multiple authorities and wide-ranging knowledge. While modernity had the effect of condemning tradition, a collaboration between modernity and tradition was crucial to the establishment of organised modernity – the period during which risk was thought calculable in relation to external influences. However this has become much more uncertain in the context of extended liberal modernity or what Beck calls 'reflexive modernisation' (1992; 1994).

Alternative 'Social Constructionisms' of Child Maltreatment

What I have suggested then is that the move to define child abuse as a socially constructed phenomena in official discourse is something which is of real significance, but not in terms of whether such an approach captures the phenomena more accurately, poses more pertinent questions for investigation or is likely to inform more appropriate research methodologies. All of these are possible. My central concern however has been to argue that such an approach needs to be understood in its social and political contexts. Rather than see socially constructed approaches as posing a challenge to the conventional I should consider how far they both represent uncertainties and tensions which lie at the heart of the second crisis of modernity and the emergence of extended liberal modernity, while at the same time presenting technical possibilities for resolving them. In conclusion I want to consider not only how social constructionist approaches to child abuse go about resolving the problems posed for the advanced liberal state in terms of policy and practice but also how, in the process, we are offered only a very limited version of social constructionism which strips it of its critical potential.

For it is my view that while it is of real significance that the official discourse on child abuse has taken a constructionist turn I am also of the view that it has not exploited the opportunities available to it to explore child abuse in these terms in any thoroughgoing way. It seems that the *Messages from Research* (DOH, 1995) was so keen to make some resolution of the issues so that practitioners could get on with the job of child protection that it has not developed the potential for analysing the nature of policy and practice made available by a more fully developed social constructionist methodology.

Messages from Research takes on a very restricted interpretation of a social constructionist perspective. The central concern is that a large number of cases are filtered out of the child protection system at an early stage without their needs being addressed. The document and subsequent official policy (DOH, 1998) is keen to reconstruct the system so that these receive services and support. However, it seems that this only becomes feasible if it is assumed at the outset that certain cases are inherently severe and thus self-evidently abusive: for example, '*with the exception of a few severe assaults and some sexual maltreatment . . .* where the decision is clear cut, as a society we have to decide which of the several million potentially harmful situations that occur each year require intervention' (DOH, 1995, p. 53, my emphasis). It is assumed that the problems associated with defining, in practice, what constitutes 'severe assaults and some sexual maltreatment' can be easily resolved. The net result is that while the vast majority of child protection cases are conceptualised as resulting from social construction and can therefore be *reconstructed* as *children in need*, for the severe cases this is not so – they are clearly and unambiguously child maltreatment. The notion of social construction is used as a metaphorical device for differentiating *real* cases of child maltreatment (severe assaults and some sexual maltreatment) and the rest which are *socially constructed*. The problem of child welfare agencies being submerged by increasing numbers of child protection cases can thus be resolved, practically, by ensuring *only* the *real* cases are defined as maltreatment while the rest should be defined as children in need thus requiring a very different and more welfare orientated response from professionals. The practical resolution thus resides with reorienting the definitions, priorities and interventions of front line practitioners and child welfare agencies. Social constructionism becomes simply concerned with issues of labelling, mis-labelling and operational practices (Parton, 1996).

However, the research studies summarised in *Messages from Research* would have provided a methodologically rich opportunity to treat the definition of child abuse as problematic and to examine how its construction, by different professionals, by parents, by children, by policy and guidance, impacted on the way responses, effects, consequences and outcomes were constructed (Wattam 1996). Rather than do this, *Messages from Research* sought to arrive at a consensus about definition by introducing the notion of a continuum. For it is argued that this:

> complex situation is clarified by introducing the idea of a *continuum of abuse*. Several research teams concluded that abuse was better understood if the focus of concern was on behaviour which children ordinarily encountered but which in certain circumstances could be defined as maltreatment. *Once this step has been taken, questions for researchers and practitioners tend to be about chronicity and severity of behaviours, such as how much shouting at children can be said to be harmful* (p. 14, my emphasis).

The point of my emphasis is to demonstrate that *Messages from Research* rejoins the orthodox professional child welfare community. Having argued that maltreatment is socially constructed, it then goes on to reconstruct for practical purposes, to arrive at an apparently all-encompassing, neutral definition so that both research and practice can get on with the job of deciding when and where to intervene. Similarly *Messages from Research* is littered with terms such as 'abuse', 'allegation', 'perpetrator', 'needs', 'neglect' and so on as if they are simple descriptions for well-established and taken for granted elements of professional practice. Any sense of the contestable and highly negotiated nature and use of these terms is lost.

In contrast, my approach to social constructionism is quite different. In research I carried out with Dave Thorpe and Corinne Wattam (1997) the central question is *how is child protection work accomplished?* Child abuse for official organisational accounting purposes is not only in the eye of the beholder (a subjective definition), it is an inter-subjective phenomenon whose meaning and import can only be understood in the cultural and organisational contexts in which it is negotiated and constituted.

This is much more than being concerned with issues of labelling, mis-labelling and operational practices. We have to understand the nature and significance of child abuse and the way this is made sense of by lay people and professionals and acted upon. Our concern (Parton, Thorpe and Wattam, 1997) was with the way child abuse and child protection had been constituted, developed and changed, in both the policy and practice spheres. A key difference between our approach and that of the

Department of Health research was that we moved beyond recognising that child abuse is a social construction (all phenomena are social constructions) to analyse the significance of the term and consider what work it does in both contemporary culture and organisational practices. Only then will we be in a position to gauge how far and in what ways policy and practice might change and to envision alternatives. This is not simply a question of trying to change individual professional attitudes and day-to-day operations for much wider issues are at stake.

One of the central concerns of our research which analysed child protection files (Parton, Thorpe and Wattam, 1997) was to make social work decisions and judgments about individual cases transparent. What quickly became apparent was that in the vast majority of cases the level and form of intervention was not based on whether the allegation or concern was substantiated or not. Invariably there were no identifiable harms or injuries and it was impossible to establish what 'really' happened. As a consequence, methods for resolving the practical concerns for agency accountability were substituted and the primary focus was that of making judgments about *risk* – its assessment and management. We demonstrated that discussions of *child abuse* were rarely mentioned in the files only by those referring or reporting cases. Similarly children were virtually absent and their voices were only present if they helped resolve disputes about the allegations, usually from adults, under investigation. The voices of children were virtually absent from *Messages from Research*. The body on whom all the attention of child protection is supposedly focused, both the practices directed specifically at protecting it, and the research which is concerned with finding out how appropriate and effective those practices are, is mute. The child's voice is missing in *Messages from Research* in the same way as it is missing from our child protection files. Such silences are of considerable import.

For one of the potential attractions of social constructionism as a contribution to social work research and practice is as a method of *critique*, where particular attention is paid to the politics of subjectivity and the ways in which meanings, cultural codes and knowledge production are entangled in the construction and maintenance of unequal power relations (Parton and Marshall, 1998). Not only does the appropriation of 'the social construction of child maltreatment' in the official discourse, via *Messages from Research*, miss this politics it also pointedly misses the position or perspective of the 'subjective' knower and attempt to recover the histories and voices of those who have been excluded particularly the child and the survivor.

Messages from Research focuses on the child protection system and those children and families referred to it. There is no serious attempt to incorporate the views of adults and children who claim to have experienced child abuse but who do not enter the system. Yet research on incidence and prevalence, particularly in relation to child sexual abuse, suggests these are considerable (La Fontaine, 1990; Queen's University, 1990; Kelly et al, 1991; Wattam and Woodward, 1996).

The problem of what to do about the problem is thus far more fundamental than *Messages from Research* would suggest. It is not simply a question of rationalising and recategorising cases that come into the system for many potential cases go unreported. There is very little evidence to suggest that children who are harmed or injured will necessarily tell someone and even less to support a view that this will be reported. Even those children and young people who find their way into the child protection system do not feel they are listened to or responded to in the ways they would wish. They are not guaranteed confidentiality and are unable to trust the professionals with whom they come into contact (Butler and Williamson, 1994; Macleod, 1996).

Yet I would argue that a crucial part of social constructionism should be to demonstrate how certain versions become dominant and taken for granted and certain voices become marginalised and lost altogether. Critique and reflexivity should be central. In the process we are offered a much more creative and challenging approach to both research and practice and provided with insights into how this might be changed in a much more fundamental way if the 'voices' and 'versions' of the marginalised and silenced are interrogated and made central.

Bibliography

Abrams, P. (1968), *The Origins of British Sociology 1834-1914*, University of Chicago Press, Chicago.
Aldridge, M. (1994), *Making Social Work News*, Routledge', London.
Beck, U. (1992), *Risk Society: Towards a New Modernity*, Sage, London.
Beck, U. (1994), 'The Reinvention of Politics: Towards a Theory of Reflexive Modernisation', in U. Beck, A. Giddons and S. Lash (eds) (1994), *Reflexive Modernisation: Politics, Tradition and Aesthetics in the Modern Social Order*, pp. 1-56, Polity Press, Cambridge.
Butler, I. and Williamson, H. (1994), *Children Speak: Children, Trauma and Social Work*, Longman, Harlow.
Department of Health (1995), *Child Protection: Messages from Research*. Her Majesty's Stationary Office, London.
Department of Health (1998), *Review of Working Together?*, Her Majesty's Stationary Office, London.
Donzelot, J. (1979), *The Policing of Families*, Hutchinson, London.
Ewald, F. (1991), 'Insurance and Risk', in G. Burchell, C. Gordon and P. Miller (eds), *The Foucault Effect: Studies in Governmentality*, pp. 197-210, Harvester and Wheatsheaf, London.
Franklin, B. and Parton, N. (eds) (1991), *Social Work, the Media and Public Relations*, Routledge, London.
Fuchs, S. and Ward, S. (1994), 'What is Deconstruction and Where and When Does it Take Place: Making Facts in Science, Building Cases in Law', *American Sociological Review*, vol. 54, no. 4, pp. 481-500.
Gibbons, J., Conroy, S. and Bell, C. (1995), *Operating the Child Protection System*, Her Majesty's Stationary Office, London.
Hacking, I. (1991), 'How should we do the history of statistics?' in G. Burchell, C. Gordon and P. Miller (eds), *The Foucault Effect: Studies in Governmentality*, pp. 181-196, Harvester and Wheatsheaf, London.
Hollis, M. (1985), 'On masks and men', in M. Carrithers, S. Collins and S. Lukes (eds), *The Category of the Person: Anthropology, Philosophy, History*, pp. 25-38, Cambridge University Press, Cambridge.
Howitt, D. (1992), *Child Abuse Errors: When Good Intentions Go Wrong*, Harvester and Wheatsheaf, London.
Kelly, L., Regan, L. and Burton, S. (1991), *An Exploratory Study of the Prevalence of Sexual Abuse in a Sample of 16-21 Year Olds*, University of North London, London.
La Fontaine, J. (1990), *Child Sexual Abuse*, Polity Press, Cambridge.
Lash, S., Szerszynski, B. and Wynne, B. (eds) (1996), *Risk, Environment and Modernity; Towards a New Ecology*, Sage, London.
O'Neill, J. (1995), *The Poverty of Postmodernism*, Routledge, London.

Macleod, M. (1996), *Talking with Children about Child Abuse*, ChildLine, London.
Norris, C. (1990), *What's Wrong with Postmodernism*, Harvester and Wheatsheaf, London.
Parton, N. (1985), *The Politics of Child Abuse*, Macmillan, London.
Parton, N. (1991), *Governing the Family: Child Care, Child Protection and the State*, Macmillan, London.
Parton, N. (1996), 'Child Protection, family support and social work: a critical appraisal of the Department of Health research studies in Child Protection', *Child and Family Social Work*, vol. 1, no. 1, pp. 3-11.
Parton, N. (ed) (1997), *Child Protection and Family Support: Tensions, Contradictions and Possibilities*, Routledge, London.
Parton, N. (1998a), 'Risk, Advanced Liberalism and Child Welfare: The Need to Rediscover Uncertainty and Ambiguity', *British Journal of Social Work*, vol. 28, no. 1, pp. 5-27.
Parton, N. (1998b), 'Advanced Liberalism, (Post) modernity and Social Work: some emerging social configurations', *Social Thought*, vol. 18, no. 3, pp. 71-88.
Parton, N. and Marshall, W. (1998), 'Postmodern and Discourse Approaches to Social Work', in R. Adams, L. Dominelli and M. Payne (eds), *Social Work*, pp. 240-249, Macmillan, London.
Parton, N., Thorpe, D. and Wattam, C. (1997), *Child Protection: Risk and the Moral Order*, Macmillan, London.
Queen's University Belfast, The Research Team (1990), *Child Sexual Abuse in Northern Ireland: A Research Study of Incidence*, Greystone, Belfast.
Rose, N. (1993a), 'Government, authority and expertise in advanced liberalism', *Economy and Society*, vol. 22, no. 3, pp. 283-299.
Rose, N. (1993b), 'Disadvantage and Power "after the Welfare State"', Finnish Translation, *Janus* (Journal of the Finnish Society for Social Policy), vol. 1, no. 1, pp. 44-68.
Rose, N. (1996), 'The Death of the Social?: Re-figuring the territory of government', *Economy and Society*, vol. 25, no. 3, pp. 327-356.
Secretary of State for Social Services (1988), *Report of the Inquiry into Child Abuse in Cleveland*, Cmnd 412. Her Majesty's Stationary Office, London.
Simons, J. W. and Billig, M. (eds) (1994), *After Postmodernism: Reconstructing Ideology Critique*, Sage, London.
Swaan, A. de (1988), *In Care of the State*, Polity Press, Cambridge.
Wagner, P. (1992), 'Liberty and discipline: Making sense of postmodernity, or, once again. towards a sociohistorical understanding of modernity, *Theory and Society*, vol. 22, pp. 467-492.
Wagner, P. (1994), *A Sociology of Modernity: Liberty and Discipline*, Routledge, London.

Wattam, C. (1996), 'The social construction of child abuse for practical policy purposes - a review of Child Protection: Messages from Research', *Child and Family Law Quarterly*, vol. 8, no. 3, pp. 189-200.

Wattam, C. and Woodward, C. (1996), '. . . *And do I abuse my children? No!': Learning About Prevention from People Who Have Experienced Child Abuse*, in Childhood Matters: Report of the National Commission of Inquiry into the Prevention of Child Abuse, vol. 2, Her Majesty's Stationary Office, London.

Williams, F. (1996), 'Postmodernism, feminism and the question of difference, in N, Parton (ed), *Social Theory, Social Change and Social Work*, pp. 61-76, Routledge, London.

Woolgar, S. and Pawluch (1985), 'Ontological Gerrymandering: the anatomy of social problems explanations', *Social Problems*, vol. 32, no. 2, pp. 214-27.

9 Constructing Child Welfare Practice in Ontario, Canada

EVELYN KHOO

Introduction

In the social work profession, the child is often the focus of intervention both as an individual and within the wider contexts of the family system and the community. While intervention draws upon an eclectic theoretical knowledge base, one prevailing view of childhood is embedded in all of these mainstream theories. Childhood is considered to be a relatively universal process, and thus children are slotted *en masse* into one social category. Although it is acknowledged that children may be socialized into very different social and cultural milieus, much of child welfare training stresses the importance of child development.

The emphasis on childhood as a social category currently dominates the discourse in work carried with abused or neglected children. What is often overlooked is the notion that childhood is essentially shaped by powerful adults but is lived by children. Furthermore, the meaning ascribed to childhood is not the same for all children. It means something very different to the relatively powerless children of the lower socio-economic classes who are the 'meat and potatoes' of the child welfare system. Thus, social constructions of childhood are influential in determining the kinds of intervention carried out. Since the knowledge base underpinning social work is so tied to meanings of childhood, once childhood is defined one way, other definitions and other modes of intervention are discarded.

The purpose of this paper therefore is to uncover some of the social constructions of childhood which are of particular significance in the area of child welfare, and to then explore the implications of these in professional practice. A case vignette will be presented to illuminate key points on a practical level. Although this vignette is derived from a child welfare agency (Children's Aid Society) in Ontario, Canada, many of the points to be discussed here should also be relevant from a cross-national perspective. We know from previous research that child abuse and neglect are considered to be significant social problems in most western industrialized societies (e.g. Trocmé et al., 1995; Finkelhor, 1994). Yet, the application of social programs in response depends on how the problem or issue is defined. In examining the social constructions of childhood and social work in one context, the reader mist reflect critically on practices occurring in one's own context. Finally, the impact of social class on the construction of practice will be highlighted.

Childhood as a Social Construction

The idea that childhood is socially constructed is to say that it is a product of the *time* and *space* in which it is experienced. As stated by Qvortrup (1994), 'childhood is the life-space which our culture limits it to be, i.e. its definitions through the courts, the school, the family, the economy, and also through philosophy and psychology'.

The space of intervention in child welfare is filled by those dominant views which portray childhood, first and foremost, as a transparent developmental stage or as progressive series of steps. These biologically-based views present all children as belonging to one category. As such, this uses those tools which complement the prevailing definition of childhood. Thus, it is through a social worker's observations and assessment that it is possible to determine whether a child is developing 'normally'. For example, child protection intervention has emphasized the importance of workers acquiring an understanding of child development based on the perspectives of Erikson (1963), Bowlby (1973) and Steinhauer (1983). In addition to looking for indicators of physical or sexual abuse, it becomes easier to discover a child who is 'abnormal', 'at risk', or 'in need of protection' since normalcy has already been established.

Origins If childhood is a stage, where do children fit in relation to the rest of society? The traditional and still dominant view of childhood as a developmental stage places children in a dependent position vis à vis their parents and the state. In Canada, the notion that children are the property of their parents remains a widely held belief traceable to Roman law, and later to Roman Catholicism and Calvinism (See: Harris and Melichercik, 1986 and Hyvönen, 1989). In contemporary Canada, a child's parents are still expected to carry out the task of child-rearing. It is only when harm has been committed or if there is a substantial risk that a child will be harmed that the state will intervene in what is considered to be the natural order of things.

In this sense, children are not exclusively dependent on their parents but are also dependent on the state. The doctrine of *parens patriae* has been at the foundation of child welfare legislation and has given social workers – as agents of the state – the legal authority to act to protect children. Nevertheless, the debate over whether the state should have the power to intervene in the life of the family has continued unabated from the 19th Century to the present (Swift, 1995).

Most recently, there have been much stronger calls to broaden the powers of the state in the name of a 'children first' approach to the delivery of child protection services. Interestingly, this new approach has not been met by much criticism because it is commonly understood that any changes that take place will be primarily directed at 'bad' families – the poor and chronically deprived who have no other resources to turn to in times of need and who, because of their position in society, cannot evade or avoid contact with the child welfare system.

Changes In advanced industrialized societies such as Canada, modernization and individualization can be regarded as two key processes which have influenced our understanding of childhood and have impacted the lives of children (Ester et. al, 1994). At a social level, modernization is reflected in the development of the so-called welfare state, where there is a degree of acceptance of the government's intervention in such areas as health care, education, and income maintenance.

Individualization has shifted society away from traditionally shared beliefs, attitudes and behaviours toward a more individualistic, autonomous and secular view of the self in society (Ester et. al, 1994). This trend has its roots within the relatively modern ideology of liberalism where the individual reigns supreme (Goodwin, 1992).

Although adult society may have benefited from modernization and individualization, it is less clear whether these changes have had an equally positive effect on the children. O'Neill (1994) is highly critical of the value placed on individualism by liberal ideology in Canada. In his view, children have no voice in such a society and have the potential to be irreparably harmed by a blind emphasis on the superiority of the individual.

Qvortrup (1994) further highlights some of the negative impacts of these major social changes. He describes childhood as becoming feminized, institutionalized, pauperized, and marginalized. He argues that there are larger numbers of single parents (mostly women) who are forced into the labour force at low wages in order to provide for their children. The declining numbers of adults who *are* having children place their children during working hours in institutions, schools, clubs, or organized and supervised time 'islands'. Finally, the declining number of children, means that children as a group have less of a voice compared to older people who are a more vocal, special interest group.

Child Welfare Work Social changes necessitate a re-categorization of childhood as a social class distinct from adulthood (Oldman, 1994). This position goes beyond saying that children are a social or developmental category. Oldman argues that children are an economically significant social class because they create 'childwork' or work organized and done by adults on or for children who are the objects of this work activity. This 'childwork' can be most obviously seen within the context of day care settings and schools. Child protection has become a specialized form of 'childwork' because the prevailing view is that children need protection as an 'endangered species' in the face of societal problems, family breakdown, and moral decay. Oldman goes on to argue (and not without controversy) that the prevalence rates of abuse are not really rising but that the growth in child welfare statistics is due to changes in the labour market.

Along a similar theme, Swift (1995) discusses various child welfare work processes from the framework of various historical, political, organizational and professional contexts. Child neglect is constructed as a social problem caused by a mother's personal deficiencies. The way that child neglect has been socially constructed (cause: 'bad mothers') has produced a child welfare system in which problems are continually being reproduced rather than help being provided in a meaningful way. Real resolution of the problem requires that the problem be redefined and, unless that happens, social workers will be confined to reproducing ultimately damaging concepts of childhood.

Whether childhood is flourishing or decaying, evolving or 'disappearing' (Postman, 1982), it is surely undergoing significant change and will continue to do so. One consequence of these societal changes is that there has been a decreasing emphasis on children as dependent beings and a greater tendency to see them as citizens. As consumers of child welfare services, they remain in a dependent position but have more power over their own lives than before. This is especially true of older children and youths. The movement leading to children being viewed as special citizens has gained momentum over the past decade in part because of the rise of individualism but also because it has become more difficult to deny children the same human rights as adult citizens.

Fundamental human rights are those rights claimed by all members of society. They include those rights applicable regardless of age to life, freedom from pain or torture, to basic food and shelter, and a degree of freedom of thought (Goodwin, 1992). Beyond this, many societies have more difficulty specifying which human rights should be universal because these more complex rights may be highly culturally, religiously, or philosophically dependent.

In Canada, as elsewhere, children have not themselves laid claim to full citizenship or to the rights that accompany citizenship. Their position has been bestowed upon them by adults. Whereas women have continued to fight for and claim full human and civil rights equal to those held by men, the special rights of children are given to them because they are seen to have certain innate limitations and disadvantages which place them at a degree of risk. These rights are limited in definition and are not meant to place children on an equal status with adults.

It has been argued that the installment of full rights for children is fraught with dangers. Should the child who has been seriously physically or sexually abused have the right to determine for himself or herself whether or not to remain in contact with the perpetrator of the abuse? Presumably, in cases of severe abuse, the safety of the child would be paramount and stronger children's rights would facilitate a child's disclosure of abuse. While improving children's rights can act as a safeguard in giving children more power to speak out if they have been harmed, a sweeping hand over of rights can reproduce abuse as well. For example, at what age do children have the right to consent to sexual contact with another person? And who decides – adults or children? Obviously, these issues are complex and should not be given a perfunctory, all-or-nothing response. As we shall see, the Ontario child welfare system has attempted to bring children into the equation during child protection hearings while taking into account their relative degree of dependency.

Social Work Intervention and Child Protection

In the Canadian context of child welfare, the social worker confronted by a case of child abuse or neglect will carry out a number of tasks required by

178 *Constructing Social Work Practices*

the state child welfare apparatus and the local child welfare agency (Falconer and Swift, 1983). These tasks can be broken down as follows:

1. Child protection work following provincial government guidelines (laws) and specific agency requirements. This work emphasizes the investigation of suspected cases of child abuse.

2. Applications before the Provincial Court.

3. Placement of children outside the family home when necessary.

4. Supervision of children in their own homes or when in foster care.

5. Ongoing social work assessments.

6. Advocacy for a client(s) who needs services beyond the scope of the Children's Aid Society (CAS).

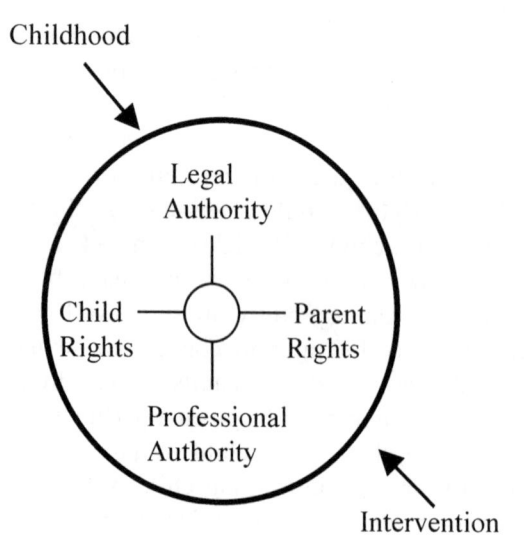

Figure 9.1 Intervention in cases of child abuse and neglect

What is not evident in this listing of social work tasks is the fact that the worker is often pulled into competing directions because of the ways in which intervention has been socially constructed and has interacted with social constructions of childhood. First, the child protection worker must juggle two kinds of authority – legal and professional. Second, the worker must balance parental versus children's rights. Figure 9.1 demonstrates graphically how the worker is at the centre of these often competing forces and must somehow negotiate all of these with the ultimate aim of protecting a child from harm.

To further illustrate what is happening when a social worker begins the task of child protection, a factual case vignette will be presented. Figure 9.2 illustrates the case of one family. Although the P. family is fictitious, the scenario draws upon the author's own experiences working as a child protection worker in the Canadian child system. The P. family is, in fact, a collage of 4 empirical cases known to the author and this collage presents many of the features of a typical child welfare case. This case is therefore presented as a snapshot of one occasion in which a family is referred to the CAS.

```
Sandie - - - 27    Children: Jamie - - - 6
Dave   - - - 29              Karen - - - 4
                             Leia  - - - 3
```

Figure 9.2   Case Vignette The P. Family

The following referral was made to the CAS, a child protection agency in an Ontario, Canada municipality. Jamie's teacher had noticed that the young boy had frequently been coming to school hungry and tired. He had been placed in the school's 'Breakfast Club'. The teacher was growing concerned about Jamie's poor concentration and because he was becoming irritable and angry toward other children in the class – sometimes even swearing and hitting. Jamie's parents had not attended two parent-teacher meetings to discuss these concerns. Today, his teacher noticed that when Jamie sat down at his seat, he did so hesitantly and placed himself at the edge of his seat. When probed by the teacher, Jamie responded that he had been 'smacked' for misbehaving and that his back and buttocks hurt. Jamie voluntarily lifted his T-shirt out of his trousers and the teacher was able to observe bruising along the small of his back.

When this report was received by the CAS, the worker, in consultation with a supervisor, determined that immediate action was required both by provincial requirements and agency protocol. Investigation and assessment brought out additional information which, when taken as a whole, was used to implement a social work plan.

Jamie had numerous ribbon-like bruises to his back and buttocks but there was no physical evidence of older bruises. Dave acknowledged having strapped the child with his belt because Jamie had repeatedly awakened in the middle of the night and had made a disaster of the kitchen, spilling food on the floor and smearing honey onto cupboard doors.

The social work investigation determined that Sandie and Dave had lived together periodically since the birth of Karen and that he is the biological father to the girls. The adults' relationship is described as chronically poor and punctured by physical altercations. Neither adult is working and Sandie has been on social assistance for several years. Sandie and her children have moved repeatedly and have been evicted on several occasions from sub-standard housing for failure to pay the rent.

Sandie expressed worry for Jamie because he was socially isolated. She said that she had become increasingly fatigued with the need to continually be mindful of his activities and for that reason relied on Dave for help. Sandie stated that Dave had never disciplined any of the children in such a way before though he had been frequently frustrated with Jamie too. During the course of the investigation, Jamie expressed some anxiety about 'getting mom into trouble' and about the possibility of being taken away from the home.

Although there was no evidence that Karen and Leia had been abused, there was some concern regarding the condition of the children in relation to their home environment. Both girls appeared not to have been bathed in some time, their clothes were not clean and there were piles of dirty clothes in the home. There was a limited amount of food in the home and it was questionable whether the children's nutritional needs were being met. Sandie reported that it could sometimes be difficult to keep a supply of nutritious food in the home particularly toward the end of the month when the family would be waiting for their benefits cheque. Nevertheless, the girls appeared attached to their mother and received warmth and affection from her.

Professional Considerations

The above vignette presents the so-called facts of the P. family in brief. In order to carry out the various tasks required in child protection work, the identified problems are systematically reduced in such a way as to key in on those areas which are within the mandate of the CAS. Other potential problems or ways of understanding the problem are buried. However, the role of the social worker still involves the mediation between two conflicting sets of beliefs and two competing styles of intervention.

Parental Rights The social worker cannot intervene in a value-free way when it involves decision-making about the P. family. First, the worker must deal with the issue of parents' rights. And, at the same time, the social construction of childhood as reflected in the discourse of the family, plays an important part in this decision-making process.

The decision-making process following a child abuse referral is rooted in the idealization of the family as the primary institution in society and is constrained by the view that parents are the arbiters of society's rules and values. In the case of the P. Family, the social worker is faced with the societal value that the parents have the fundamental right to decide for themselves, and free from state interference, how to raise Jamie. Thus, Jamie not only belongs to a family (which gives him identity) he belongs to his parents in a proprietal sense. Parental rights are deeply rooted in traditional values about the family and have been upheld even in the face of other value changes. This can make the task of balancing parental rights and the rights of the child a complex one. This task becomes an increasingly complex one if we consider the multicultural makeup of Canadian society which produces a multitude of ideas about proper child-raising.

According to the Declaration of Principles in the Child and Family Services Act (CFSA) (Government of Ontario, 1989), services should be provided, wherever possible on the basis of mutual consent of the parents and the service provider, and that 'least restrictive or disruptive' measures should be followed.

Parental rights are at the surface in the case of the P. family where the social worker first must decide whether the occurrence had derived from the excessive 'discipline' of Jamie by his step-father (the act of disciplining being a right and obligation); whether there was an intent to harm Jamie (considered an illness or defect in the perpetrator); and whether Jamie's mother failed to protect him (protection often being the duty of the adult female). Since physical injury could be easily documented, verification of physical abuse is quite possible. In deciding the least intrusive course of action, however, the social worker must still assess whether this appears to have been an isolated incident, or whether there are other indicators of a pattern of abuse.

In this case, the legalization and bureaucratization of the decision-making process makes it appear that all families are treated equally. Either Jamie has been physically harmed as defined by injuries resulting from excessive or inappropriate discipline, or he has not been harmed. Thus, guidelines state that the CAS will intervene on the basis of Jamie's bruising. But, *how* we intervene is not the same for all families.

In a middle class family, we are less likely to impose a court order or other involuntary interventions. We would look at the entire family situation and other signs of a 'bad' family may not be evident. Nutrition would not be a concern, at least one parent would have a decent job and income, and the incident may be attributed to some interpersonal relationship difficulties in the family. The worker may be inclined to approach the case by referring the family to a therapist and perhaps would include a psychological assessment of Jamie because of his aggressive behaviour. Even the duration of the agency's involvement may be shorter. In every way, such a family would have greater power in relation to the CAS than the P. family.

Thus, we see Jamie as being at higher risk of future abuse and may even suspect that physically abusive incidents had gone on undetected in the past. Jamie's behaviour in and out of the home may be classified as bordering on 'out of control' and there would be much consideration of whether or not his parents could cope with him. The likely outcome would be that the agency would take the case to court – asking for and, in all likelihood, obtaining a finding that Jamie is in need of society's protection in the form of a supervision order. Indeed, his sisters would likely be included in such an order because they would be found to be "at risk" of physical harm.

Given children's position in relation to parental rights, we see that in some families the state has greater power to intervene in the lives of children. The state has, in such cases greater power to intervene in the lives of poor children because their power is directly connected to that of their parents. That is, they are relatively powerless.

Children's Rights Whereas the rights of parents have dominated the discourse on parent-child and family-state relations, in recent years the rights of the child have begun to be heard. Thus, even the poorest of children now have some power in the child welfare system. The movement to bring forward children's rights has gained momentum as children have increasingly been viewed as individuals and because it has become increasingly difficult to deny children the same human rights as adult citizens. Therefore, society's changing conceptualization of childhood has resulted in children being given increasing individual rights. To illustrate, Jamie has now entered into the position of a potential third party in child protection hearings. But, it must be recognized that this is a relatively recent phenomenon and that the rights afforded to him and children in similar circumstances are still quite limited.

The rights of the child have evolved in the form of official decrees and legislation as well as in the ideology of society. For example, the United Nations Declaration of the Rights of the Child (1959), to which Canada is a signatory, states that children in addition to other fundamental rights:

> shall enjoy special protection...to enable him [sic] to develop physically, mentally, morally, spiritually, and socially in a healthy and normal manner.

and that they:

> shall be protected against all forms of neglect, cruelty and exploitation.

The declaration also states that the 'best interests of the child' shall be paramount but that, 'responsibility lies in the first place with his parents'. This non-binding declaration is indicative of both earlier and current attempts to articulate and establish boundaries around the rights of the child. It is possible to see in the text of this declaration that children remain first and foremost the responsibility of their parents and that adults will be the ones to define what the best interests of the child are.

In spite of being a signatory, the Canadian state continues to have legislation which apparently contradicts UN principles. Section 43 of the Criminal Code of Canada has given parents, teachers or other standing in the place of a parent, the right to use corporal punishment as long as the physical force used, 'does not exceed what is reasonable under the circumstances'. As of 1997, this legislation had still not been repealed and no political party had stood strongly against this section of criminal law.

At the same time, the Charter of Rights and Freedoms which is a part of the Canadian Constitution Act (1982), states that all individuals are equal before the law and, in particular, without discrimination based on age. This seems to contradict Section 43 since, the latter would appear to condone behaviour by adults which would be considered physical assault if it were perpetrated against another adult rather than a child.

Jamie's rights become explicit only if the CAS begins protection hearings in the Provincial Court. Under the CFSA it is the court's responsibility to determine if a child would benefit from legal representation to protect his or her interests. A ruling appointing a Children's Lawyer (formerly Official Guardian) is therefore not automatic.

Part five (V) of the Act is entirely devoted to the definition of the rights of the child. These rights are only applicable to children who reside in the care of the CAS or who are in a detention facility under the Young Offenders Act. If Jamie were to reside in foster care, he would have a right not to be kept in locked premises, and not to receive corporal punishment. He would also have a right to speak with his lawyer, the Ombudsman of Ontario, or a representative of the Office of Child and Family Advocacy. The Act goes into great detail about other individual rights. Some of the most important of these are Jamie's right to a plan of care, and to participate in and express his views regarding any significant decisions concerning himself.

While not intending to diminish the importance of the gains made in the area of children's rights, we should consider whether these rights could be made more explicit outside of court proceedings. For example, the conciliation process, in which children have a chance to express themselves during their parent's divorce, has proved to be a useful process for children (Garwood, 1992). Keeping the child's view in focus in child protection work is vital if we expect the child to emerge intact from the consequences of either having disclosed abuse/neglect or it being uncovered in some other way.

Legal Authority In exercising legal authority, every act by the child protection worker is influenced by social constructions of childhood. From the doctrine of *parens patriae* which continues to reinforce the notion of the state taking over the caretaking role from 'bad' parents, to the current Child and Family Services Act, the child's destiny still remains in the hands of adults.

Many people in the field of child protection and in the larger society would argue that the parents of Jamie had clearly crossed the line from appropriate discipline and had thus physically abused their son. The ultimate consequence for this breech of parental responsibility is that they should no longer continue to have the right to exercise care and control over their child. The fact that a report was received concerning the possible abuse of a child is sufficient to require the CAS to investigate and gives the child protection worker the legal authority to do so. But, intervention does not necessarily mean the immediate removal of Jamie from his parent's care. The legal mandate establishes the power of the state to intervene in the family on an involuntary basis. However, it also sets limits on this intervention so as not to abrogate the rights of the parents.

Under the CFSA, the legal mandate under which the CAS can impose involuntary intervention in a family has been considerably narrowed. Analysis of this document shows that definitions of child abuse and neglect have been more narrowly defined to include certain acts of commission or omission by parents. And, to obtain an order compelling intervention with the family system, a child must first be found 'in need of protection' according to these narrowly interpreted concepts of physical, sexual or emotion harm or substantial risk of harm. Interestingly, the terms 'child abuse' and 'neglect' are not currently not used in the legislation. The Act does, however, specify additional grounds for a finding of a 'child in need of protection' based on the emotional, mental or developmental condition of the child. In these cases, the conditions of the child must be 'serious' and the parent must also be unwilling, or unable to do what is necessary to remedy the situation.

Although there are other principles specified in the legislation, two key principles guide the court's legal interpretation of the Act. These are: i) the recognition of 'least intrusive measures' (CFSA, sec. 37, 3) and ii) the 'best interests of a child' (CFSA, sec. 55, 3). When deciding the case, the court must decide whether the child protection worker made every possible consideration to secure the protection of the child through voluntary means. The sequence of possible court-ordered interventions from least intrusive to most intrusive are supervision orders followed by temporary wardship, to crown wardship where all parental rights are eliminated. When deciding a child's best interests, consideration must be given to a child's need for a secure and loving family, a sense of stability, the need for parents, and the opportunity to reside within his own culture (a right particularly important to Native children whose parents, as children, were often removed and placed in non-Native communities).

Assuming for the moment that Jamie was found to be a 'child in need of protection', the child protection worker can use her legal authority and the CFSA in developing a casework plan. Legal tools at the worker's disposal include: supervision orders (in which the social worker can specify specific terms and conditions that must be met before involuntary services can be terminated), placement of the child in foster or institutional care as a society ward (for up to a maximum of 24 months), a permanent custody order, and, if a child is placed in the care of a CAS, orders establishing, limiting or denying access between Jamie and his parents.

While it is ultimately the court which decides whether a child is in need of protection and what plan of care will be accepted, the social worker has a tremendous amount of responsibility and power in presenting the situation of the family and the planned intervention to the court within the limits of the society's legal mandate. This power is checked by the parents' right to legal representation and the child's potential to be appointed a Children's Lawyer particularly if the case will be argued and the child is old enough to express his views.

It is significant, however, that the child is not automatically appointed a children's lawyer. Furthermore, even in the case of a lawyer being appointed for the child, it is not always clear that the child has an independent and equal voice in child protection hearings. If the child is too young to speak, the Children's Lawyer will represent the child's best interests. If the child is somewhat older but not over the age of 12, the Children's Lawyer may act on a combination of best interests and the child's expressed wishes. It is only the older child (over the age of 12) who can actually be present in court and who can instruct the Children's Lawyer to represent his or her wishes alone.

The aforementioned discussion of features of legal authority demonstrates how conceptualizations of childhood and children pervade legislation. It is evident that children are not yet equal partners in the legal process. But, the legislation is meant, in theory, to be a guide with checks and balances built in to prevent abuses of power by the child welfare system.

Professional Authority Professional authority in child protection work is shaped in part by the body of knowledge which comprises the social work profession. Authority is attached to offices (such as the CAS) and requires a deferential attitude on the part of citizens (or clients) to be fully established, whereas power is the ability to influence others or cause them to do what we want (Goodwin, 1992). In child protection work, professional authority is derived from the knowledge and values of the social work profession. When carrying out the many tasks of child protection work, there are certain ways in which the worker's decisions are informed. The worker is generally formally educated from a social work perspective and therefore has a degree of professional authority stemming from her professional knowledge. The social worker also has received specific training in child welfare practice and thus has specialized knowledge about the role of a social worker in this specific setting. Specialized training in child welfare also shapes the worker's understanding of specific problems in the family so that she will be able to effectively assess a family's strengths, weaknesses and needs, the level of risk for a child, and to develop a social work plan (Falconer and Swift, 1983).

Professional authority in child protection work rests on the ability of the social worker and client to establish a positive relationship in which the rights and responsibilities of all parties are recognized (Institute for the Prevention of Child Abuse, I.P.C.A.). To apply authority in child protection requires a worker to act humanely and with genuineness while keeping to the guidelines of social work professionalism. What supposedly makes social work different from other professions is its concern for both the individual and the individual in relation to his or her social environment. As a values-based profession, social work focuses on maintaining a respect for the inherent dignity of the individual. Social workers should not presume to know what is best for the client. Therefore, in child protection, social workers must also be able to tame our wish to impose our beliefs on clients.

However, the profession's knowledge base still focuses more on the flaws of the parents who have presumably not provided the proper care for a child. Society's failings are rarely discussed.

Thus when we use our professional authority in all of its forms (e.g. knowledge of human behaviour, development of children, family dynamics, problem-solving techniques, communication, service advocacy, relationship, and understanding of resistance) we must be cognizant of the fact that it would be impossible to do all of this and not be influenced by societal constructions of childhood.

In some ways, the use of professional authority can be a double-edged sword. This form of authority is derived from the knowledge base of the profession and puts the social worker in the position of 'expert' in relation to her client(s). If we take the example of the P. Family, this expertise can be one tool available to obtain compliance by Sandie and Dave on matters regarding so-called appropriate child-management techniques. While the worker-client relationship is arguably the most important change-producing force in social work (Morén, 1994), genuineness and positive-regard for the client are not often prioritized in the social work plan with clients of the CAS. And, what of Jamie in this interaction with an authority figure? Not only is the child protection worker an 'expert' based on professional knowledge. She is an 'expert' because of the wisdom that supposedly comes with age.

Discussion

Child welfare services in Canada have gradually evolved and been shaped by changing societal values and conditions as well as changing social constructions of childhood. The social welfare system has evolved into an entity which recognizes two classes of needy people – the worthy and the unworthy. Health care, education, care for the elderly, the handicapped and to a lesser extent, programs for the unemployed are distributed on the principle of universal need. All in society are seen to have a right to health care, and education. The elderly and handicapped are considered a worthy group of recipients of public aid because they have special needs through no fault of their own. The public recognize the inevitability of aging and are sympathetic toward those with disabilities. Because workers do not control the employment market themselves, they contribute to unemployment insurance while working and, thus, have a right to receive support if they are laid off.

The P. family, and other recipients of child welfare services, however, would be classified as the unworthy poor. Dave 'should' be working to support the family regardless of the unemployment statistics and the fact that he is an unskilled labourer. Although the laws against spousal abuse are clear, Sandie remains with Dave because the traditional values on which she was raised are stronger than her ability to protect herself and her children. The family as a whole is unworthy because the parents have failed in their role as care-takers. And, Jamie is also unworthy because his behaviour can be seen as contributing to the stressors which lead to his abuse.

In Canadian society, Jamie's chances for success are limited due to the fact that he has been born into a poor family. He does not have the same chances in life even though certain features of his life are shared with children from upper classes. While he may have the opportunity to receive a basic education through the school system, he will not have the freedom to participate in sports and other extra-curricular activities. And, when he is at home, he is still confronted by a lack many of the things that other wealthier children take for granted such as decent clothes, adequate meals, the stability of a reasonably secure home life, and hope for the future.

Jamie's experience of life is one of increasing frustration as he lashes out against those around him. He sees his own family's poverty on the one hand but is inundated primarily through television with images of wealth, consumption, and power. These images, replete with sport and entertainment heroes, provide him a totally distorted picture of what it means to be successful and yet, who can blame him for wanting the same tokens of wealth and success as his wealthier classmates? But, without having access to an equal playing field, Jamie's odds of becoming a successful individual as defined by these media images are very limited.

When Jamie's worker begins to develop a social work plan, aside from the obvious need to protect him from future harm, she will try to put in place some services that are meant to give him more opportunities. These programs are provided on an individual basis and may include finding Jamie a Big Brother, finding a community services program that offers after-school activities for needy children, and obtaining sponsorship for Jamie and his family to receive a Christmas 'hamper' with toys and food. But, seemingly little can be done to change the structural arrangements in society which keep Jamie's family in poverty and which place Jamie at risk.

Statements that child abuse and neglect can be found among all socioeconomic classes imply that these problems are distributed proportionately among the total population (Peyton, 1980). Evidence is to the contrary even if the media sometimes would have us believe otherwise. Violent crime is far more prevalent amongst the lower classes, and child abuse indicators also demonstrate that this is true. It's not just a question of abuse being hidden more by the middle classes although this is probably also true to some extent. Upholding the myth of the classlessness of abuse serves functions for those who accept the view. Abuse can thus be treated as a disease or character flaw in the parents rather than a poverty related problem.

We do a disservice to poor people in not recognizing this because it limits the effectiveness of approaches we use to deal with the problem. We never really deal with the real, difficult poverty associated issues. According to Peyton (1989), poverty may not just be associated with child abuse, it may actually be a causative agent in the parents abusive or negligent behaviours which result in harm to their children.

In child protection work, it can be difficult to find the extra time and energy necessary to fight for remedies to the health and safety hazards which attend poverty and thus place children in danger of harm and abuse. Similarly, attendance or adherence to the myth of the classlessness of abuse diverts us from tackling the real problems and also diverts resources away from finding a solution to the problem.

In the present revisionist climate in which many aspects of the provision of personal social services are being rethought, child protection services have also been under scrutiny and continue to be the focus of ongoing re-examination. Indeed, right now Canadian society seems to be at the apex of significant change regarding the way childhood is being defined and in the way child welfare services are to be delivered. Our media has in recent years provided a conflicting view of childhood. It has been called everything from a dangerous time to a breeding ground for predators (Ehrenreich, 1996). In recent years, however, most of what the media has focused on has been the failures of the child welfare system.

Much has been said and written about the failure of the system to protect society's children. However, there is a *double entendre* in the message being presented. The media mentions children generally and the assumption is that all children are at stake. But, the hidden message is that child victims of abuse are the progeny of both killer parents and a system which has placed too much emphasis on the rights of the parents.

A series of seven Coroner's Inquests recently investigated the deaths of children who were under the supervision of the CAS. These inquests were intensively followed by the media and a number of recommendations were recommended first by the media and then officially by the Office of the Coroner. Two key recommendations were made and are currently under consideration by the Government of Ontario. First, is the call for a definition of neglect under the Child and Family Services Act. This omission in the Act was considered a major flaw and danger to children as the vast majority of cases held by the CAS included elements of neglect which, if not properly addressed could lead to the deaths of children. Second, it was recommended that the Child and Family Services Act take a 'children first' first approach rather than a 'least intrusive approach' to intervention.

But, are these approaches truly going to help? And, are there alternatives to the conventional way of *doing* child protection work or are social workers with critical views about child welfare destined to "burn out" or get out of the system? It is easier to focus on the idea that bad children or child victims are created by individual parents with a variety of character flaws. And once these children get old enough to become the predators, we can easily convince ourselves that they are either inadequate or evil. Notwithstanding, we must remember that we are all responsible for creating the conditions which lead to child abuse and neglect.

On the other hand, there is a positive message in the notion that childhood and intervention are socially constructed. This is that everything that is created by humans can be changed. Although the tasks may be difficult, the potential for change remains.

Bringing in other definitions of childhood and reconstructing social work intervention in child welfare requires a lot of us. We can, as individuals begin to work differently with clients in the way that we define the client's problems or other identified problems. We can begin to use other powers beyond the professional and legal to empower our clients. This involves thinking differently about cases and about the way we intervene on the frontlines.

We need to broaden our view on what childhood is and on the ways it is experienced differently by different groups of children. This understanding can form the basis for broadening child-focused social work research and practice to include structural or critical analyses which address the independent interests of the child.

Bibliography

Bowlby, J. (1973), *Separation: Anxiety and Anger*, vol. II of *Attachment and Loss*, Penguin, U.K.
Child Protection Part I: Investigation and Assessment (1990), Institute for the Prevention of Child Abuse, Resource Material, Toronto.
Ehrenreich, B. (1996), 'Oh, Grow Up!', *TIME Magazine*, Nov. 4, pp. 68.
Erikson, E. H. (1963), *Childhood and Society* (2nd ed.), Norton, New York.
Ester, P. Halman, L. and de Moor, R. (eds) (1994), *The Individualizing Society: Value change in Europe and North America*, Tilburg University Press.

Falconer, N. and Swift, K. (1983), *Preparing for Practice: The fundamentals of child protection*, The CAS of Metropolitan Toronto, Toronto.
Finkelhor, D. (1994), 'The International Epidemiology of Child Sexual Abuse', *Child Abuse and Neglect*, vol. 18, no. 5, pp. 409-417.
Garwood, F. (1992), 'Conciliation: A Forum for Children's Views?', *Children and Society*, vol. 6, no. 4, pp. 353-363.
Goodwin, B. (1992), *Using Political Ideas (3rd ed.)*, John Wiley and Sons Ltd, Rexdale, Canada.
Government of Canada (1982), *The Constitution Acts, 1867 to 1982*, Canadian Government Publishing Centre, Ottawa, Canada.
Government of Ontario (1989), *Child and Family Services Act, 1984*, Ministry of the Attorney General (publisher), Ontario, Canada.
Harris, J. and Melichercik (1986), 'Age and State-Related Programs', in J. Turner, and F. Turner (eds), *Canadian Social Welfare*, Collier, Macmillan, Toronto.
Hyvönen, U. (1989), *The Concept of Childhood in Modernity*, Paper presented at the IUC seminar, Sociology of Science: Controversies in Science and Sociology, Dubrovnick, Former Yugoslavia.
Morén, S. (1994), 'Social work is Beautiful', *Scandinavian Journal of Social Welfare*, vol. 3, pp. 158-166.
Oldman, D. (1994), 'Adult-Child Relations as Class Relations', in J. Qvortrup, M. Bardy, G. Sgritta, and H. Wintersberger (eds), *Childhood Matters: Social theory, practice and politics*, Avebury, Ashgate, Hants, England.
O'Neill, J. (1994), *The Missing Child in Liberal Theory: Towards a covenant theory of family, community, welfare and the civic state*, University of Toronto Press, Toronto.
Peyton, L. (1980), 'Child Abuse and Neglect: The Myth of Classlessness', in J. Cook, and R. Tyler Bowles (eds), *Child Abuse: Commission and Omission*, Butterworths, Toronto.
Postman, J. (1982), *The Disappearance of Childhood*, Dalcourt Press, New York.
Steinhauer, P. D. (1983), Assessing for Parenting Capacity, *American Journal of Orthopsychiatry*, vol. 53, no. 3, pp. 468-481.
Swift, K. (1995), *Manufacturing Bad Mothers: A critical perspective on child neglect*, University of Toronto Press, Toronto.
Trocmé, N., McPhee, D. and Tam, K. K. (1995), 'Child Abuse and Neglect in Ontario: Incidence and Characteristics', *Child Welfare*, vol. 74, no. 3, pp. 563-586.
Turner, J. and Turner, F. (eds) (1986), *Canadian Social Welfare*, Collier Macmillan Canada, Toronto.
Qvortrup, J. (1994), 'Childhood Matters: An Introduction', in J. Qvortrup, M. Bardy, G. Sgritta, and H. Wintersberger (eds), *Childhood Matters: Social theory, practice and politics*, Avebury Ashgate, England.
Qvortrup, J., Bardy, M., Sgritta, G., and Wintersberger, H. (eds), *Childhood Matters: Social theory, practice and politics*, Avebury Ashgate Hants, England.

10 Constructing Juvenile Delinquency: The Socio-Legal Control of Young Offenders in Israel, 1920-1975

MIMI AJZENSTADT

Introduction

In 1996, a taxi-driver was shot to death in a middle-class neighborhood in Israel. Very quickly, it was found that this murder was committed by two high-school children who had planned it for some time. They admitted their guilt and were sentenced to detainment in a juvenile prison. This unusual event drew public attention and the daily newspapers published articles attempting to understand the motives for the murder. Most reports related the boys' criminal behavior to some pathological traits: one of them was depicted as a victim of his parents' divorce, and of the instability of his family life. The other was described as suffering from a weak personality and other emotional problems. A few months later, a new article was published describing the daily activity of one of the boys in the prison. In a television program on issues relating to media coverage of the week, the moderator asked the victim's daughter to respond to the article. She attacked the use of the medical-welfare approach and claimed that while the media showed the murderers as victims, it neglected the real victims of the case: the taxi driver's family. She claimed that the boys should be punished and remain behind bars without being given a public stage, which presents them through a medical focus, causing feelings of pity and in some way even forgiveness.

194 *Constructing Social Work Practices*

Medicalization of Crime and Social Control

While her criticism was mainly ignored, this was probably the first time the dominant discourse around juvenile delinquency in Israel has been challenged. This discourse is characterized by its highly medical-welfare approach (cf. Conrad and Schneider, 1980) which sees young offenders as sick children who are victims of psychological or social forces they are unable to control and thus have to be treated and rehabilitated. This medicalized approach is manifested, mainly, in the power allocated to probation officers who supply the juvenile courts with a medical-social report about the minor, and recommend a sentence. Almost 80 per cent of these recommendations are fully accepted by the court (– Ministry of Labor and Social Affairs, 1996, p. 32). It is important to note that in most cases juvenile delinquents who come mainly from families belonging to the lower strata in Israeli society (– Ministry of Labor and Social Affairs, 1996, p. 18), appear before the courts without being represented by an attorney. This is because the judicial process is treatment oriented and not a legal process, even though charges are placed, formal criminal files opened and minors penalized. However, in cases of juvenile Arab minors who are charged with terrorist activities (burning cars, throwing stones at soldiers and policemen) this medical approach is not invoked.

During the last two decades, various sociologists, criminologists, social workers and lawyers in Europe and the USA have criticized the medical model, highlighting abused human rights, the vagueness of definitions used to classify offenders and the power of the medical-welfare profession. This criticism, however, had almost no influence on the medical model in Israel. In this paper, I will follow the evolution of the discourse around juvenile delinquency in Israel from the 1930s, when it started to be promulgated and professionals claimed the 'ownership' of the problem (cf. Gusfield, 1981; 1989) until the 1970s, when this discourse was formally institutionalized – a situation which has not changed until today.

In order to investigate these issues, this paper utilizes recent developments in the sociology of social control, sociology of law and sociology of deviance and criminology (Chunn, 1992; Cohen, 1985; Donzelot, 1979; Edwards, 1988). Those 'revisionist' theories of social control which introduce critical and feminist thinking about law, control, and the management of social deviance challenge the traditional assumption that saw in the prosperity of treatment agencies and methods a linear progressive development, a step forward in the attitudes of society toward criminals and offenders (see Cohen and Scull, 1983). In contrast, the revisionist approaches refer to changes in the penal, medical and welfare responses to crime which occurred in North America, Canada and Europe in much broader structural terms, emphasizing social, economic and political forces causing it and influencing its pattern (see for example Melossi, 1990; Simon, 1993a; 1993b). The construction of these control mechanisms and their focus has engendered a rethinking of theories of control, away from individualist approaches toward more historically-oriented explanations of the field. Thus, the new theories stress that the investigation of these policies should examine the various political, ideological, social, financial and even practical forces which influenced the processes leading to the adoption of treatment models and their implementation while responding to criminal behavior.

Scholars such as Garland (1985) and Valverde (1992) have shown that the emergence of law and welfare policies in the period between the end of the 19th century and the mid-20th century, was the product of a combination of liberal political thought, a vigorous form of social Christianity associated closely with middle class Protestantism, and the development of human sciences. Emergent ideologies were allied with the perception that there were detectable differences in individual and collective behavior within society which in turn were dependent on distinctions deriving from social class, gender, ethnicity and race. The solution to deviance, mainly among the lower orders, was seen as inherent in the inculcation of middle class, patriarchal, white Anglo-Saxon values – hard work, thrift and moral commitment. Toward the 1950s those strong elements of moral judgementalism had combined with a growing confidence in the ability of science to explain so-called deviant behavior and to provide a rationale for the use of law and other controls as a key instrument of social management and change.

Following those theories and locating the construction of juvenile delinquency in Israel within general political changes and developments, this chapter focuses on two main periods of time: 1930-1948 (the pre-state period) and the years 1949-1975, when a civil society was formed. It traces the societal reaction to juvenile delinquency in Israel and examines the claims (cf. Spector and Kitsuse, 1977) made by various social actors involved in public, official and professional debates about crime, control, and the social order of Israeli society. Archival material including official reports, private correspondence, relevant newspaper articles and articles published in professional magazines was examined in order to allow a reconstruction of the ways in which the socio-legal reaction to juvenile delinquency was established and employed.

Crime and the Zionist Discourse, 1930–1948

The Zionist movement was established at the end of the 19th century in Europe calling for the creation of a specific Jewish collective entity in a natural, national, territorial and collective environment. At the beginning of the 20th century, the Zionist movement developed into a full-fledged political platform, soon translated into action by the first settlers who came to Palestine as idealists, ready to devote themselves to achieving the goals of nationhood. The pioneers, who came mainly from Europe, saw themselves as developing and creating a new physical and political Jewish entity. They imagined a new, strong, muscular, natural human being, living and working in a modern community administered by modern ideas and knowledge.

Between 1920 and 1947 Palestine was governed by the British Mandate. Parallel to the Mandate regime, local economic, cultural, educational and welfare institutions were established to deal with the ongoing life of the Jewish community in Palestine. Within this structure, issues relating to wayward youth began to emerge, mainly among professionals who came to Israel from Germany during the 1930s. Among those newcomers there were medical practitioners, social workers, psychologists and educators who established schools, health facilities and units aiming to care for the welfare of the citizens. Very soon, they became part of the financial elite in the Jewish community, being key influential actors in debates and practices about the appropriate social order which was to prevail in the country. They were involved in the welfare, health and educational departments of various municipalities and the Vaad-Leumi – National Council – the main autonomous Jewish organ established to deal with various aspects of daily life of the Jewish community.

Similarly to the 'child-saver' movement (cf. Platt, 1969), a paternalistic view adopted by those professional groups saw young offenders and abandoned youth, those who lived outside their families, youth who did not attend schools, as being 'at-risk' and thus having to be cared for and saved by society. As a result, The *Young Offender Act*[1] was enacted in 1922 and was amended in 1937.[2] The acts marked a major change in the society's reaction toward juvenile delinquency. Prior to this Act, young offenders were whipped and imprisoned (Naaman, 1939, p. 9). With the introduction of the 1937 Act, judges were required to consult a personal report written by probation officers appointed by the British government.[3] This report included descriptions of the family of the accused, assessment of his/her psychological and physical developments and a recommendation for punishment or treatment. The judge was empowered to order juvenile delinquents to be supervised by suitable persons and treated by experts. Moreover, the Act widened the clientele of the juvenile court, enabling the judge to order deserted and wayward children to be treated by welfare agencies.[4] These Acts altered the field of the penal response toward crime and deviance and led the way in Palestine, and later in the State of Israel, to the creation of a whole range of agencies, institutions and treatment techniques aiming to use scientific developments, allowing experts to identify, treat, and even prevent delinquency (see for example Elad and Wiener, 1995).

In this reaction to juvenile delinquency three inter-related main trends began to emerge: the promulgation of a discourse of pathology, the focus of the discourse on youth from 'Oriental' families, the merging of this concern within a wider 'master' discourse.

The Promulgation of a Discourse of Pathology

Following the then popular positivist 'Lombrosian' paradigm, physicians and representatives of professional groups saw children's involvement in crimes as originating in biological or psychological pathological deficiency of certain individuals. Medical knowledge concerning criminality was seriously limited in a number of ways at this time and was recognized by the profession to be so. There was ample scope for dispute and controversy regarding the extent of the criminal behavior, the ability of the profession to control its spread, and questions of etiology, diagnosis, and classification. In spite of expert dispute most physicians claimed that criminals suffered from a variety of physical illnesses. In an article published by Dr. Kraus (1936), in the official bulletin of the Palestine Physicians Association (*Harefua*) for example, young offenders were described as suffering from: 'mental deficiency, psychopathy, brain disease in childhood or were children of mentally abnormal parents' (p. 641).

The involvement of physicians with the mental and physical attributes of criminality was manifested at the time mainly in the development of the mental hygiene movement. Similarly to their counterparts in the USA (Valverde, 1991), Canada (see Ajzenstadt, 1994) and England (see discussion in Garland, 1985), physicians in Palestine established a Hygiene Movement active in areas of education, crime, deviance, mental and physical hygiene and mental sickness. The key figure in this area was Dr. Brachiyahu (Borochov) who immigrated to Palestine immediately after receiving his degree in medicine in Switzerland in 1910. He established the School Hygiene Department in Jerusalem in 1919 and fought against contagious diseases such as trachoma, ringworm and pollution. As early as 1923, Dr. Brachiyahu established a Child Guidance Clinic in Tel Aviv and Jerusalem. During the following years similar clinics were opened in other cities (see Prat, 1950, p. 137). In November 1943, Brachiyahu started the *Mental Hygiene Journal*. He published numerous articles and books and became an authoritative figure in the area of mental hygiene and juvenile delinquency (see Brand, 1950). Brachiyahu's observations and studies led him to conclude that feebleminded children comprised between 70-80 per cent of the children involved in crimes.[5] He claimed that since they were not being cared for and were not being educated in special classes and institutions, they were used by psychopaths or deserted youth who socialized with these children in violent activity and sexual criminal behavior (Brachyahu 1935a, p. 205). In other studies he diagnosed 6-8 per cent of the Jewish children in the country as being mentally retarded, and another 25 per cent as marginal cases who without proper treatment would deteriorate to criminal life (see Brachyahu, 1935b, p. 276, see Glikson, 1950, p. 137).

Ideas of abnormality, mental health and involvement in crime were discussed heatedly by the supporters of the Eugenic theory. Importing ideas mainly from Europe, various physicians recruited Eugenic ideas to promote the achievement of health and welfare of the Jewish community. As early as 1928 Dr. Shimon Einhorn lectured to the Tel Aviv branch of the Medical Association on the subject of: 'Sterilization of mentally ill persons and habitual criminals' (Einhorn, 1929). After reviewing the major themes of the Eugenic Movement and Eugenic legislation enacted in the western world, Dr. Einhorn explained that most researchers tend to allow sterilization when a patient is mentally disturbed, lecherous and prone to involvement in sexual crimes (p. 43). He went on to explain in length how such sterilization should be performed.[6] A year later, Dr. Rabinowitz

(1929) continued with a similar line of thought and warned the public against imbeciles, schizophrenics, and people suffering from mental disorders leaving the mental hospital, getting married and giving birth to mentally-ill, idiots and epileptic children. He claimed that this phenomenon should be corrected by disseminating the idea of selective breeding and the search for means to prohibit people of this type to get married (p. 12). As late as 1944, Dr. Loewenstein lectured at a meeting of neurologists and psychiatrists in Tel Aviv, where he called for the de-politicizing of Eugenic ideas by praising its objectivity and scientific contribution to the 'peace of the nation' (p. 65). Supporting the Eugenic ideas which began to decline among the scientific community around the world at this time (McLaren, 1990), he acknowledges the fact that the Nazi regime used this doctrine in a 'biased and distorted way for political purposes. But this use should not prevent us from seeing real Eugenic ideas in the appropriate objectivity which it deserved' (p. 66). The physician called upon his colleagues to prevent the birth of certain offspring by various means, among them prohibition of marriage, prevention of pregnancy, forced abortion and sterilization (ibid.).

Similarly to the European and North American progressive reformers (Chunn, 1992; Garland, 1985; Platt, 1969), professionals in Palestine monopolized the societal responses to juvenile delinquency. They claimed that they could utilize their expertise and scientific ability to predict, identify, treat and prevent physical and environmental situations causing youths/minors to be involved in criminal activity. Thus, Dr. Kraus (1936), for example, claimed that physicians experienced in psychiatry and medical pedagogy should 'diagnose each case and direct the person along the proper path' (p. 642). Physicians and members of other professional groups saw themselves as responsible not only for the treatment of certain youth who went astray, but as being placed in the forefront of those paving the way to the creation of a new Jewish society in Palestine. Issues raised by practitioners were not simply technical ones of how to best identify and control certain forms of deviant behavior, but they saw themselves as participating in the development of an 'absolutely new Psycho-physical Jewish type' (Rivkai, 1932, p. 218). This new Jewish youth would be cured of the Diaspora's degenerative slovenly affects to become healthy strong human beings (Nordau, 1955, pp. 117-118).

Moreover, in order to enable the new Jewish person to develop, physicians claimed that they should lead the battle against primitives among the citizens who used traditional non-scientific medical practices.

Thus, for example, Dr. Brand (1950) reflected that 'the population needed not only medical assistance, but a minimum of guidance ... overcoming this malady must be carried out not by oaths, charms and amulets, burning by white-hot iron or crushed coral but by medical means' (p. 129). In order to carry out this medical-national aim, physicians called upon the British government authorities and the welfare, health and educational agencies of the Vaad Leumi to initiate a series of 'pedagogical-physical means' among which were the development of physical and mental examination of kindergarten and elementary school children and for those identified as sick (physically or mentally) to be placed in special classes, in schools, where they could study manual or agricultural work (Brachiyahu, 1935a, p. 209). Such medical disciplining, whether as an educational means or as rehabilitation, was justified not in terms of the doctor's obligation to a sick individual, but in terms of social order, and in terms of the greatest good for the greatest number.

The pathologization of juvenile delinquency was advanced by the discipline of social welfare which started to emerge in Palestine during the 1930s, mainly through the work of Henrietta Szold who was appointed as the Director of the Vaad Leumi's Welfare Department. Claiming the ownership (cf. Gusfield, 1981) of the juvenile delinquency phenomenon, Szold and her colleagues argued that only through the use of 'scientific methods of social work knowledge and practice' (Cohen, 1936, p. 70) would this behavior be prevented. While social workers called for the location of delinquency in social circumstances such as pathological families and neighborhoods, they nevertheless continued to individualize the behavior and saw the deviant as sick and thus requiring to be the target of control and regulations. Such a point of view was put forward by Szold who stated that 'criminals are sick, distorted and deformed by their life circumstances or they are miserable persons who were born feeble' (Szold, 1937, p. 7).

The pioneering society which emphasized values of hard work, individual commitment and responsibility, did not always welcome the discipline of social work that demanded public responsibility and care for the disabled. Thus, social workers claimed incessantly in their official organs that social work is as productive as agriculture and industry since both aim to process raw material to a new shape suitable for the newly-established Jewish community (Dushkin, 1935, p. 112). In addition, Szold demanded that the Jewish authorities force school principals who did not trust her new methods to allow social workers to direct them with preventative measures in order to 'erase the public disgrace [juvenile delinquency] from our community'.[7]

The Focus of the Discourse

While the discursive claims were cast in universal terms, the main focus of the discourse was youth from the so-called 'Oriental' communities, sometimes called Sepharadi Jews – those families who comprised 20 per cent of the Jewish population in Palestine prior to the establishment of the state (Lissak, 1994, p. 192) and who had immigrated from Islamic countries. Others inhabited the old city of Jerusalem or other cities and were descendants of Sepharadi Jews who had lived in Palestine for centuries. The majority lived in poverty and were mainly considered as the lower strata of the community (Gelber, 1992, p. 344). They were portrayed by the elite groups, among them members of newly-formed organizations of professionals, as primitive and as endangering the smooth development of the new society if they were not treated and normalized. For Dr. Rabinowitz (1929) who worked in the Ezrat-Nasheem mental hospital in Jerusalem, Bukharans and Persians as members of 'primitives societies make no special demands of their environment, and are submissive to external conditions' (p. 10). He warns that while until now, they had a relatively low rate of mental illnesses, when our 'cultural life begins to have its effect on these communities, it will give rise to significant percentages of neurotics and psychotics' (ibid.). Juvenile delinquents in Jerusalem, were described by Dr. Kraus (1936) as coming from Moroccan families whose parents were 'manual laborers, unskilled workers, water-drawers, and beggars' (p. 639). Dr. Brachiyahu (1936a), was even more specific. He claimed that 'academicians, teachers, farmers, clerks, merchants do not breed criminals. But, the children of unskilled workers become young offenders' (p. 206). For him, this difference in origins did not result from socio-economic differences, but originated in the ignorance and primitiveness of the Oriental families (see similar claims in Frankenstein, 1944).

These claims pointing to cultural inferiority of Oriental Jews were supported by various statistical analyses revealing that the slum areas, mainly near the developing big cities and the old city of Jerusalem where most Oriental people live, had become a breeding ground for abnormality and an ecological disaster as they were inhabited by 'poor, inferior families, with retarded children' (Thon, 1937, p. 174). For Brachyahu, there was a difference in the 'biological material of the poor children and of the wealthy' (see Brand, 1950, p. 129). Without proper professional intervention, these urban areas would rapidly become a health hazard, as they could contaminate the entire society and in turn destroy the potential for a Zionist renaissance.

In the dominant expert account for juvenile delinquency only scant voices were heard attempting without success to challenge it. Thus, Dr. Pirst (1936) suggested an alternative explanation to the involvement of Oriental youth in crime. In an article published in the official journal of social workers, titled: 'Delicate Questions', he proposed to look for the reasons for this phenomenon not in the Oriental cultural environment and habits but in the structural political and economic circumstances which drove those children to crime as a result of poverty and even hunger (p. 182). His claims, however, were absorbed within the hegemonic mode of reasoning of the time, when seeds for the distinction between 'them' and 'us' were planted. In Said's words, members of the Asian and African families were defined as the 'problematic other' who must be disciplined, following the European claim that: 'Europe is powerful and articulate; Asia is defeated and distant' (Said, 1978). The behaviors of youth of 'Oriental' origin in Israel and their involvement in the work force from an early age were not seen as a reason for their involvement in crime, rather they were interpreted as a sign of their degeneration.

The Marginality of Delinquent Behavior

The existence of the phenomenon of wayward, neglected and criminal youth was perceived by the professionals as a symbolic threat to the national goal – the establishment of a new Jewish society. They were portrayed as endangering the Zionist dream since it was assumed that they would not develop a commitment to the Jewish collective and in turn would harm the creation of the new human being who should be committed to the collective entity. Such an idea was expressed by a judge in a juvenile court who in 1963 wrote that during the 1930s, 'the existence of wayward neglected youth and juvenile delinquents who lack any commitment to the Yishuv [Jewish community in Palestine] was seen as potentially bringing disaster to our social and national project' (p. 10). Faced with such a danger, the professionals saw themselves as responsible for providing a solution. Their resolution was influenced by the Zionist, pioneer ideology: youth defined as being at-risk were referred to various educational institutions where they were trained for agricultural work and prepared for collective living. The aim was to 'normalize' the youth, socializing and disciplining them to become citizens able to contribute to the new Jewish society. An analysis of the various programs points to the class, ethnic and gender dimensions included in such an aim. Attempting to secure the 'proper' working of the nation, professionals set out to save the youth from the lower strata (economically and culturally) who were mainly of 'Oriental' origin. Such an approach is evident in the explanation of a social worker Mrs. Reha Freier who immigrated to Palestine from Germany in 1941 and established a program which sent 'Oriental' youth from poor families to the kibbutzim, attempting to expose them to a Western lifestyle. Freier wanted to turn those youth who are abandoned and neglected, being exposed to evil, into 'conquerors of our land ... [Our aim is] to unite the Oriental community, with their large families and who are isolated, living a degenerate life, with the entire nation in Zion bringing them to a life of regeneration'.[8]

The solutions for the phenomenon of wayward youth were gender-based: girls were portrayed as potential victims of police officers and soldiers in the streets. In such an environment, 'girls can be led astray'[9] and become a disgrace to their families and the nation. In order to prevent the downfall of girls, Henrietta Szold suggested the establishment of an institute which would treat girls 'at risk'. In such an institution girls would be socialized to fulfill their gender role and 'be trained in manual work, mainly agriculture and domestic.'[10]

In this way, the rhetoric and practice regarding juvenile delinquency was absorbed into the Zionist master discourse. This was based on the assumption that the process of regeneration and national revival in which the professional would play a central role, youth from 'Oriental' families would be taught to live according to 'proper' Western modern values.

Crime and the Zionist-Modernist Discourse, 1949–1970

Between 1949 and the 1970s, the phenomena of youth delinquency continued to be marginalized, being absorbed within a wider master discourse. During this time, the three themes (the discourse of pathology, the focus on 'Oriental' youth, and the absorption of the concern into a master discourse) which started to emerge in the earlier period, continued and were consolidated. The social construction of crime during these years was influenced by social and demographic changes within Israeli society. The establishment of the State of Israel in 1948 brought a major influx of immigrants. In 1948, the population numbered 650,000 ; in 1973 the State of Israel had 3,000,000 inhabitants. While until 1948, 89.6 per cent of the newcomers came from Europe and America and 10.4 per cent from Asia and Africa, after 1948 only 48 per cent of the new immigrants came from America-Europe and the majority, 51.6 per cent came from Asia and Africa (Smooha, 1993). In most cases, the education level and professional skills of these new immigrants were lower by Euro-American standards and they were seen by the representatives of the authorities and the hegemonic establishment as being undeveloped. The new immigrants were granted full citizenship, but were required to assimilate into the existing economic and cultural structure of Israeli society. Over the first two decades, Israel underwent economic development which had a differential influence on the various ethnic groups. The veteran and the newly-arrived European citizens constituted the middle class, working as professionals, in managerial jobs and owning small businesses. At the same time, the 'Orientals' worked in unskilled or semi-skilled jobs in agriculture, construction and industry. This differential entry into the work-force led to the consolidation of 'Orientals' in the lower strata of the social hierarchy (Smooha, 1993, pp. 180-181).

Against this social background, members of the elite groups were concerned at the phenomenon of wayward youth cut off from society, among them young offenders. The discourse of pathology which started to emerge in the earlier period expanded and began to include new ideas and new psychological and sociological explanations were imported to Israel from Europe and the USA.

The Discourse of Pathology

Similarly to the earlier period, no distinction was made between deserted youth and juvenile delinquents. Such an approach was manifested in the report of a special inquiry commission, appointed in 1953 by the Justice Minister and chaired by Supreme Court Judge Agranat, for the investigation of juvenile delinquency and the suggestion of legal and administrative ways to deal with the problem. The commission concluded that there is no need to distinguish between 'the young offender who has already committed a crime and between the child who is neglected or deprived and thus might become a criminal in the future' (p. 6). According to the commission the aim of the criminal procedure is 'to correct the young offender, to watch over him and to protect him ... so he will become a useful and law-abiding citizen' (ibid.).

During this time, the definition of criminality and negligence as an individual pathology was supported with new concepts from biology and psychology. On the one hand, crime and in particular, juvenile delinquency were considered as infectious diseases. The general medical explanation, was combined with environmental explanations which saw these behaviors as dangerous since they appear first as isolated cases and then multiply and spread in the environment (Naddad, 1956). Such an explanation introduced to the discourse of pathology a more sophisticated classification notion, distinguishing between various types of individual and environmental sicknesses. Unconventional behavior and criminality were likened to a large pond. In its center are the very sick youth and in the ripples surrounding it are found the less sick, the temporarily sick and the ones who are only potentially ill: 'the inner circle radiates its influence and infects those in the periphery until it reaches those who have not yet been infected' (Naddad, 1957, p. 334). It was left to university-based and trained experts to provide the detailed knowledge to identify and treat these sicknesses. Such an opinion was expressed by the Legal Advisor to the government, Mr. Ben-Zev, who in 1967 stated that: 'with the help of the social sciences and in the age of omnipotent science with its unlimited powers, experts will be able to determine methods to explain the reasons for delinquency and to suggest ways to deal with it' (p. 32).

On the other hand, juvenile delinquency started to be 'monopolized' by psychiatrists who saw this behavior as originating in a range of personality disorders and mental illnesses (see Tsur, 1991). Thus, Prof. Winik, the Director of the Talbia Hospital for the Mentally Insane in Jerusalem, claimed that most delinquents are mentally ill and thus require psychiatric treatment (Winik, 1960; 1961). Similarly, for Brachiyahu (1956), 'criminality is not a specific illness, but it is only one of the many forms of deviation from normal mental health' (p. 11).

Using this medical reasoning, professionals and experts saw themselves as producing scientific knowledge to solve individual and social pathologies. Indeed from the 1960s, a whole range of laws, welfare and educational programs were set up to help, protect and prevent youth from becoming involved in criminality and deviant nonconformist behavior.

Similar to the earlier period, ideas opposing this medicalization of deviance were heard. Such an opposing voice was raised in a professional journal of psychiatry. Using a poem-format, the author challenges this conception:

> Who is the mentally ill?
> What can be said to he who seeks
> Features common to the burglar, embezzler, rapist and he who solves problems by the knife?
>
> In former times, when wisdom reigned
> The answer was: They are criminals, deviants,
> And warrant punishment of imprisonment and hard labor.
>
> But today, times of "changed values"
> – And wisdom cast by the wayside
> A new impassioned definition arises,
>
> Amazing in its stupidity, claiming:
> All tormented in vain
> Victims of our society are they.
>
> They are psychopaths – their fate decided
> Their place in an institution, for examination and treatment
> Their past veiled in a screen of secrecy.
>
> Will every criminal, sex deviant and rapist
> Who do their foul deeds under an extinguished lamp
> To trial not be brought under the guise of mental illness?
>
> And will the embezzler, pickpocket, knife-wielder and burglar
> Serve as the source of an insurgent crime wave?
> And as the psychopath be dragged out of the mire?
>
> Scenes of pity arising so
> At times lead to a morose conclusion:
> – Are we all mentally ill?
> And well only those whose way is deviant!
> (Kashtan, 1958, p. 268).

The Focus of the Discourse

As in the earlier period, the discourse of pathology focused mainly on 'Oriental' youth. This was manifested in the report of the Agranat Inquiry Commission, which was mainly devoted to the 'problem of the new immigrants' (Ministry of Justice, 1956). The Commission saw the etiology of their involvement in nonconformist behavior as originating in their 'tendency not to understand the meaning of the laws and rules aiming to regulate the public order in the areas of finance and hygiene' (ibid. 19). According to the Commission, those families 'brought with them cultural values, different habits, traditions and life styles, which they were not prepared to give up' (p. 21) and were not willing to sacrifice their traditional norms or to adapt themselves to a productive life in Israel. They were not flexible and resisted change culturally, socially and professionally (p. 22). For Dr. Winberg (1950), those families brought with them an array of mental diseases leading to involvement in criminality (p. 145). He encouraged Israeli authorities to set up a broad preventive plan in which new immigrants would be examined to detect mental illnesses and suggest ways of treatment designed by experts (ibid.).

These perceptions, which targeted 'Oriental' youth and families, expanded the distinction between the 'Oriental' and Western ethnic groups which started to develop in the pre-state period. Such a cultural and political differentiation was now supported with more sophisticated scientific rhetoric. One of the most prominent scholars advancing such classification was the psychologist Professor Frankenstein. In 1952, he wrote: 'youth delinquency originates in the gap between the primitiveness of the 'Orientals' and the civilization of the new Israel' (p. 350). This primitiveness is manifested in a range of psychological disorders and personality problems: a primitive person lacks his 'self', he is not capable of abstract thinking, he cannot identify with other people, he lacks social responsibility. Such a person suffers from a 'primitive mentality' and comes from a society which is characterized by cultural retardation (Frankenstein 1964). When those 'Levantine or rural' (Frankenstein, 1952, p. 356) people immigrated to Israel, they were transferred to a middle place, located between their original primitiveness and a modern civilization, they are required to adapt themselves to complex social demands and then their primitiveness becomes salient. Moreover, he claimed that they 'lack a mature mentality as a result of their parents' inability to educate them ... [and] the influence of traits such as impatience, lack of diligence and instability' (Frankenstein, 1951, p. 242).

During the 1960s, this mix of psychological and environmental explanations with their ethnic manifestations was combined with sociological theories which adopted 'cultural conflict' explanations. According to various researchers, crime, deviance, gambling and the use of alcohol, the involvement in prostitution, primitive beliefs and superstitions, dropout from school of 'Oriental' students originated in a culture conflict between newcomers and the veteran residents of the country. The involvement in such behaviors was seen as an inevitable byproduct of the contact between traditional and modern societies. For some investigators, this macro-sociological level of analysis was accompanied by a micro level explanation which saw Sepharadic families as reacting negatively to cultural transformations due to their personal inability to internalize Israeli values (Shoham, 1962; 1970).

The Marginalization of Juvenile Delinquency

While explanations for the involvement of 'Oriental' youth in a variety of deviant and nonconformist behaviors broadened during this time, involving a whole range of scientific interpretations, and plans for intervention, it nevertheless continued to be supplementary to the wider Zionist discourse which became more concise after the establishment of the state. The behaviors of 'Oriental' youth were interpreted once again as challenging the harmony of the Jewish community, through their inability and sometimes unwillingness to adjust to and identify with the Western, Jewish, Israeli life style. 'Oriental' youth who resided near the border and smuggled food and petty equipment to enemy Arab countries, for example, raised the concern of the Agranat Inquiry Commission members who warned that 'in this way, youth establish contact with Arabs from across the border, and thus their identity with the Israeli community, its values and laws would weaken' (p. 20). Similar alarmed voices were heard at the end of the 1960s, after the Six Day War, with the reunification of Jerusalem, when claims were made that Jewish girls in Jerusalem were involved in prostitution with Arab clients. The Welfare Minister at that time, Dr. Burg, stirred up national feelings, stating in the Israeli Parliament (Knesset) that relations between Jewish girls and Arab males are:

the anti-image of Israel. This is a bad phenomenon, especially in a nation that aims to set an example for other nations. We came here with ideals. The foundations of this country were laid by idealists, pioneers, Zionists... These phenomena of deviant girls are simply awful (Israeli Knesset Reports, 1969, p. 2708).

This Zionist discourse which continued to highlight the creation of a nation according to Jewish, idealist values was combined now with a modernist discourse which emphasized the significance of science, technology and rational thinking. Expressing such a view, Professor Hanani of the Israeli Technion, claimed in 1967, that: 'Israeli society accepted Western culture as the guiding culture, determining our life in Israel. If we want to build a modern nation, we need to base ourselves upon the Western world' (p. 21). In face of such danger, groups of professionals (medical practitioners, psychologists, social workers and educators) who belonged to the Western middle-class group saw themselves as being required and able to rescue the youth and society in general. Being committed to the 'melting-pot' ideology, which believed that various social problems are the natural outcome of the immigration process and would be resolved with the absorption of these communities into Israeli society, they set out to re-socialize 'Orientals' into Israeli values. Such plans exposed 'Oriental' youth to a disciplinary welfare, educational, legal and medical structure of controls which attempted to force new immigrants to give up their traditional beliefs and customs and to adapt to Israeli norms, in order to merge into Israeli society. These perceptions paved the way for the development of a welfarist ideology legitimizing state intervention into family life, regulating daily activities of youth, mainly from 'Oriental' families defined as being 'at risk' through an expanding framework or through a hybrid regulatory mode which includes educational, welfare, mental health and legal agencies.[11] These perceptions have continued to exist from the 1970s and until now, and are manifested in the proliferation of programs and plans legitimizing experts' intervention and control.

Conclusion

As we have seen, crime and control did not emerge as an autonomous social problem in Israel. Throughout the years, they were constructed as a part of wider and central social problems. Criminal behavior was perceived as social and political differences typical of a society of immigrants – a notion existing even now, 45 years after the major waves of immigration to Israel. Believing in the power and ability of groups of professionals to 'socialize' these new immigrants, the medical model which came under major criticism in Europe and the USA, is still dominant in Israel today (Ajzenstadt, 1998; Cohen 1990). This attitude is evident in the power allocated to probation officers in the existing youth laws[12] and the rehabilitative, educational ideology directing the juvenile court in Israel (Raifen, 1972). The strong belief in professionals who would eventually bring about the long-anticipated aim of the creation of a hegemonic Jewish, Zionist, modern society did not allow for the critical evaluation of the power of professionals. Thus, the reliability of the medicalization of deviance and the welfarist ideology itself rarely became issues of dispute within Israeli society, where there is a strong consensus that expert knowledge will 'normalize' youth from various ethnic groups to follow a specific normative framework designed by the dominant groups in Israeli society.

However, recently, this strong medical conception is starting to be challenged in various arenas. A few academic studies criticize the monopoly of the professionals in such areas of the treatment of mental health (Aviram, 1990) and girls considered to be in distress (Ajzenstadt and Steinberg, 1995). Moreover, civil liberty organizations and NGO groups focusing on human rights and especially children's rights have begun to be actively involved in the socio-legal response toward youth in the welfare and penal areas. This is part of a greater sensitivity to human rights in Israel during recent years – a sensitivity which is evident in the passing of various rights-oriented legislation (Sebba, 1996, p. 271). Thus, while juvenile delinquency still remains absorbed within wider discourses, it might be shifted now toward a legal rather than a medical-therapeutic construct.

Notes

1 The 1922 Young Offender Act.
2 The 1937, Young Offender Act.
3 Ibid, section 8(7).
4 Ibid, section 16.
5 A lecture by Brachyahu in the Scientific Conference of the Jewish Medical Association in Palestine, News from Hadassa, 15.10.1944.

6   A further study should examine the prevalence of those procedures, the reason and the rationale given them.
7   A memo from Szold to the Secrecy of the Vaad Leumi, 2.6.1936, The Central Zionist Archive j1/3592.
8   Freier, Reha, 15.10.1944. Report concerning problems of abandoned children in Palestine, and their solution, Jerusalem: The central Zionist Archives, J7579.
9   A letter from Szold to Dr. G. Lubinski, Vaad Leumi, 3.11.1941, The central Zionist Archive, J. 3947.
10 Szold, A memo regarding the establishment of an institute for wayward girls, 4.6.1942, The central Zionist Archive, J 7535.
11 Described by Pond as 'socialized justice', by Garland as the 'welfare sanction', and by Donzelot as the 'tutelary complex'.
12 The Youth (Care and Supervision) Law, 1960 and the Youth (Trial, Punishment and Modes of Treatment) Law, 1971.

Bibliography

Ajzenstadt, Mimi (1994), 'The Changing Image of the State: The Case of Alcohol Regulations in British Columbia', *The Canadian Journal of Sociology*, vol. 19, no. 4, pp. 441-460.

Ajzenstadt, M. (1988), 'The Study of Crime and Social Control in Israel: Some Theoretical Observations', in R. R. Friedman (ed), *Crime and Criminal Justice in Israel: Assessing the Knowledge Base towards the Twenty-First Century*, Suny, Albany, pp. 3-25.

Ajzenstadt, M. and Steinberg, O. (1995), '"The Elasticity of the Law": Treating Girls in Distress in Israel through the Shadow of the Law', *The British Journal of Criminology*, vol. 35, no. 2, pp. 236-247.

Aviram, U. (1990), 'Care or Convenience: On the Medical Bureaucratic Model of the Mentally Ill', *International Journal Of Law and Psychiatry*, vol. 13, no. 13, pp. 163-177.

Ben-Zev, M. (1967), 'Juvenile Delinquency, in the Eyes of a Jurist', in The Welfare Ministry (ed), *The Youth for the Prevention of Youth Delinquency*, Proceedings of the 5th Conference of the Council for Prevention of Delinquency and Treatment of Delinquency, The Welfare Ministry, Jerusalem, pp. 31-36, (Hebrew).

Brachiyahu, M. (1935a), 'Juvenile delinquency in Palestine', *Harefuah*, vol. 9, pp. 205-209, (Hebrew).

Brachiyahu, M. (1935b), 'Juvenile delinquency in Israel', *Harefuah*, vol. 28, pp. 274-294, (Hebrew).

Brachiyahu, M. (1956), 'Juvenile delinquency in Israel', *Harefuah*, vol. 51, pp. 11-13, (Hebrew).

Brand, A. (1950), 'Thirty years of the Hygiene Department of the Schools', *Harefuah*, vol. 39, pp. 129-131, (Hebrew).
Chunn, D. (1992), *From Punishment to Doing Good: Family Courts and Socialized Justice in Ontario 1880-1940*, Toronto University Press, Toronto.
Cohen, R. (1936), 'Five Years of Organized Welfare Work', *Bulletin on Social Work in Palestine*, vol. 2, nos. 5-6, pp. 68-71, (Hebrew).
Cohen, S. (1990), 'Politics and Crime in Israel: Reactions from the Home Front', *Social Justice*, vol. 17, no. 1, pp. 5-13.
Cohen, S. (1985), *Visions of Social Control: Crime, Punishment and Classification*, Polity Press, Oxford.
Cohen, S. and Scull, A. (1983), 'Social Control in History and Sociology', in S. Cohen and A. Scull (eds) *Social Control and the State*, Basil Blackwell, Oxford, pp. 1-12.
Conrad P. and Schneider, J.W. (1980), *Deviance and Medicalization: From Badness to Sickness*, Mosby Company, St. Louis.
Donzelot, J. (1979), *The Policing of Families*, Pantheon Books, New York.
Dushkin, Alexander M. (1935), 'The Basics of Social Welfare in Palestine: As seen by Henrietta Szold', *Bulletin on Social work in Palestine*, vol. 1, 6, pp. 111-114, (Hebrew).
Edwards, A. (1988), *Regulation and Repression: The Study of Social Control*, Allen and Unwin, London.
Einhorn, Shimon (1929), 'Castration of Mentally Ill and Potential Criminals', *Harefuah*, vol. 3, pp. 42-43, (Hebrew).
Elad, N. and Weiner (1995), *The History of Youth Probation and Services for Disadvantaged Delinquent Children in Israel*, Ramot, Tel Aviv University, Tel Aviv, (Hebrew).
Frankenstein, C. (1952), 'About the Primitiveness Concept', *Megamot*, vol. 2. no. 4, pp. 339-360, (Hebrew).
Frankenstein, C. (1944), 'Delinquency among Jewish Youth in Jerusalem', *On behalf of children and youth*, vol. 19, pp. 4-21, (Hebrew).
Frankenstein, C. (1964), *Man in Distress: Elements of Social Educational and Therapeutic Treatment*, Dvir, Tel Aviv, (Hebrew).
Frankenstein, C. (1951), 'A New Type of Juvenile Delinquency', *Megamot*, vol. 1, pp. 237-249, (Hebrew).
Garland, D. (1985), *Punishment and Welfare: A History of Penal Strategies*, Gower, Vermont.
Gelber, Y. (1992), 'The Consolidation of Jewish Society in Eretz-Israel, 1936-1947' in M. Lissak, A. Shapira and G. Cohen (eds), *The History of the Jewish Community in Eretz-Israel since 1882*, The Israeli Academy for Sciences and Humanities and The Bialik Institute, Jerusalem, pp. 303-461, (Hebrew).
Glikson, Naomi (1950), 'The care of the mentally retarded child', *Harefuah*, vol. 39, pp. 137-139, (Hebrew).

Gusfield, J. R. (1989), 'Constructing the Ownership of Social Problems: Fun and Profit in the Welfare State', *Social Problems*, vol. 6, no. 5, pp. 431-441.
Gusfield, J. R. (1981), *The Culture of Public Problems: Drinking - Driving and the Symbolic Order*, The University of Chicago Press, Chicago.
Kashtan, Haim (1958), 'Who is mentally ill?', *Eitanim*, vol. 3, pp. 268-269, (Hebrew).
Kraus, S. (1936), 'The Social-Hygiene Condition of the Children of the Old City and the Reasons for the Increase of Offenses', *Harefuah*, vol. 11, pp. 637-643, (Hebrew).
Lissak, M. (1992), 'Immigration, Absorption and Society Building in the Jewish Community in Eretz-Israel (1918-1930)', in M. Lissak, A. Shapira and G. Cohen (eds), *The History of the Jewish Community in Eretz-Israel since 1882*, The Israeli Academy for Sciences and Humanities and The Bialik Institute, Jerusalem, pp. 173-213, (Hebrew).
Loewenstein, K. (1944), 'Eugenic Problems in the Field of Psychotic and Mental Illnesses', *Harefuah*, vol. 26, no. 4, pp. 65-67, (Hebrew).
McLaren, A. (1990), *Our Own Master Race: Eugenics in Canada, 1885-1945*, McClelland and Stewart, Toronto.
Ministry of Labor and Social Affairs (1996), *Juveniles Treated by the Juvenile Probation Services, 1995*, The Central Library of Social Work, Jerusalem, (Hebrew).
Ministry of Justice (1956), *A Report of the Inquiry Commission of Juvenile Delinquency*, Ministry of Justice, Jerusalem, (Hebrew).
Markman, R. A. (1966), 'Juvenile Delinquency in Israel', *American Journal of Psychiatry*, vol. 123, no. 4, pp. 463-469.
Melossi, D. (1990), *The State of Social Control: A Sociological Study of Concepts of State and Social Control in making of Democracy*, St. Martin's Press, New York.
Naaman, H. (1939), *Juvenile Delinquents*, Jerusalem, (Hebrew).
Naddad, A. (1956), 'The Unity between the Individual and the Environment: Treatment Principles of Deserted Youth', *Megamot*, vol. 5, no 3, pp. 199-226, (Hebrew).
Naddad, A. (1957), 'The Individual Treatment of Deserted Youth', *Megamot*, vol. 5, no. 4, pp. 333-362, (Hebrew).
Nordau, M. (1955), *Zionist Writings*, vol. A., The Zionist Organization, Jerusalem, (Hebrew).
Pirst, A. (1936), 'Delicate Questions', *Bulletin on Social Welfare in Palestine*, vol. 9, pp. 180-183, (Hebrew).
Platt, A. M. (1969), *The Child Savers: The Invention of Delinquency*, University of Chicago, Chicago.
Prat, M. I. (1950), 'The History of the Psycho-Therapy Work in the School Hygiene Department in Palestine,' *Harefuah*, vol. 39, pp. 136-137, (Hebrew).

Pound, R. (1943), 'The Rise of Sociological Justice', *National Probation Association Yearbook,* New York, pp. 3-24.
Rabinowitz, Abraham (1929), 'The Situation in Palestine and Aid to the Mentally and Psychologically Ill', *Harefuah,* vol. 3, pp. 8-14, (Hebrew).
Reifen, D. (1963), *The Juvenile Court,* Szold Foundation, Jerusalem, (Hebrew).
Reifen, D. (1972), *The Juvenile Court in Modern Society,* University of Pennsylvania Press, Philadelphia.
Rivkai, Y. (1932), 'Cooperation between Doctors and Teachers in Palestine', *Harefuah,* vol. 6, pp. 217-220 (Hebrew).
Said, E. (1978), *Orientalism,* Penguin, Harmondsworth.
Sebba, L. (1996), 'Sanctioning Policy in Israel - An Historical Overview', *Israel Law Review,* vol. 30. nos. 1-2, pp. 234-275.
Simon, J. (1993a), 'From Confinement to Waste Management: The Postmodernization of Social Control', *Focus on Law Studies,* vol. 8, no. 4, pp. 6-7.
Simon, J. (1993b), *Poor Discipline: Parole and the Social Control of the Underclass, 1890-1990,* University of Chicago press, Chicago.
Smooha, S. (1993), 'Class, Communal and National Gaps and Democracy in Israel', in U. Ram (ed), *Israeli Society: Critical Perspectives,* Breirot, Tel Aviv, pp. 172-202, (Hebrew).
Spector, M. and Kitususe, J. I. (1977), *Constructing Social Problems,* Cummings, Melno Park, CA.
Szold, Henrietta (1937), *On Behalf of Children and Youth in Palestine,* Jerusalem, (Hebrew).
Thon, H. L. (1937), 'Social Work in Neighborhood Locations', *Bulletin on Social work in Palestine,* vol. 2, 9-10, pp. 173-176, (Hebrew).
Tsur, A. (1991), *Discourse on Mental Health in Israel as a Product and Producer of Knowledge/Power,* Unpublished Ph.D. Thesis, The Hebrew University of Jerusalem, Jerusalem, (Hebrew).
Valverde, M. (1991), *The Age of Light, Soap, and Water: Moral Reform in English Canada, 1885-1925,* McClelland and Stewart, Toronto.
Weinberg, A. A. (1950), 'Psycho-Hygienic Problems in the Adjustment of New Immigrants', *Harefuah,* vol. 38, pp. 144-145, (Hebrew).
Winik, H.Z. (1960), 'The Psychiatrist's Role in the Judgment of Mentally Ill Criminals', *Harefuah,* vol. 25. no. 2, pp. 35-38, (Hebrew).
Winik, H.Z. (1961), 'Psychiatric Comments on the Problem of Delinquency', *Saad,* July, pp. 131-135, (Hebrew).

PART IV:
PRACTICAL RELEVANCE

11 Financial Counseling at Norwegian Social Offices: Lessons for Constructing Social Work Practice

MICHAEL SELTZER AND SVEIN ALVE

Introduction

The choice of the word 'lessons' in the title of this chapter is an intentional one. As we will try to show here, the formal education of social workers in Norway – and elsewhere we strongly suspect – has long ignored areas involving money matters and related financial problems presented by clients. This we found in a 3-year study focusing on how social work agencies dealt with the consequences of the Debt Crisis of the 1990s. In the responses to questionnaires sent to all of Norway's 512 social work offices, we found almost no social workers who could recall receiving any lessons and practical training in their education's for dealing with money problems presented by clients. Though many remembered receiving instruction focused on macro-economic issues such as GNP and state budgetary allocations, few could recall their training touching upon money matters in client work. This area, our data clearly showed, had not been part of the lessons plans for generations of social work students in Norway. There were many reasons for this omission. However, a major one clearly involved the psychodynamic tradition in social work: one allotting little space to money and finances in its discussion of the meetings between social worker and client. A key element of this tradition was the belief that the core of the social work task was supposed to be a personal, face-to-face relationship between social worker and client – a nexus ideally characterized by openness and trust. This, it was felt, enhanced the independence and problem-solving skills of the client. In this way of thinking, money had a negative role: its presence in the social worker-client relationship was seen as detracting from – or at worse being directly harmful to – the proper practice of social work.

This orientation would have made perfect sense if social work students in Norway upon graduating assumed positions as therapists. This, however, has never been the case. Only a small minority of social workers work in therapeutic milieus, while the overwhelming majority are employed at social offices where they are required by law to meet persons in need of financial aid and there to decide whether these helpseekers are to receive assistance and if so, how much. As shown by many researchers, (Ranger, 1986; 1993; Stjernø et al 1988; Stjernø 1982; 1983; Guttormsen and Høigaard, 1978), most clients coming to social welfare offices in Norway have not been seeking therapeutic relationships: the arriving needing material help – most often in the form of money. Thus a perennial dilemma faced by newly graduated social workers employed at Norway's social offices involved complicated attempts to combine negotiations about money with building relationships to make possible personal change and the solving of problems.

Client narratives have shown that these kinds of highly problematic situations were often resolved by what can be understood in a Goffmanesque sense as 'the deal'. According to one long term client interviewed in one of the first research project focused on the day to day operations of a Norwegian social office, the 'deal' was comprised of a simple, but degrading, exchange: As he put it, 'It's all right at the social office. Your spread out your soul to them for one hundred crowns a week' (Guttormsen and Høigaard 1978, p. 161).

In retrospect, it appears that two additional factors helped maintain the kind of status quo in which money matters were traditionally dealt at social offices prior to the debt crisis of the 1980s. One feature was the relatively low status of client populations at social offices during much of the postwar period. As long as clients were drawn from low status groups possessing relatively few resources and little 'cultural capital' (Bourdieu and Passeron 1977), such as transients, alcoholics, drug addicts, and unmarried mothers, the path of least resistance for many clients appeared to be to various forms of trading disclosures of self for money from social workers. The second feature maintaining this system involved social workers. As long as many chose the path of least resistance at social offices and replaced therapeutically influenced social work ideals with more agency oriented 'people processing' goals (Prottas 1979), the system could function through this combination of tradeoffs and shifts in orientation.

The Debt Crisis in Norway

In the late 1980s, this way of handling client money troubles in social work practice in Norway was challenged dramatically. At that time social work offices in Norway were confronted – sometimes massively – by clients presenting problems involving debt default and mortgage arrears. For many experienced social workers, meetings with these clients and their problems represented unfamiliar situations. For the first time, they encountered in ever increasing numbers middle class persons much like themselves. Social workers soon found that considerations of money and personal finance no longer could be relegated to peripheral roles in these meetings. The debt crisis of the late 1980s finally forced money and its problematic relation to social work on to the centerstage of the Norwegian welfare state.

Increases in debt defaulters at this time can be understood historically in relation to the radical relaxation of what had been austere and tightly regulated financial and housing markets. This reflected a shift in the political leadership of Norway towards the rights as well as the rise of free market policies during the 1980s throughout the West. These changes presented many Norwegians with their first opportunities to take part on the growing consumer market of the early 1980s. For young adults in particular, this period was unique in the history of modern Norway. For the first time, persons establishing households could borrow money relatively easily to finance home, automobile and other major purchases. This situation contrasted dramatically with what previous generations had experienced on much more restrictive housing and consumer markets. The transformations coincided with what appeared to be expanding job markets in Norway (NOU 1989).

But the final years of the 1980s witnessed the beginning to the end of the expanding credit, housing and job markets of the early years of this decade. At the individual level, these changes were often exemplified by money troubles experienced by young couples who had purchased apartments and houses at a time of easily obtainable mortgages with high interest rates. One measure of these changes was that one quarter of Norway's population purchased homes during 1985 – 1989 period. A consequence of this, however, was a corresponding inflation in prices on the housing market (NOU 1989). For many couples, the maintenance of these and other loans with high interest rates demanded the employment of both spouses.

As unemployment began to make its impact felt in Norway, it was these groups of young families with the greatest debtloads who most often experienced joblessness (Lunde and Poppe, 1991: 104).

Statistics compiled on persons experiencing debt problems showed that the percentage of Norwegian households with these kinds of problems increased from 6 to 19 per cent in the period 1985 – 1990. In 1990, a total of more than 300 000 households reported experiencing payment problems in the previous year. These figures also indicated that at least 120,000 households in this group were in severe debt crisis. The three groups experiencing the most pronounced problems were unemployed persons, young families under the age of 40 and single-parented households (Lunde and Poppe, 1991).

While there was considerable debate among researchers about the scope of the debt problem in Norway (Gulbrandsen, 1991; Lunde and Poppe, 1991), there was more or less general agreement about its rapid growth. As debtor clients in rapidly growing numbers began to make their presence felt at Norwegian social offices, it soon became apparent that there were a number of difficulties involved with fulfilling those sections of the Norwegian social welfare law (LOSO) requiring social offices to provide information and counseling services to clients. One obvious problem, as already discussed, was related to the deficiencies in the educational backgrounds of social workers who were to provide debt counseling. The arrival in great numbers of debtor clients, however, forced social offices lacking formal competence to put together various financial counseling programs to deal with these 'new' sets of problems.

Some offices reassigned office personnel with mercantile background to deal with debtor clients, while many offices hired persons possessing educational and occupational experience from banking and other financial institutions. In a few cases, social work offices retained the services of external economic counselors often hired as consultants. A consequence of these attempts to cope with the problems meant that persons with debt troubles arriving at Norwegian social offices in 1990 could expect to meet three kinds of financial counselors. These were: 1) social workers lacking formal training in money matters; 2) social workers or social work office employees possessing some background in finance;

and 3) trained economic counselors, many of whom had been previously employed by banking and credit institutions.

The period from 1989 to 1993 witnessed a rapid growth of financial counseling services at social work offices. By 1993, more than 20 per cent of all parishes in Norway had established specialized counseling services for clients with debt problems. Many of these – especially in the most hard pressed urban areas where problems with mortgage arrears were a major problem – were staffed by persons with backgrounds in banking and finance and little to no knowledge nor experience with social work theory and practice.

The question of what happened in the face to face encounters between these counselors lacking social work training and clients arriving at social offices seeking help with debt problems was a central concern of our research project. Accordingly three social offices serving an area characterized by high levels of mortgage defaults and persons experiencing serious financial problems were selected. Personnel at these offices were interviewed and 11 observations of client-counselor interactions were carried out our multidisciplinary research team (psychology, social work, sociology and cultural anthropology). These observations took place throughout the working day and evening. Though always involving one financial counselor and at least one client, the observed sessions included other actors as well. In some sessions, social workers charged with receiving new clients were also present. In other sessions, various members of the client's family were present. In one session, an interpreter accompanied an immigrant client. Before presented a summary of the results of the qualitative analysis of this observational data, it is important at this point to make some observations about how debt default is constructed in the wider society.

Constructing Debtors: Dominant Discourse and Alternative Constructions

To begin with, it is clear that being unable to repay debts is *not* simply a problem involving relations among debits and credits. Perhaps more than anything else is this a situation involving assaults on the debtor's feelings of self-worth and sense of identity. Research on debtors in default others experiencing financially related stress provide clear indications of the psychological and social costs for borrowers unable to repay debts

(Caplovitz, 1974; Rock, 1973; Parker, 1985; Brusdal, 1988; Ford, 1988; Solheim, 1992; Stolanowski, 1990; Poppe and Borgeraas, 1992; Ilstad, 1989). These findings show clearly the massive negative consequences these experiences have for the identities of debtors. The data indicates that being unable to repay creditors involves experiencing feelings of diminishment of self. For the debt defaulter, being in financial arrears means exposing one's self to feelings of inadequacy, shame, guilt, worthlessness, anxiety, confusion, anger and despair. Clearly such feelings do not develop in a vacuum and are bound up by how dominant discourse in society defines and explains debt default and those failing to fulfill their contractual obligations as debtors.

Central to these constructions are the ways in which debt default is related to the moral character and other personality traits of the defaulter by the media and society at large. In one of the few empirical investigations of public attitudes toward debtors, debt default and indebtedness carried out by the sociologist Paul Rock in Great Britain, more than fifty per cent of those interviewed cited 'not enough self-control' as the main reason for people being in trouble over debt (1973, p. 17). In addition, more than two thirds of the respondents strongly agreed or agreed with a depiction of debtors as 'People who. . .do not know how to run their lives properly'.

In Norway, the findings of a nationwide sampling of public opinion conducted in 1992 by SIFO (State Institute for Consumer Research) were represented in *Aftenposten,* the country's most prestigious daily newspaper under the headline 'Blame the debt victims: Most people mean debt problems are self-inflicted' *(Aftenposten,* May 25, 1992, p. 48). This negative media portrayal supplemented an earlier highly publicized characterization made earlier in a newspaper interview by the Norwegian Minister of Family Affairs who characterized persons in debt trouble as 'messes' (in Norwegian, *'rotekopper') (Dagbladet,* March 23, 1992, p. 2). Her comments were made about a proposal for a law providing assistance to debtors being drafted by the ministry she headed. In response to a journalist, the minister, Grete Berget, stated straightforwardly that she did not wish to head a ministry proposing laws to help those incapable of ordering their financial affairs. This negative characterization of the Norwegian debt defaulter in the vernacular complemented a more formal, yet equally damning, construction presented by one sociologist researcher who concluded that debt troubles were due to a deficient or poor payment morality together with deficiencies in 'persons with exaggerated beliefs

Financial Counseling at Norwegian Social Offices 223

and opinions about what are reasonable financial dispositions' (Gulbrandsen, 1989, p. 15).

The debt crisis as well took place in a Norwegian society where the ideal of self-reliance as a key moral virtue long has been a key feature of dominant ideology. As shown in a number of research reports on the social political implications of this notion in Norway (Halvorsen, 1993; 1994; 1996), self-reliance is valued most highly as a character trait both by the public sector as well as society at large. The notion that an individual with good character should be self-reliant and not dependent on others is not only an ideal in extremely individualistic societies like the United States (see, for example, Goodin, 1988). It has been shown that self-reliance is also extremely influential in societies possessing welfare states with social democratic orientations. In Norway, for example, a legislated central goal for social work practice since its beginnings has been the promotion of 'help to self help' among social clients (Halvorsen 1996; Terum, 1986). The intense debate in Norway about the propriety of legislation to help the victims of the debt crisis can be understood in part as public discourse about whether state intervention on behalf of debt defaulters would have a detrimental effect on their character by making them dependent and hence undermine their self-reliance. As noted, this debate also focused on various constructions of alleged character flaws and deficiencies among debt defaulters. As such it was a moral debate focused on the alleged character deficiencies of those unable to steer their own finances and subsequently failing in their contractual obligations to creditors. Given the moral dimensions involving the alleged character and behavioral flaws of the debt defaulters by dominant ideology in Norwegian society, there were many potentials present for reinforcing these constructions in the meeting between this group and financial counselors at the social offices. Even if it could be assumed that counselors were aware of the potentially harmful consequences of these meetings, this by no means guaranteed that they would act to counteract dominant definitions of clients. Research findings from many settings have long demonstrated that increased deviancy is often an unintended consequence of the actions by those, such as probation officers and social workers, who have been entrusted by society with the task of changing deviant identities (Wilkins, 1965; Bondesson, 1977; Young, 1971).

Resisting and Counteracting Dominant Constructions of the Debt Defaulter

In analyzing our observational data – especially against the background of the forces already impacting negatively on the identities of debtors entering the counseling situation – it was remarkable how few actions on the part of counselors could be identified as amplifiers and reinforcers of deviant identity. On the contrary, many acts by counselors that could be understood as positive reframings of identity-related problems presented by clients.

Our analyses suggested that related processes of *normalization* and *rationalization* – in particular – appeared to function in positive ways to help clients with upgradings of self-image. Nearly every session observed contained sequences where counselors responded to clients' descriptions of debt and default problems, with reference to others in similar situations. This kind of response was almost invariably linked to comments about how easy it was for even the best managed budgets to slide into arrears if a partner became sick, daycare for a child became unavailable, or a plant or business closed.

Thus, in one session, a client expressed fears that she had been blacklisted by banks and credit institutions for 'failing' in some way to deal with the financial chaos she inherited from her estranged spouse. After examining the letter refusing a loan sent the client by her bank, the counselor commented:

> They quite simply believe another loan is too much. This is not blacklisting. It's simply standard banking practice.

In two different sessions, clients framing financial problems in terms of their own failings were told by counselors that many persons shared these kinds of problems owing to forces outside their control which had caused sharp drops in housing prices coupled with and steep increases in monthly rents.

In terms of reframing, these and similar comments seemed to transform what initially appeared to have been accepted by clients as proof of individual incompetence to a much less stigmatizing problems involving many 'normal' persons. This kind of transformation, viewed from a classic sociological perspective, thus became an act on the part of the counselor drawing a crucial distinction for the client between personal troubles of milieu and public issues of social structure (Mills, 1959). Defining *in* such issues appeared to function as a counterweight to character-related explanations of debt troubles defining clients *out* by society at large.

For most persons in debt crisis, the points of reference to which they can relate default to outside the counseling sessions were few in number. Furthermore, these almost overwhelmingly define being in debt arrears as reflecting the debtor's own shortcomings and failures. When reinforced still further by public opinion focused on the irresponsibility of debt defaulters, clients entering financial counseling tended to have a low opinion of themselves as money managers. Thus the role of the counselor was unique in that it represented a single voice of financial expertise *not* necessarily reflecting the interests of the creditor and the prejudices of the wider social arena. The observational material showed counselors using this independent expertise in economy, personal finance and banking to provide clients with informed and rational explanations for debt problems having little to do with personal failings or other shortcomings on the part of the clients. A recurrent rationalization noted in the observations was represented by explanations presented by counselors linking problems presented by clients to structural factors and processes in society and outside the control of clients.

Among these rationalizations, counselors were witnessed reassuring clients by with the following statements:

Housing expenses today are generally far too high.

You have much debt owing to the high housing expenses.

The costs of repaying the housing loan will grow now
and then go down. That's the way SIFBO mortgages are.

In one instance, a client blaming herself for not waiting long enough before purchasing a flat prior to a drastic drop in the housing market was told by the counselor:

Well, I know of people who have had to pay even higher prices for the same kind of flats.

At the beginning of one counseling session, a client who expressed fears about being unable to meet a mortgage payment was told by the counselor:

It's only natural that you want to stop repayment on the principal to the bank during a crisis like this.

Similarly, one client fearful of losing her home was provided time out to cry and upon finishing was reassured by the counselor who commented:

Almost every (creditor) understands acute problems. The problem is due to the fact that you simply don't have the money because of problems with social security payments.

Another distraught client was told by a counselor:

Creditors can talked with.

The data show that clients entering the counseling situation more often than not presented two major sorts of problems involving disorder. The obvious presenting problems involving default was inevitably accompanied by difficulties related to disordered household economies and other financial aspects of client life. For many clients, the inability to repay debts appeared to produce ripple effects disturbing and disarranging other aspects of their lives. It was therefore not uncommon for clients to arrive at counseling sessions jumbles of paper, tax returns, unpaid bills, receipts and sealed notices opened in the presence of counselors which threatened eviction or foreclosure. One social work student whose placement put her in contact with a debtor client described to us using a snow shovel to clear a passage in the masses of unopened letters piled in the entrance to the client's apartment. Though not witnessed in our observations, persons arriving traumatized at their first counseling sessions in possession of plastic sacks filled with eviction notices, unpaid bills and collection agency threats were described as archetypal by Norwegian and Swedish counselors interviewed during the project.

Our observations showed that it was very often necessary for counselors to sort, to assess and to order the various problems of these kinds during the sessions. Typically, financial counselors devoted the beginnings of sessions to help clients identifying differences between major and minor debts, classify debts and finally assign priorities to debts and debt repayments. As measured by client commentary as well as observations of client non-verbal behaviour, it was reckoned that the act of transforming a disarrayed personal economy into an ordered and systematized form had positive impact on the client.

One client made what could be interpreted as a characteristic declaration about this kind of ordering. Upon concluding the first counseling session, the client thanked the counselor by exclaiming:

> It's been great to go through our finances! Now we have
> a much better startingpoint for deciding what to do.

At another and more concrete level, the ordering processes observed in the sessions appeared to result in several substantial changes. In one observation, this ordering appeared to reduce visibly the confusion expressed by the client about what was thought to be two different debts. The counselor in this instance discovered, to the client's obvious relief, that there was in point of fact only one debt. In another observation, a counselor sorted out a complex income tax problem and showed the debtor couple how they could save money by filing separate income tax returns.

Mediation and its Place in Financial Counseling: An Anthropological Interpretation

Data from our observations supplied strong evidence for the centrality of the mediator/negotiator role in financial counseling and the importance of this in resisting and counteracting negative constructions of debtor client identities. In all sessions witnessed by the team, counselors were observed either negotiating directly with creditors on behalf of clients or discussing past and/or future negotiations with creditors.

Among those creditors with whom these negotiations took place were commercial and savings banks, the State Housing Bank, credit and collection agencies as well as various private landlords and other housing bodies to whom clients owed money, back rent and mortgage payments. The activities of the counselors vis-à-vis these creditors assumed several forms. These included written and oral communications between counselors and creditors about: loan repayment scheduling, temporary reduction or suspension of interest and principal repayments, scheduling of future meetings with creditors, and discussion with creditors about threatened evictions, repossessions and mortgage foreclosures. In relation to eviction and foreclosure notices, the observers witnessed two instances wherein counselors postponed threatened legal actions.

On the surface, acts of negotiating performed by counselors appeared to be rather straightforward services on behalf of clients involving negotiating with bureaucratic organizations. But when negotiation is framed as communication with a perspective provided by cultural anthropology, acts involving debtors, creditors and mediating financial counselors become transformed into something more complex.

Framed in terms of communication theory, the normal relationship between a debtor and a creditor is a dyadic one (Watzlawick et al., 1967). In the course of everyday life, creditors present bills for services rendered or moneys owed and debtors repay these amounts. Reciprocal expectations are fulfilled, especially in terms of mutual rights and duties, and thus the dyadic relation between both parts can be characterized as stable. In one way, the stability of the debtor-creditor dyad is insured by the shared meanings both parts attach to the important elements of their relationship. Theoretically, the relation existing between actors in the dyad is a complementary one: i.e. each part behaves in a manner that pre-supposes, while at the same time provides reasons for, the behavior of the other part (Watzlawick et al., 1967, p. 69). However, when the debtor defaults on these obligations, the dyad becomes unstable along several key dimensions. Firstly, what could have been conceptualized as a shared universe of meaning in the dyad dissolves into what could be understood as two worlds of different meanings: where creditors inhabit one world and debtors another. Secondly, the kind of complementarity which once provided considerable stability in the dyad is replaced by a kind of complementarity functioning to promote increasing instability in the dyad. Communications theory posits that if allowed to function unchecked, this kind of complementarity will eventually destroy the relationship (Bateson, 1958; Ruesch and Bateson, 1951; Hoffman, 1971).

When the debt crisis of the late 1980s first manifested itself, the crisis was compounded by a cognitive problem experienced by creditors. Long conditioned to attach 'bad faith' and breach of contract meanings to a relatively few defaulting debtors, creditors – especially banks – expressed experiences of discomfort and dissonance when forced to front a rapidly growing legion of defaulters who did not fit into the traditional 'bad debt' niche. This situation was complicated still further by the reactions of these 'new' debt defaulters.

For the debtor unable to repay loans, default frequently takes on the meaning and dimensions of a personal tragedy. Research in other settings, too, has demonstrated that the experience of being unable to repay loans, to fulfill mortgage obligations and to honor rental agreements is attached to a multitude of largely negative symbolic meanings involving – feelings of inadequacy, guilt and shame (Rock, 1973; Ford, 1988).

Framed in this way, the breakdown of the debtor-creditor dyad triggered by default appears to manifest in several stages or phases. As described here, the first phase appears to be one where a cognitive crisis develops among creditors whose cognitive maps of debt default do not fit the terrain of the new environment they find themselves in. Simultaneously, an affective crisis develops among defaulting debtors whose membership in a society morally condemning default opens them to translate quantitative failings involved credits and debits into qualitative failings of personal character.

In the second phase, reports from bankers and financial counselors indicate that creditors attempt to contact defaulting debtors. Since default takes place most often without prior notice (cf. Chilman et al., 1988; Rock, 1973; Ford, 1988), creditors are caught unawares and are thus eager to find out the reasons for the default. Often, in attempting to establish contact with debt defaulters, creditors tend to frame their messages both in legalistic terms symbolizing the obligatory nature of the dyadic relation and in moralistic terms symbolizing the tradition of treating 'bad debts' with considerable firmness. For debt defaulters on the receiving end of this communiqués, this phase is often one characterized by inaction. Our findings as well as data from research on defaulting debtors elsewhere (cf. Caplowitz, 1974; Ford, 1988) reveal that debtors who default experience a kind of paralysis: the research picture shows them responding to this situation by withdrawing and by saying and doing nothing.

This reaction, familiar to persons trained in the psychology of crisis, has been shown by several researchers to be interpreted in other ways by creditors. Unfamiliar as they are in working with persons in crises, creditors interpret this patterns of inaction and silence as further signs of bad faith, irresponsibility and unwillingness on the debtors' part to deal with their financial obligations (Poppe and Borgeraas, 1992; Ford, 1988). As one researcher on the debt problem in Norway put it, the cognitive confusion experienced by banking personnel is exemplified in one of their common complaints about these 'new' debt defaulters:

> We know they are in crisis, but why don't they answer our letters (Stolanowski 1994b).

As creditors receiving little to no response from debtors then reintensify their efforts to contact them only to be met again with continued inaction on the part of these debtors, the process enters its final phase. Here the radically different interpretations of default held by the parts of the dyad join to produce a rapidly intensifying self-reinforcing process. This process is a cyclic and well known in other settings. First termed schismogenesis by the anthropologist Gregory Bateson, it has been assigned a variety of names by other researchers. 'Mutual reaction processes' and 'deviation-amplifying mutual casual processes' are two terms often used to refer to these self-reinforcing cycles in the literature of communications theory, mathematics, sociology, conflict and family therapy research (Richardson, 1960; Boulding, 1963; Hoffman, 1971; 1981).

Reformulated in terms of Bateson's original conceptualization, the state of affairs existing between a persistent creditor actively seeking contact with a increasingly withdrawn defaulting debtor is an example of 'complementary schismogenesis' (Bateson 1958, pp. 176-77). Stated more simply, this process is one exemplified by a vicious circle where the behavior patterns of each actor become progressively accentuated, the defaulting debtor withdrawing more and more as the contact-seeking creditor becomes more and more assertive. As Bateson noted in the first edition of *Naven*, self-reinforcing cycles of this type if not checked ultimately led to the collapse of the dyads and larger social systems where they took place. For Bateson and his students in later years (e.g. Haley, 1971; 1977; Hoffman, 1981; Watzlawick et al., 1967) as well as other researchers in a range of disciplines (e.g. Barth, 1959; Boulding, 1963), there developed a prime concern with identifying those rituals, institutions and roles which functioned to prevent runaway processes of this sort from destroying human relationships and systems.

Given a research perspective informed by the theoretical considerations presented thusfar, the negotiating functions of the financial counselor appear in a different form than earlier noted. In the first place, the counselor assumes a nearly anthropological role in mediating between the different worlds of meaning occupied by creditors and defaulting debtors. Understood in this way, the counselor as a mediator is both observer and translator of two cultures. One major task of this role is thus to make the meanings of the cultural categories borne by one group understandable to another group bearing a different culture, and vice versa. In a number of sessions observed, counselors devoted considerable time and attention to making the contents of letters from creditors intelligible to clients. On the other hand, several counselors interviewed about their activities noted that telephone negotiations with creditors often included making intelligible the situations of clients.

Perhaps even more important than this aspect of negotiations are those interventions performed by counselors to break the schismogenetic processes entrapping both creditor and debtor in potentially destructive cycles. There is material from Norway (Poppe and Borgeraas, 1992) and Great Britain (Ford, 1988) indicating that debtor withdrawal and passivity ultimately creates so much insecurity among creditors that they demand instant foreclosures and forced auctions to minimize their feared losses. Creditors thus act 'rationally' and extract themselves from the dyad and in the process of doing so destroy the relationship.

Seen against the background of what is known about crisis and its various stages, the behavior of the debtor, too, has a 'rational' character. The actors in this as in other schismogenetic processes exhibit rational choices. There is, as Bateson and others have noted, a fiendishly simple logic about the actions of actors in situations such as these. As we have seen, the classic debtor-creditor situation is one where the more the creditor attempts to establish a dialogue with a debtor, the more the creditor withdraws into passivity and silence which in turn stimulates the creditor to even greater efforts to establish contact. One part of the research on the pathologies of the mode of schismogenetic communication have been oriented towards finding socially appropriate ways of intervening in these cycles. In one way, the development of family therapy as a discipline can be traced to the impetus of Bateson's ideas about schismogenesis and ways of stopping its processes of destruction (Hoffman, 1981; Haley, 1977).

In light of some of the objections raised about the propriety of financial counseling and mediation in social work, it is interesting to note that similar objections seldom have been voiced about social workers functioning family therapists. What makes this even more interesting is that both the family therapist and the financial counselor share a near identical role in relation to intervening in the schismogenetic processes they encounter at their respective worksites. The family therapist working with couples and larger systems is constantly required to function in the role of a third party in relation to dyads experiencing schismogenesis. In these situations, the intensity of these processes have been amplified to such an extent that only the intervention by a third party – the therapist –

can prevent a 'runaway' and in this way stabilize the dyad (Haley, 1963). Though the dyadic relation between creditor and debtor is of course of a different quality than that of the relationship between spouses, the financial counselor, too, is required to intervene in the same kinds of processes threatening its stability. As already noted in this discussion, there is ample evidence that interventions performed by counselors acting as mediators between anxious creditors and defaulting debtors have managed to create situations favorable to renegotiation and thus help stabilize relationships which initially had scarce chances for survival.

Lessons for Social Work

Space does not permit more than a cursory set of reflections on the lessons to be learned from financial counseling. Our data suggest that there are two areas where social workers could be doing a better job for debtor clients. In the first place, it is doubtful whether a person in crisis is especially receptive to appeals to become more self-reliant – 'help to self help' as it is called in Norwegian social work ideology. Further, given the ideological implications of self-reliance and its links to doctrines blaming victims for their own situations (see, for example, Gans, 1995), tactics aimed at promoting self-reliance can lend themselves to transformations of troubles having social structural origins into problems involving personal and moral character deficiencies. By adopting a 'self-reliance' approach to clients, the social worker counselor may end up performing functions paralleling those of the 'mark cooler' described by Goffman (1952) as well as the 'social pathologist' of individual troubles parodied by Mills (1943). Rather than assisting clients by intervening on their behalf with creditors and thereby counteracting schismogenetic processes, social workers preferring to stressing self reliance may serve to reinforce subtly dominant ideological constructions of defaulting debtors as morally and otherwise deficient persons. As already noted, debt troubled clients arriving at the social offices are also burdened by considerable ideological baggage assigning blame to them for situations structurally produced by a host of economic forces over which they have had almost no control. The obvious classic parallel to this is the finding by Jahoda and Bakke among others that unemployed person during the depression of the 1930s blamed themselves rather than the workings of the capitalist system for their joblessness (Jahoda et al., 1971; Bakke, 1933).

The second area calling for improvement in the way social workers provide counseling to debtor clients is closely linked to the first – namely, increased expertise in mediating between debtors and creditors. As described earlier, the arrival of middle class clients at these offices created a serious crisis for social workers. In the beginning, this crisis was understood as being one involving the inability of social workers to help these clients. This inability was seen as resulting from deficiencies in social work education and lack of experience in dealing with financial matters.

This understanding of the crisis was then used as a rationale for employing financially trained counseling staff at social offices – especially where the debt crisis was widespread. In one way, our research findings support this linking of the crisis at social offices to deficiencies in social work education and training. Indeed, in the final chapter of our research report, we make a number of suggestions for improving social worker training programs and curricula. But in another way, our findings also suggest that the crisis may have involved a much more basic problem in social work practice. The presence of this 'new' client group, it could be argued, produced a crisis principally because it disturbed the traditional formulae for transactions at social offices based on extreme power differentials between middle class professionals and clients located beneath them in the Norwegian class system.

Understood in this way, upgrading mediation and negotiation in social work education will work to break down traditional 'one up – one down' molds recorded in research reports on social work – client interaction in Norway (e.g. Guttormsen and Hoigaard, 1978; Ranger 1986, 1993; Ohnstad, 1993). The role of the mediator as observed by us and others (e.g. Bar-On, 1990) do not reveal these kinds of traditional power differentials. Indeed, in many instances where power differentials come into play, it is the financial counselors who most often was in the 'one down' position in relation to a powerful creditor, such an official of a national bank or mortgage institution. In many respects, the financial counseling sessions observed by us often had the character of meetings between social equals.

Several features underscored this. For example, financial counselors often sat on the same side of the desk with clients while going through figures, letters and the like. Another illustration of the lack of power differentials in the counseling sessions is worth mentioning here. As the research progressed, team members were first surprised and then accustomed to hearing counselors with non-social work backgrounds use the term 'customers', rather than clients, to refer to those persons they met in counseling sessions. The infectiousness of this kind of redefining, though difficult to gauge, provides still another example of a manner of dealing with people not normally associated with social work agencies and other 'street-level bureaucracies' (e.g. Prottas, 1979; Lipsky, 1981).

Clearly, the arrival of personnel trained to relate to customers, rather than clients, represented a shift from traditional practices at social offices. One consequence of this was that there thus existed few traditions and very little ideology about conducting this kind of work at the social offices. The result of this may have created situations whereby it was left to the discretion of individual financial counselors to explore anew how best to cope with problems presented by clients experiencing financial troubles. Since middle class debtor clients were newcomers to social office, there was an absence of tradition and ideology about how they should be dealt with. This, too, may have functioned to allow counselors to deal with debtors in the kinds of positive ways we witnessed in the sessions. The general impression we gained from our study was that social work could benefit greatly from the lessons to be drawn from the ways counselors tackled the problems presented by these victims of the debt crisis – especially in the manner in which debt default was externalized, freed from judgments of moral character, and dealt with in an atmosphere enhancing mediation and the solving of money troubles in matter-of-fact ways.

Finally, it is paradoxical that clients in our study as well as research reports from elsewhere report extremely positive if not outright therapeutic results from their meetings with financial counseling personnel having no therapeutic training. A follow-up study of persons with debt problems who had received financial counseling at a project carried out by consumer affairs counselor in two Swedish cities found that 95 per cent characterized their experiences as being beneficial – one and one-half years after completing the project (Konsumverket 1989).

We can only speculate at this time why therapeutic results arise from these encounters. It may be that if situations are formally defined as non-therapeutic this then paradoxically frees participants from the constraints of therapeutic agendas – often heavily ritualized – and thus allows clients to engage in dialogue with persons having legitimized expertise about issues impacting on their identities. If these dialogic encounters then lead to the creation of new and positive meanings clients can then attribute to their situation, life and identity, these non-therapeutic meetings clearly have functioned in therapeutic ways. Until such time as further research is done on this extremely important issue, we can only offer conjecture as to how these redefinitions reconstructed in such encounters. Clearly, the patterns of financial counseling we have witnessed have much to teach social work teachers as well as practitioners. A major question remains, however, whether they are ready and willing to learn from these lessons.

Bibliography

Aftenposten (1994), 'Oslo gjeldsofre høyt utdannet', 24 februar, page 2 (evening edition).
Aftenposten (1992), 'Skylder på gjeldsofrene', 25 mai, page 48 (morning edition).
Ahl, K. (1976), *Lyftet*, Bokförlaget Prisma, Stockholm.
Bakke, E. (1933), *The Unemployed Man*, Nisbet, London.
Bar-On, A. (1990), 'Organizational Resource Mobilization: A Hidden Face of Social Work Practice', *British Journal of Social Work*, vol. 20, pp. 133-49.
Barth, F. (1959), 'Segmentary Opposition and the Theory of Games', *Journal of Royal Anthropological Institute*, vol. 89, pp. 5-21.
Bateson, G. (1958), *Naven* (revised edition) Stanford University Press, Palo Alto.
Bondeson, U. (1977), *Kriminalvård i frihet*, Liber, Stockholm.
Boulding, K. (1963), *Conflict and Defense*, Harper and Row, New York.
Bourdieu, P. and Passeron, J-C. (1977), *Reproduction in Education, Society, and Culture*, Sage, London.
Brusdal, R. (1988), *En kvalitativ studie av hushold i økonomisk krise*, NEK rapport 2, København.
Caplovitz, D. (1974), *Consumers in Trouble: A Study of Debtors in Default*, Macmillan, New York.
Chilman, C., Cox, F. and Nunnally, E. (eds) (1988), *Employment and Economic Problems. Families in Trouble. Volume 1*, Sage, London.
Dagbladet (1992), interview with Grete Berget, 23 mars, page 2.
Denzin, N. (1970), *The Research Act: A Theoretical Guide to Research Methods*, Aldine, New York.
Erlandson, D., Harris, E., Skipper, B. and Allen, S. (1993), *Doing Naturalistic Inquiry*, Sage, London.
Ford, J. (1988), *The Indebted Society: Credit and Default in the 1980s*, Routledge, London.
Gans, H. (1995), *The War Against The Poor*, Basic Books, New York.
Goodin, R. (1988), *Reasons for Welfare: The Political Theory of The Welfare State*. Princeton University Press, Princeton.
Goffman, E. (1952), 'On Cooling the Mark out: some aspects of adaption to failure', *Psychiatry*, vol. 15, pp. 451-63.

Gulbrandsen, L. (1989), *Gjeldsekplosjon og gjeldsreduksjon. Låneopptak i norske husholdninger i 1980-åra*, INAS Rapport 89:7, Oslo.

Gulbrandsen, L. (1991), *Fra forbrukerfest til gjeldskrise*, INAS Rapport 91:9, Oslo.

Guttormsen, G. and Høigaard, C. (1978), *Fattigdom i en velstandskommune: en undersøkelse av sosialomsorgen i Bærum*, Universitetsforlaget, Oslo.

Haley, J. (1977), 'Toward a Theory of Pathological Systems', in P. Watzlawick and J. Weakland (eds), *The Interactional View*, W. W. Norton: New York.

Haley, J. (1963), *Strategies of Family Therapy*, Grune and Stratton, New York.

Haley, J. (ed) (1971), *Changing Families*, Grune and Stratton, New York.

Halvorsen, K. (1996), 'Symbolic Purposes and Factual Consequences of the Concepts 'Self-reliance' and 'Dependency' in Contemporary Discourses on Welfare', paper presented at Scandinavian Journal of Social Welfare Symposium, University of Stockholm, Stockholm.

Halvorsen, K. (1994), *Arbeidsløshet og arbeidsmarginalisering. Levekår og mestring*. Universitetsforlaget, Oslo.

Halvorsen, K. (ed) (1993), *Sosialpolitisk årbok: 1993*, Universitetsforlaget, Oslo.

Hoffman, L. (1971), 'Deviation-Amplifying Processes in Natural Groups', in J. Haley (ed), *Changing Families*, Grune and Stratton, New York.

Hoffman, L. (1981), *Foundations of Family Therapy*, Basic Books, New York.

Ilstad, S. (1989), 'Økonomisk stress hos familier: Årsaker og virkninger, og mestring', *Tidsskrift for Norsk Psykologforening*, vol. 26, pp. 238-44.

Jahoda, M., Lazersfeld, P. and Zeisel, H. (1971), *Marienthal: The Sociography of an Unemployed Community*. (American edition). Aldine, Chicago.

Konsumverket (1989), *Ett og ett halvt år senara...*Rapport 1988/89:9, Vallingby.

Lipsky, M. (1981), *Street-Level Bureaucracy: Dilemmas of the Individual in Public Services*, Russel Sage, New York.

Lunde, T. og Poppe, C. (1991) *Ny-fattigdom i velferdsstaten*, SIFO Rapport: 3. Oslo.

Mills, C. (1959), *The Sociological Imagination,* Oxford University Press, New York.

Mills, C. (1943), 'The Professional Ideology of Social Pathologists', *American Journal of Sociology*, vol. 49, pp. 165-80.

NOU (*Norske Offentlig Utredning*) (1989).

Ohnstad, A. (1993), *Den gode samtalen*, Det norske samlaget, Oslo.

Parker, G. (1985), *Problems and Courses of Indebtedness: A Study of Clients of the Birmingham Money Advice Centre*, Unpublished Ph.D. thesis, University of Birmingham, England.

Poppe, C. and Borgeraas, E. (1992), *Økonomisk rådgivning overfor personer med betalingsvansker*, Statens institutt for forbruksforskning, Lysaker.

Prottas, J. (1979), *People-processing. The Street-Level Bureaucrat in Public Service*, Lexington Books, Boston.

Ranger, M. (1993), *Er det bare meg som roter sånn?*, (second revised edition), Universitetsforlaget, Oslo.
Ranger, M. (1986), *Er der bare meg som roter sånn?*, Universitetsforlaget, Oslo.
Richardson, L. (1960), *Arms and Insecurity*, Boxwood Press, Pittsburgh.
Rock, P. (1973), *Making People Pay*, Routledge and Kegan Paul, London.
Ruesch, H. and Bateson, G. (1951), *Communication: The Social Matrix of Society*, W. W. Norton, New York.
Seltzer, M., Hjelmvedt, V., Ohnstad, A. and Ranger, M. (1995), *Økonomisk veiledning ved sosialkontor: en tverfaglig rapport*, Nota Bene, Høgskolen i Oslo, ØKS Rapport 3.
Solheim, S. (1992), foredrag om økonomisk rådgivning, NKSH.
Stjernø, S. (1983), *Stress og utbrenthet*, Universitetsforlaget, Oslo.
Sternø, S. (1982), *Omsorg som yrke*, Universitetsforlaget, Oslo.
Stjernø, S., Hezlien, A. and Terum, L. (1988), *Et bedre sosialkontor!*, Universitetsforlaget, Oslo.
Stolanowski, P. (1994a), *Tilstrekkelig til livets opphold: grunnlag og metoder for økonomisk rådgivning på sosialkontor*, Bedriftsøkonomen forlag, Oslo.
Stolanowski, P. (1994b), foredrag om økonomisk rådgivning, NKSH.
Stolanowski, P. (1990), *Økonomisk rådgivning i sosialt arbeid*, Bedriftsøkonomen forlag, Oslo.
Terum, L. (1986), *Penger eller behandling*, INAS notat 86:5, Oslo.
Watzlawick, P. and Weakland, J. (eds) (1977), *The Interactional View*, W. W. Norton, New York.
Watzlawick, P., Jackson, D. and Beavin, J. (1967), *Pragmatics of Human Communication*, W. W. Norton, New York.
Wilkins, L. (1965), 'A Behavioural Theory of Drug Taking', *Howard Journal*, vol. 11, pp. 6-17.
Young, J. (1971), *The Drugtakers The Social Meaning of Drug Use*, Paladin, London.

12 A Model for Constructivist Social Work Practice: The Product of a Clinician-Researcher Dialogue

JACLYN MILLER AND MARY KATHERINE O'CONNOR

Introduction

This chapter is a true consequence of a constructivist process. For about two years the authors, one a researcher and the other a clinician, were involved in what Guba and Lincoln (1989) have called a hermeneutic dialectic. Through this process we have co-constructed meaning for our work together. We began our dialogue from very different orientations and perspectives which led to different initial understandings of what might constitute social constructivist practice. While our personal dialogue, conflict and resolutions must necessarily remain unseen, our consensus is represented by the model of practice highlighted in the case material we will present.

This chapter then, is both a product of the hermeneutic dialectic of constructivism we hope to elucidate, and an example of the process itself. To aid the reader in understanding the elements of this process, we will present a comparison framework which separates two distinct approaches to ontology (what is to be known), and epistemology (how it can be known). While these terms are most at home with philosophers and 'scientists', the questions they represent are fundamental to all realms of knowing, including clinical practice.

Constructivism in Context: The Epistemological Debate in Social Work

The epistemological debate, or the debate on how we know what we know in social work, has gone in many directions. The complexity of the activities social workers are involved in, combined with the range of client populations served, challenge the definition of social work as a profession and the development of empirically based social work theories. In the United States, the debate is embedded in the history of social work becoming a profession. The formal debate began in 1915 when Abraham Flexner, an authority on professional education, declared that social work was not a profession. He found it did not have a body of knowledge that could be taught and could guide practice; social work was not scientific.

Mary Richmond, Jane Addams, Charlotte Towle, Virginia Robinson and other American social work foremothers took up Flexner's challenge and produced definitions and theoretical models (see for example, Addams, 1916, 1930; Richmond, 1917; Robinson, 1930; Towle, 1936) that were reflective of the social science of the early 1900s. They helped to shape social workers' thinking about the scientific study of social work practice. These early social work leaders embraced logical positivism as a means of framing activities and garnering credibility and respect. This represented a move away from social work's early roots in religion, philosophy, and humanism, a legacy that gave social work 'its wisdom about the worth of individuals and fostered a commitment to the importance of values in the practice of social work' (Weick, 1987, p. 218). The struggle continued at the 1929 Milford Conference (1974); was further explicated in the Hollis-Taylor Report of 1951; and is seen in the *Working definition of social work practice*, 1958. The move toward positivism was formalized in the 1950s when the profession adopted the Social Work Research Group's commitment to 'basic science' (Gordon, 1951; Mass and Varon, 1949). The emphasis on knowledge through observation and measurement meant foresaking intuition and other less scientifically rigorous, potentially 'biased' ways of knowing, including practice wisdom. This ratified social work's acceptance, not only of Freud and the medical model, but also of operationalization for measurement and control for generalizability. It also engaged the profession in what has become an endless balancing act of embracing both knowledge and values in social work education and in social work practice.

In the late 1970s and early 1980s (Austin, 1978; Beckerman, 1978; Fischer, 1981; Gordon, 1983; Haworth, 1984; Heineman, 1981; Hudson, 1983; Imre, 1984; Karger, 1983), mirroring the public professional dialogue in other disciplines and professions such as education, sociology, and psychology (see Adams, 1979; Blalock, 1979; Chronbach, 1975; Eisner, 1979), the debate reemerged in social work. The limits of research findings, the inability of research to address complex social issues, and the problems with effectiveness measures caused many to question the usefulness of a positivist perspective in guiding social work practice (Haworth, 1984; Heineman, 1981; Imre, 1984).

Logical positivist and empiricist roots continue to be questioned. Some, like Roberta Imre (1982), call for a return to our philosophical roots. Others call for more flexibility in pursuing ways of knowing (Berlin, 1990; Fraser, Taylor, Jackson and O'Jack, 1991). Many suggest that quantitative evidence counts, but does not and should not stand alone (Dean, 1989,1993; Heineman-Peiper, 1989; Scott, 1989; Tyson, 1992). At the same time, the social work profession in the U.S. is challenged from without for its' lack of defined activities and effective measures and from within for its' lack of good science for good practice (Gilbert, 1977; Grinnell et al., 1994; Thyer, 1986). Howard Goldstein (1992) recently suggests that if our profession has not made progress as science, then perhaps social work is art.

Constructivist research in social work can be seen as a bridge between traditional views of art and science. It fits in the realm of rigorous, systematic knowledge building possible from science while recognizing the magical and visceral knowing that comes through art. The controversy for social work, and most of social science, is not between art and science. Rather, it involves ontological and epistemological questions about what social reality is like: how we know and how this knowledge is transmitted. The paradigmatic debate concerns the assumptions made about the essence of any phenomena under investigation. For example, is reality external to the individual or is it the product of the individual's consciousness? There are questions about how knowledge can be obtained. Is it hard, true, real, and capable of being transmitted in tangible form? Or is it soft, subjective, spiritual, and of a unique and personal nature that can only be acquired or personally experienced? What of human nature? Do humans relate to the environment in a mechanistic, deterministic way? Or do humans with free will create their environments?

Different answers to the above questions are grounded in different philosophical perspectives that incline the researcher/practitioner toward different methodological assumptions about what constitutes good research and knowledge-guided practice. These answers create different paradigms for analysis of social theory, different assumptions for analysis of social phenomena, and different concepts and analytic tools for social research.

Table 12.1 Contrasting Positivist and Constructivist Positions

CONTRASTING POSITIVIST AND CONSTRUCTIVIST POSITIONS

Assumptions About	Positivist Perspective	Constructivist Perspective
Ontology: The nature of reality	Single, tangible, fragmentable, convergent. 'realist'	Multiple, constructed, holistic, divergent. 'relativist'
Epistemology: The nature of knowing	Dualistic; objective	Monistic; subjective
Purpose: Generalization	Context and time-free generalizations; nomothetic statements; focus on similarities; prediction	Context and time-bound working hypotheses; idiographic statements; focus on differences and similarities; understanding
Explanation: Causality	Real causes, temporally precedent or simultaneous	Interactive mutual shaping
Objectivity: The inquirer-respondent relationship	Independent	Interrelated
Axiology: The role of values	Value-free	Value-bound

Table 12.1 provides a comparison of the assumptions underlying the positivist and constructivist paradigmatic perspectives detailed elsewhere

by Rodwell (1990). In brief, positivists believe in the existence of universal laws. Therefore, the purpose of research is to analyze relationships and regularities between various elements of the entity being investigated.

Constructivists believe in the relativistic nature of the world, so the focus of research is on the context-embedded, subjective experience of the person in the creation of her/his social world.

These assumptions have dramatic impact not only on the conceptualization and implementation of a research process, which has already been develop and explicated (see Guba and Lincoln, 1989; Rodwell, 1998), but also on the conceptualization of a clinical process, which has not yet been explicated. As can be seen from Table 12.2, these two perspectives give rise to practice models that differ along key dimensions.

Table 12.2 Comparative Practice Perspectives

CONTRASTING POSITIVIST AND CONSTRUCTIVIST POSITIONS

	Positivist Perspective	Constructivist Perspective
The nature of the problem	Disease or condition needing treatment; person centered; pathological	Viability, fit between client system and the environment; interactive; situational; consensus-based focus
Role of clinician	Neutral, distant, expert with knowledge and skills necessary to effect a cure; powerful, in control; responsible; active; directive	'Sides' with all involved; teacher/learner of coping patterns in the client system and environment; offers/ uncovers/constructs options; pragmatic and empowering
Role of client	Target of treatment by expert; passive recipient; incompetent, lacking understanding of problem; defined in isolation	Co-creator of information for problem definition, resources and outcomes; powerful, strong; active decision maker; client role and who is client, broadly defined

(continued)

	Positivist Perspective	Constructivist Perspective
Client/clinician relationship	Unequal; clinician leads, client follows; clinician 'treats' client	Collaborative, shared expertise; mutual shaping of reality and each other; respect
Nature of assessment/diagnosis	Context free; conclusions from 'facts'; professional language using collective categories	Meaningful, co-constructed; making sense; linked to physical, spiritual, social, structural contexts; reflective of unique complexity
The nature of the problem-solving process	Value free; result of deductive thinking; linear; expert diagnosis of problem followed by the application of techniques designed to treat symptoms	Value-embedded; result of inductive thinking; tacit; mutual exploration of of conditions; collaborative search for resources that will strengthen client ability to meet needs; cyclical and circular
Nature of outcomes	Change is in client; unifocused; 'fixed' or 'failed' based on the competence of clinician and determined by experts	Change affects all participants including clinician; unpredictable; joint evaluation of outcomes; more tentative; multiple resources and results client owned

Similar discussions and debate in other disciplines also have resulted in shifts in the conceptualization of clinical interventions (see Beck, 1993; Berger and Luckmann, 1973; Doise, 1989; Neimeyer, 1993; Owen, 1992; Palazzoli, Boscolo, Cecchin and Prata, 1978; Schotter, 1975). Within these shifts, the focus is on meaning (Kracke, 1987; Von Glasersfeld, 1979), problem-determined systems (Boscolo, Cecchin, Hoffman and Penn, 1987; Imber-Black, 1985), the narrative (Fish, 1993; Neimeyer and Neimeyer, 1994; Schotter and Gergen, 1989), discourse analysis (Braten, 1984), and the theoretical prominence of the epistemological assumptions of both constructionism and constructivism.

Table 12.3 Contrasts between Constructivism and Constructionism

CONTRASTING CONSTRUCTIVIST AND CONSTRUCTIONIST POSITIONS

Constructivism	Constructionism
Nature of Knowledge	
Cognitive schemas	Linguistic negotiation (conversation)
A construction of the subject's experience and action	Generated between individuals who judge and correct
An invention of new interpretive frameworks or structures	Agreement regarding meaning
Evolutionary to more comprehensive interpretations	Product of claims-making, labeling and other constitutive definitional processes
Human Beings	
Proactive, goal-directed, and purposive organism	Personality and identity socially constructed and potentially changing from situation to situation
Human Interaction	
Structural coupling - fitting together structures and coordinating behaviors of self-organized systems	Linguistic coupling - negotiating meaning across cognitive, social, moral structures
Processes Relevant to Constructivist Research	
Schemas for analysis	Discourse analysis
Purposeful questioning	Stories
Managing paradox	Problems understood within the social network or context
Experiential data collection	Circular questioning and emergent processes
Restructuring of cognitive meaning	
Conceptual frameworks	Narrative reconstructions
Hearing the multiple voices	Opening spaces for conversation

While these terms are often used interchangeably in the literature, they are not identical and clarification of assumptions is crucial in the development of a conceptually rigorous framework for constructivist practice. Comparing and contrasting elements of constructionist and constructivist theories is a useful baseline. A portion of this task has been accomplished in an article by Franklin (1995) who compares and contrasts constructionism and constructivism as theories and then compares how they can be used in *thinking* about clinical practice. While this leads to interesting ideas about practice interventions, what is missing is a model that can be used to guide behavior in all aspects of the clinical process. As can be seen in Table 12.3, constructionist and constructivist theories have come together in the model of constructivist research. What we propose is the same integrative effort, informed by this constructivist research model, for constructivist clinical practice.

Basically, both constructionism and constructivism emphasize human agency and assert that reality is socially and psychologically constructed. Both hold an interactional view of human behavior and a connectedness between the individual and the social environment. Both assert reflexivity in understanding and meaning making. Both reject the 'received view' of reality: i.e., there is no single, objective reality 'out there' to be received/perceived and understood through sensory perceptions, but many possible ways to understand behaviors, interactions, or events. Both assert that structures (cognitive or social) that exist beyond oneself cannot be objectively known due to the nature of language and social processes. Radical constructivists such as Maturana (1988), Varela (1989), Watzlawick (1984), and Keeney (1983) go even further to suggest that it is impossible to know anything except what is in one's own mind.

However, the two theories diverge in conceptualizing how reality is shaped, formed, or constructed. Constructionists emphasize language, narrative, socio-historical, and cultural processes as primary factors in meaning making and in understanding our own constructions, our own knowledge-base. Constructivists, on the other hand, emphasize cognitive structures, or schemas, such as organizing principles, deep structures, and interactive feedback from the environment. In a constructivist interpretive framework, knowledge is validated through internal consistency with existing knowledge structures and through social consensus among observers. In both theories, however, there is a belief in the diversity of possible meanings and alternative interpretations that makes contextual relativity, if not true relativity, possible.

For the purposes of creating a theoretical linkage to constructivist research, it would be best to view constructivism and constructionism as a fuzzy set of frameworks with mainly indistinct boundaries. Within each we will find diversity and contradictions. Within each we will find similar contributions to a very distinct way of being with clients that focuses on their own constructions of reality and their own strength and possibilities.

Their commonalities are present in the constructivist research model. Their differences are also part of the research process. From the constructivists come schemas for analysis, purposeful questioning, managing paradox, experiential data collection, and restructuring of cognitive meaning (Franklin, 1995, p. 397). From constructionism, discourse analysis, stories, problems understood within the social network or context, circular questioning and emergent processes, narrative reconstructions, and opening spaces for conversation will emerge (Franklin, 1995, p. 397). Both theories give meaning to the research process. Both are congruent with the goals and procedures of constructivist research. In fact, both are necessary for the logic of the constructivist research methods.

As was demonstrated by Franklin (1995), the ideas inherent in this alternative way of being with clients are not foreign to social workers engaged in clinical practice. For example, when Hoffman (1988, p. 110) suggests we change from an 'observed system reality' (the normative/positivist view) to an 'observing system reality' (the alternative/constructivist view), we are on familiar ground of the therapeutic encounter. The sole purpose of such encounters is to observe (using all senses and abilities) in order to know and understand what we can of the other and her/his world. Unfortunately, the philosophical dimensions of the alternative approach to practice have not translated into a well-developed model for constructivist interventions and practice. It is easy to think about a social construction of reality in which: development is contextual; individuals are producers of their own development; meaning making is self-evolution; reality has many forms; and, in which language constitutes reality. It is easy to think that the clinician's role is to learn how the client makes meaning and to create a social context for reconstruction through dialogue (Sexton and Griffin, 1997). However, other than the use of narrative, no clear, logically consistent, and thorough guidelines for constructivist practice or therapy have been found. Using the methodology of constructivist research as a guide, the following section presents some guidelines for constructivist clinical practice.

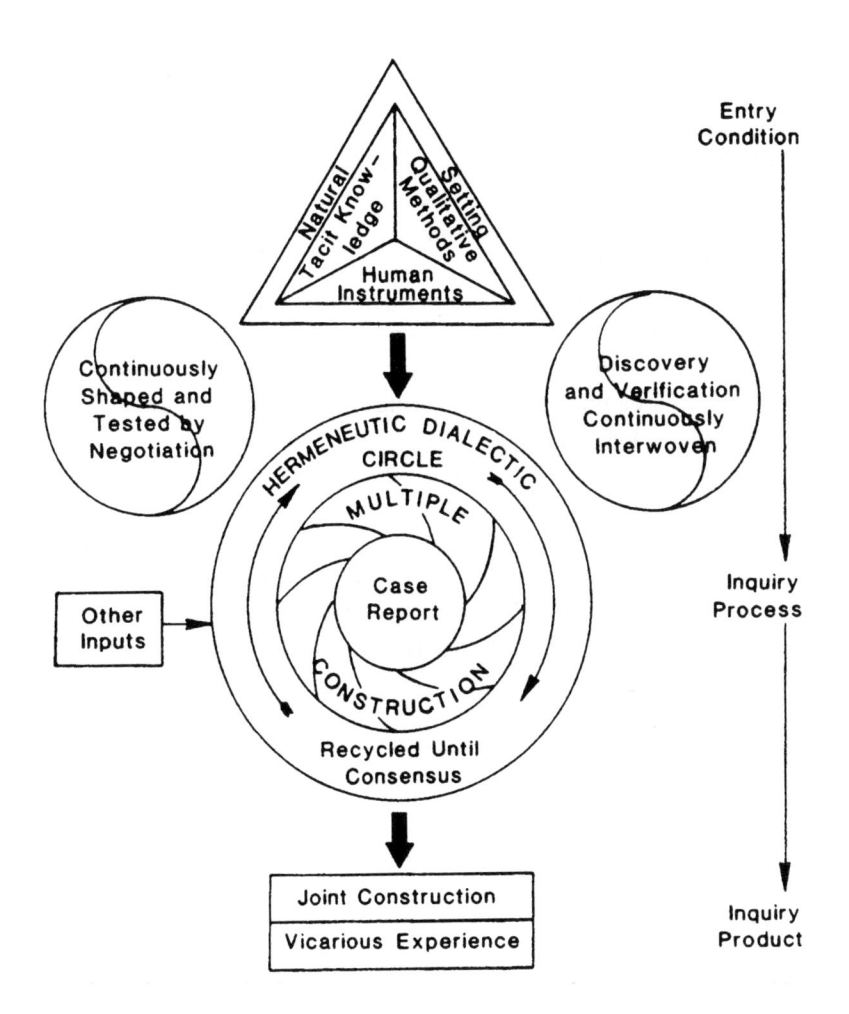

A Model for Constructivist Social Work Practice 247

Figure 12.1 The Methodology of Constructivist Inquiry
Source: Guba and Lincoln, 1989

Constructivist Clinical Practice

The methodology of constructivist inquiry describes an entry condition, the inquiry process, and the product of inquiry (see Figure 12.1) directly derived from the assumptions of constructivism. To be constructivist, the inquiry must be in the natural setting of the subject of the inquiry. The human instrument (the researcher) uses qualitative methods and relies on tacit knowledge in a discovery and verification process that is continuous. The process and the discoveries are continuously shaped and tested through negotiation with the participants. The inquiry process, then, is circular and dialectical, leading to conflict, compromise, and greater sophistication about the subject. The hermeneutic-dialectic continues until consensus is reached about the phenomena under investigation.

This framework moves us into schools of clinical practice which place subjective meaning (understanding and knowing) in a central position, where tacit knowledge already is considered a relevant and valued source of knowing. Tacit knowledge is that part of what we 'know' that remains unarticulated after we have explained all we can about the subject we are trying to understand. Elusive aspects of the clinical dialogue can be subsumed under tacit knowing, e.g., intuition, 'practice wisdom', art, unconscious processes, and the integral contributions of bodily experience. The dynamic connection between experience that is immediate (near) and experience that is mediated (distant) is brought forward in this process of inquiry.

The Entry Condition

No focus of inquiry can be engaged separate from its natural context since it is in context that the co-construction of meaning was and continues to be created. As Varela (1979) emphasizes, the observing system is not ever an individual, it is always an observer community. Human beings learn through the constructed lenses of language and culture. Many of the theoretical underpinnings of psychotherapy reflect an acceptance of this stance. Object relations theory, symbolic interactionism, role construct theory, and Sullivan's interpersonal approach are but a few examples.

The relativist ontology of constructivism requires that the context for the focus of inquiry be that which is relevant to the client. This is activated in the hermeneutic-dialectic process when the clinician quite literally 'begins where the client is' because there is no other place to start. The clinician is not an expert, but a learner. Any predetermined set of questions would be based on the clinician's construction, or on the constructions that are culturally and time-based for others, e.g., base of classifications, schemas, etc.

> A middle-aged male is referred, at his request, by his wife's therapist. He will only see a female clinician. At our first meeting, he begins by telling me that his marriage is wonderful; he and his wife love each other very much; they have great sex; and, they are both committed to the relationship. He then says he cross-dresses...that he is a transvestite. Because he feels so much more comfortable in it, he wears women's underwear all the time now.

This client presents his marriage as the first context for a conversation about his use of female clothing. So far, the stakeholders are he and his wife. As he continues to educate the clinician, he elaborates the context and talks about cross-dressing in today's society, and then in the context of his personal history. He has read a good deal about transvestism; knows what society 'thinks' of this behavior in men; discourses on the blurring of gender roles for women in recent years; and says that he is angry about the limits place on him by others' inability to tolerate difference.

The Inquiry Process

In the constructivist framework, the nature of the problem shifts significantly and classifications and diagnoses are not relevant. Instead, the unique construction of what is to be talked about (the focus of inquiry) comes from the client. In this vein, Hoffman (1988) describes how the family therapy world is struggling to conceptualize the 'problem' as a result of the shifts in perspective brought about by second-order cybernetics and other influences (all of which can be described as alternative perspectives). She has settled on calling it 'the system that is formed by a conversation about a problem' (p. 116).

> This client has been cross-dressing in women's lingerie throughout his current marriage. He says it is the 'pink elephant' in the living room that no one talks about: there have been no conversations about it. He experiences his wife as passive, although recently Prozac has made a positive change in her. He can now point things out to her about their finances, the car, and the house without her 'hiding in the closet'. Still, they have not talked about 'the elephant'.

A somewhat broader approach to describing the focus of inquiry is in Von Glasersfeld's (1979) term, 'non-viability'. Non-viability, rather than maladaptation, becomes the purpose for which social workers engage in a change process with clients. Viability and non-viability imply a conception of the world that has some norms, limits, and structures into which humans must 'fit'. There is order, but that order is unique to the person and situation. Determining the order and the viability, or lack thereof, become part of the clinical process.

> So far, in our work together, this client has only vaguely described areas of non-viability in his life. He has, however, shared 'facts' of his history as he experienced them: parents divorced early in his life; his father 'disappeared'; mother remarried several years later to a man who was 'junk-yard dog mean', the client has been married three times; he took drugs; played guitar; wrote songs; and traveled around for a number of years and does not remember much about how he survived.

There are many pieces of psychosocial information in the above description to lead one, using a number of theoretical frameworks, to make inferences about non-viability.

> In session, the client muses about these pieces of his life and how they might relate to his cross-dressing behavior. He also shrugs off this musing and says, 'that isn't the problem...the problem is how is it that I'm 'stuck' working in a mall, taking care of everyone in my life, and not allowed to cross-dress if I want'.

What the 'problem' is, is being continuously shaped and tested by negotiation. The role of the clinician here is crucial. There is a different meaning to the term 'neutral' in this framework. Here, neutral is not distant and non-responsive. It is being able to 'side with', or stand next to those involved. The clinician can bring the view of significant others into the room by the questions posed, encouraging the continuous interweaving of discovery and verification.

> This client has 'peopled' my office in just two sessions. As he talks, I realize I have immediate images of the people: his brother, best friend, current wife, first wife, mother, father, stepfather, and grandmother. And, as I review, I realize people are missing: his sister, grandfather, and second wife. I keep my images to myself, but trust that they are a mixture of his experiences and mine.

I ask recursive questions... 'tell me what your grandmother would say about this'...and... 'if she said that, what would that mean to you?'

Responsive focusing is a term used by Guba and Lincoln (1989, p. 178) to describe a major element of their methodology that facilitates multiple constructions. An example of the initiation of responsive focusing in the clinical process would be to begin by having the client tell you what question to ask and asking them to answer it. A responsive question might be, 'tell me what *you* think *I* should know'. This begins the process of gathering or constructing multiple meaning, beginning with the client's perspective.

> The client tells me that I need to know that he prefers to wear women's underclothes. It is a physical sensation that has brought him both pleasure and comfort since the first time he put on women's lingerie when he was in a play in his teens.

The emergent nature of the process proscribes a predetermined configuration of biopsychosocial data collection and, thus, a uniform assessment. Rather, the encounter is devoted to gathering information through observation, listening, and empathic responsiveness. This is the hermeneutic circle. Basch (1988) describes empathy as a process of identifying an internal affective experience in the therapeutic dyad and recognizing it as a response to or resonance with the other. This recognition leads to an idiographic interpretation of what the response might mean about the other. This is tested and shaped through interpretive questioning. With this, the meaning for the client (the focus of inquiry) is negotiated over time between clinician and client.

> The client tells me how good he felt about our first meeting. He has already thought much more about what he wants to explore and he traces this 'opening' to a word I used in response to his description of cross-dressing: 'congruent'. The word created a connection for him in a way that seemed to reflect several levels or iterations of his schemata and of our process. He had spoken of his love of math and science. We were having a dialogue about cross-dressing. We were constructing our relationship and beginning to restructure meaning.

The Inquiry Product

Listening and observing are engaged processes. They are not unidirectional processes where the information from 'out there' is taken in. Rather, they are interactive and recursive where feedback and feedforward mechanisms move toward a joint construction of what is known. For the client, this has the potential of narrative reconstruction. The responses and findings that emerge in the therapeutic dialogue must 'fit' for the client. They must be useful in making sense of his or her unique experience. To be useful, they must be relevant, they must work, and they must be modifiable. In this last element, it becomes clear that in constructivist therapy the outcome *is* the process.

> Cross-dressing faded into background and the foreground became a reconstructed narrative about the creative self: how he had used music, poetry, and dressing-up as self-expression and self-containment through difficult early family experiences and subsequent years. What he had left behind, along with the pain, was a part of himself...a part he reclaimed through the dialectic process with me. He quit his job at a shopping mall and went to work full-time in a recording studio.

Conclusions

Constructivist therapy is a learning/teaching process that is continuous, recursive, divergent, and never finalized. The clinician participates in the process from a collaborative stance. Not only does the clinician learn about different value positions and perspectives, but she also teaches the client about the position of others and how to ask better questions of one another. The wholeness of the experience, indeed, the wholeness of the individual is not fragmentable into separate parts. The focus and the process engage the mind, body, and context simultaneously, consistently, and recursively. Constructivist clinical practice, then, is a process that constructs a new contextual reality, the form and experience of which cannot be specified in advance. The process emerges as the clinical dialogue proceeds. Structure emerges only as the therapy unfolds and results emerge out of negotiated understanding. Since the results of the clinical process are embedded in the current context, the future remains unknown. However, the outcome of this type of collaborative work serves as a template for shaping that future.

The changes in perspective and process described above do not come without loss. The relativism assumed in a constructivist perspective means there can be no certainty in any state of affairs. There is no objective truth and the resultant level of ambiguity may be too much for some to tolerate. The clinician gives up even the illusion that she controls the process. The client and other significant stakeholders have equally definitive input that shapes the process, rather than a single theoretical approach shaping the interventions. In addition, practice from this perspective fully recognizes that the outcome of each therapeutic endeavor is unique and not generalizable. We forgo the expectation that interventions will be found to be globally effective.

Though many elements of constructivism seem different, the qualities necessary in the clinician to truly accomplish the shifts are very familiar and totally congruent with expectations of a clinical practitioner. A constructivist clinician must primarily appreciate diversity and respect the rights of the individual to hold different values and construct different narratives. The clinician must welcome the opportunity to air and clarify these differences, not threatened by them, but embracing them. Personally, in addition to qualities of honesty, respect, courtesy, and integrity above suspicion, the clinician must engender trust in her ethics and professional competence. This is required for the client to engage in this uncharted process. For the clinician to be comfortable in this endeavor, she must have a high tolerance for ambiguity and frustration. She must have the capacity to distance herself from the process enough to avoid undue influence while maintaining genuine involvement. Finally, the constructivist clinician must be willing to be changed by the therapeutic process, both personally and professionally. This can happen only if she is open to the risks involved in participating in an all-encompassing, unpredictable, unending process of becoming.

Bibliography

Adams, E. (1979), 'Measurement Theory in Current Research', in P. Asquith and H. E. Kyberg, *Philosophy of Science*, Philosophy of Science Association, East Lansing, Michigan, pp. 207-227.

Addams, J. (1916), *The Long Road of Woman's Memory*, Macmillan, New York.

Addams, J. (1930), *The Second Twenty Years at Hull House, September 1909 to September 1929, with a Record of a Growing World Consciousness*, Macmillan, New York.

Austin, D. (1978), 'Research and Social Work: Educational Paradoxes and Possibilities', *Journal of Social Service Research*, vol. 2.

Basch, M. (1988), *Understanding Psychotherapy*, Basic Books, New York.

Beck, A. (1993), 'Cognitive Therapy: Past, Present, and Future', *Journal of Consulting and Clinical Psychology*, vol. 61, no. 2, pp. 194-198.

Beckerman, A. (1978), 'Differentiating Between Social Research and Social Work Research: Implications for Teaching', *Journal of Education for Social work*, vol. 14, pp. 9-15.

Berger, P., and Luckmann, T. (1973), *The Social Construction of Reality*, Penguin, London.

Berlin, S. (1990), 'Dichotomous and Complex Thinking', *Social Service Review*, vol. 64, pp. 46-59.

Blalock, H. M. (1979), 'Presidential Address: Measurement and Conceptualization Problems', *American Sociological Review*, vol. 44, pp. 881-194.

Boscolo, L., Cecchin, C., Hoffman, L., and Penn, P. (1987), *Milan Systemic Family Therapy*, Basic Books, New York.

Braten, S. (1984), 'The Third Position', in F. Geyer and J. van der Zowen (eds), *Sociocybernetics Paradoxes*, Sage, London.

Chronbach, L. (1975), 'Beyond the Two Disciplines of Scientific Psychology', *American Psychologist*, vol. 30, no. 2, pp. 116-127.

Dean, R. (1989), 'Ways of Knowing in Clinical Practice', *Clinical Social Work Journal*, vol. 17, no. 2, pp. 116-127.

Dean, R. (1993), 'Constructivism: An Approach to Clinical Practice', *Smith College Studies in Social Work*, vol. 63, pp. 127-146.

Doise, W. (1989), 'Constructivism in Social Psychology', *European Journal of Social Psychology*, vol.19, pp. 389-400.

Eisner, E. (1979), 'The Use of Qualitative Forms of Evaluation for Improving Educational Practice', *Educational Evaluation and Policy Analysis*, vol. 1, pp. 11-19.

Fischer, J. (1981), 'The Social Work Revolution', *Social Work*, vol. 26, pp. 199-207.

Fish, V. (1993), 'Poststructuralism in Family Therapy: Interrogating the Narrative/Conversational Mode', *Journal of Marital and Family Therapy*, vol. 19, no. 3, pp. 221-232.

Franklin, C. (1995), 'Expanding the Vision of the Social Constructionist Debates: Creating Relevance for Practitioners', *Families in Society*, September, pp. 395-407.

Fraser, M., Taylor, M. Jackson, R., and O'Jack, J. (1991), 'Social Work and Science: Many Ways of Knowing?' *Social Work Research & Abstracts*, vol. 27, no. 4, pp. 5-15.

Gilbert, N. (1977), 'The Search for Professional Identity', *Social Work*, vol. 22, no. 5, pp. 401-406.

Goldstein, H. (1992), 'If Social Work Hasn't Made Progress as a Science, Might It Be an Art?', *Families in Society*, vol. 73, pp. 48-55.

Gordon, W. (1951), *'Toward Basic Research in Social Work'*, paper delivered at the fiftieth anniversary meeting of the Missouri Association for Social Welfare, October, 1950, St. Louis, The George Warren Brown School of Social Work.

Gordon, W. (1983), 'Social Work Revolution or Evolution?', *Social Work*, vol. 28, pp. 81-185.

Grinnell, R., et al. (1994), 'Social Work Researchers' Quest for Respectability', *Social Work*, July, pp. 469-470.

Guba, E., and Lincoln, Y. (1989), *Fourth Generation Evaluation* (3rd ed.), Sage, Newbury Park, CA.

Haworth, G. (1984), 'Social Work Research, Practice, and Paradigms', *Social Service Review*, vol. 58, pp. 343-357.

Heineman, M. (1981), 'The Obsolete Imperative in Social Work Research', *Social Service Review*, vol. 55, pp. 371-397.

Heineman-Peiper, M. (1989), 'The Heuristic Paradigm: A Unifying and Comprehensive Approach to Social Work Research', *Smith College Studies in Social Work*, vol. 60, pp. 8-34.

Hoffman, L. (1988), 'A Constructivist Position for Family Therapy', *The Irish Journal of Psychology*, vol. 9, no. 1, pp. 110-129.

Hudson, W. (1983), 'Scientific Imperatives in Social Work Research and Practice', *Social Service Review*, vol. 56, pp. 246-258.

Imber-Black, E. (1985), 'Families and Multiple Helpers: A Systemic Perspective', in D. Campbell and R. Draper (eds), *Application of Systemic Family Therapy: The Milan Method*, Grune and Stratton, New York.

Imre, R. (1982), *Knowing and Caring: Philosophical Issues in Social Work*, University Press of America, Washington, D.C.

Imre, R. (1984), 'The Nature of Knowledge in Social Work', *Social Work*, vol. 29, pp. 41-45.

Karger, H. (1983), 'Science, Research and Social Work: Who Controls the Profession', *Social Work*, vol. 28, pp. 200-205.

Keeney, B. (1983), *Aesthetics of change*, Guilford, New York.

Kracke, M. (1987), 'Everyone Who Dreams Has a Bit of Shaman: Cultural and Personal Meanings of Dreams--Evidence from the Amazon', *Psychiatry Journal of the University of Ottawa*, vol. 12, no. 2, pp. 65-72.

Maturana, H. (1988), 'Reality: The Search for Objectivity or the Quest for a Compelling Argument', *Irish Journal of Psychology*, vol. 9, pp. 25-82.

Mass, H.S., and Varon, E. (1949), 'The Case Worker in Clinical and Socio-Psychological Research', *Social Service Review*, vol. 23, pp. 302-314.

Neimeyer, G., and Neimeyer, R. (1994), 'Constructivist Methods of Marital and Family Therapy: A Practical Precis', *Journal of Mental Health Counseling*, pp. 85-104.

Neimeyer, R. (1993), 'An Appraisal of Constructivist Psychotherapies', *Journal of Consulting and Clinical Psychology*, vol. 61, no. 2, pp. 221-234.

Owen, I. (1992), 'Applying Social Constructionism to Psychotherapy', *Counselling Psychology Quarterly*, vol. 5, no. 4, pp. 385-402.

Palazzoli, M., Boscolo, L., Cecchin, G., and Prata, G. (1978), *Paradox and Counterparadox*, Jason Aronson, New York.

Richmond, M. (1917), *Social Diagnosis*, Russell Sage Foundation, New York.

Robinson, V. (1930), *A Changing Psychology in Social Case Work*, University of North Carolina Press, Chapel Hill.

Rodwell, M.K. (1990), 'Person/Environment Construct: Positivist Versus Naturalist, Dilemma or Opportunity for Health Social Work Research and Practice?' *Social Science and Medicine*, vol. 31, no. 1, pp. 27-34.

Rodwell, M.K. (1998), *Social Work Constructivist Research*, Garland, New York.

Scott, D. (1989), 'Meaning Construction and Social Work Practice', *Social Service Review*, vol. 63, pp. 39-52.

Schotter, J. (1975), *Images of Man in Psychological Research*, Metheun and Co., London.

Schotter, J., and Gergen, K. (eds), (1989), *Texts of Identity*, Sage, Newbury Park.

Sexton, T., and Griffin, B. (eds), (1997), *Constructivist Thinking in Counseling Practice, Research, and Training*, Teachers College Press, New York.

Social Case Work: Generic and Specific: A Report on the Milford Conference, (1974), National Association of Social Workers (reprint of 1929 ed.), Washington, D.C.

Thyer, B. (1986), 'On Pseudoscience and Pseudoreasoning', *Social Work Research & Abstracts*, vol. 22, no. 2, pp. 371-372.

Towle, C. (1936), 'Factors in Treatment', in *Proceedings of the National Conference on Social Work 63rd Annual Session, Atlantic City*, University of Chicago Press, Chicago, pp. 179-191.

Tyson, K. (1992), 'A New Approach to Relevant and Scientific Research for Practitioners: The Heuristic Paradigm', *Social Work*, vol. 37, pp. 541-556.

Varela, F. (1979), *Principles of biological autonomy*, North Holland Press, New York.

Varela, F. (1989), 'Reflections on the Circulation of Concepts between the Biology of Cognition and Systemic Family Therapy', *Family Process*, vol. 28, pp. 15-24.

Von Glasersfeld, E. (1979), 'The Control of Perception and the Construction of Reality', *Dialectica*, vol. 33, pp. 37-50.

Watzlawick, P. (1984), *The Invented Reality*, W.W. Norton, New York.

Weick, A. (1987), 'Reconceptualizing the Philosophical Perspective of Social Work', *Social Service Review*, vol. 61, pp. 218-230.

13 Speaking Up and Speaking Out: A Dialogic Approach to Anti-Oppressive Practice

DANIELLE TURNEY

... conversation is not just *one* of our many activities in *the* world. On the contrary, we constitute both ourselves and our worlds in our conversational activity. For us they are foundational (Shotter, 1993, Preface).

Introduction

The development of anti-oppressive practice has been a central concern in British social work education, training and practice in recent years and debate still continues about what it means and how it can be implemented. In this chapter, I suggest an approach towards theorising such practice[1], taking anti-oppressive practice (AOP) to be 'a form of social work practice which addresses social divisions and structural inequalities in the work that is done with people whether they be users ('clients') or workers. AOP aims to provide more appropriate and sensitive services by responding to people's needs regardless of their social status. AOP embodies a person centred philosophy; an egalitarian value system concerned with reducing the deleterious effects of structural inequalities upon people's lives; a methodology focusing on both process and outcome; and a way of structuring relationships between individuals that aims to empower users by reducing the negative effects of social hierarchies on their interaction and the work they do together' (Dominelli, 1996, pp. 170-171). AOP in this broad definition takes account of difference and inequality leading to oppression structured around 'race' and gender as well as addressing other significant axes of oppression. It therefore requires an ability to understand the operation of power dynamics and how they are manifested in different forms of oppression arising in 'real life' situations.

The remark from Shotter (1993) that prefaces this chapter offers a useful frame for my discussion of anti-oppressive practice in social work. It immediately highlights the importance of language and of a particular way of using language – conversation – to construct meaning. Shotter's 'rhetorical – responsive' version of social constructionism endorses a hermeneutic approach to understanding (1993, p. 6) which, I argue below, has much to contribute to social work practice. The linguistic turn implied by hermeneutics is well-suited to social work theorising as social work is essentially conversational; it is language-based activity (Rojek et al, 1988, p. 137), which depends heavily on *talk*. Indeed, within social work there is an approach to practice that suggests that the simple experience of being involved in a conversation in which one is treated with respect and acknowledged as 'conversible with' is in itself therapeutic. But I would want to take this further and suggest that a hermeneutic approach goes beyond just talking: it involves a commitment to an ethically-informed dialogue with Otherness which presupposes a respect for and willingness to engage with difference without which AOP is impossible.

I propose that a conception of practice grounded in a theory of dialogic understanding may help practitioners and educators to frame a more adequate response to issues of oppression and inequality. To support this contention, I analyse how a dialogic approach helps make sense of anti-oppressive practice as a form of ethical engagement with an Other. Such engagement is not amenable to once-and-for-all solutions, and the paper specifically moves away from a definition of AOP which suggests that there is one right answer, applicable on all occasions and in all circumstances. Indeed, from a constructionist perspective, attempts to define AOP in isolation from any context will be of limited use. The social construction of meaning comes to the fore in the idea of the hermeneutic conversation, which emphasises both the significance of each of the participant's contributions to the production of meaning, and the inevitable situatedness of any account.[2]

The dialogic model does not only apply to activities 'within' social work. Such an approach allows an engagement or 'conversation' between social work and ideas drawn from other traditions and disciplines. So in this paper, I draw on ideas put forward by a number of Black feminist writers who emphasise the importance for oppressed groups of 'finding a voice' and 'being heard'. The issue, as Henderson remarks, 'is not that black women [and other marginalised or excluded groups] in the past have had nothing to say, but rather that they have had no say' (1992, p. 151).

This suggests that marginalised groups have found ways of constructing their own perspectives and analyses and that one part of AOP may lie in the defining and legitimising of 'spaces' where those voices can be heard: 'other people can only realize themselves in the world as speakers if others are prepared to make themselves properly available to them as listeners. And to do that, they must treat what speakers say *seriously*' (Shotter, 1993, p. 163). The later part of the paper charts the possible contribution of these ideas to the development of empowering practice within social work.

Understanding in Social Work

The potential interest in hermeneutics for social work lies in their shared concern with understanding. As Henkel observes, from a hermeneutic perspective, interpretation 'is at the heart of what it means to be a human being. We become who we are in the process of understanding, which is inextricable from interpretation and application and is something in which we are engaged all the time' (1995, p. 71). Three features of understanding are pertinent here: interpretation and understanding are context-dependent; all understanding is dialogic and is based in language – meaning cannot exist 'outside of' language; and understanding has an ethical or moral-practical dimension.

Gadamer (1979) develops the idea of context through emphasising the role of tradition in achieving understanding. By 'tradition', he means the particular socio-cultural and historical matrix within which we are each placed and from which we each speak. He explores the possibilities and problems of understanding an Other given that both parties – the Self and the Other – are embedded in their own 'tradition'. Understanding does not take place in a vacuum but is always mediated by existing expectations, assumptions or 'knowledge' about experiences of the type before us which are drawn from the tradition within which we find ourselves. He refers to the frameworks or assumptions that shape our understanding as 'prejudices', using the term in a non-pejorative way to describe the 'pre-judgements' which we use to organise our perceptions of the world. So far, this is not a new or startling formulation – indeed, in social work it is a fundamental tenet of reflective practice that the worker's framework of assumptions – her values, beliefs and attitudes – has an important impact on the social work process. But Gadamer takes the ideas of 'tradition' and 'prejudice' and accords them a new significance.

We are each 'thrown' into a historical and cultural matrix that we have not chosen, and this frames our experiences of Otherness in that it provides the ground-rules for deciding which elements in that encounter should be deemed significant and the kinds of questions it is legitimate to pose about them. Understanding something or someone 'new' or Other to oneself is a complex process of appropriation and integration where each party's basic stance or orientation towards the Other is framed in the language and concepts of their own tradition. Understanding involves a 'translation' of the alien or Other in terms that make sense within one's own tradition; it is a creative or constructive process.

Gadamer explains that historical forces shape our understanding and, by drawing attention to the historicality of understanding, emphasises that our knowledge can never be complete. Our perspective on any given event or object of understanding is necessarily always partial and finite. But it is the particular situation in which we find ourselves that provides the 'horizon' from which our understanding can proceed. Gadamer maintains that involvement in a particular historical or linguistic context does not prevent us from understanding languages, cultures or past events from our own or from other traditions. Indeed, it is that very involvement that provides or suggests an orientation towards the 'object of understanding' and places it within a context.

Gadamer's particular version of hermeneutics provides an approach to the problem of understanding and interpretation based on dialogue – communication aimed at reaching an understanding through agreement about the matter in hand. For him, the hermeneutic problem 'is concerned with achieving agreement with somebody else about our shared "world"' (Bleicher, 1980, p. 3). Understanding is conceptualised as a kind of discussion or dialogue between different points of view and Gadamer looks to the conditions of conversation to illuminate those of understanding in general. Each partner in a genuine conversation devotes herself entirely to the matter at hand, and to achieving an understanding of the truth about it. This involves a recognition of the limitations of one's own knowledge and a willingness to learn from the contribution of the other party (Gadamer, 1979, p. 326).

Gadamer's epistemological stance here is quite distinctive: as mentioned before, each individual's viewpoint, and hence knowledge, is necessarily partial, limited and historically constrained; there is no position of absolute knowledge from which to judge the contributions to the dialogue, so each partner joins the conversation with the awareness that, in a certain sense, she does not know about the matter before her and therefore should allow for the possible truth of other views. Thus, each participant stands in a special relationship to the other: 'Each partner must thus be taken seriously as an equal dialogue partner, as someone who, despite heritage, quirks of expression or the like is equally capable of illuminating the subject matter' (Gadamer, 1979, p. 347) – which potentially has immediate implications for social worker / client relations, a point I return to later on.

A genuine conversation is a process of 'integration and appropriation' (Warnke, 1987, p. 101), whose outcome is a form of agreement or shared understanding. The reciprocity of conversation leads to a new position that represents neither party's original view but is, rather, an advance over the position maintained by each at the beginning. The notion of 'agreement' here allows both for a consensus between the parties about the matter at hand, and for disagreement – that is, an agreement to disagree. What is at issue is the attitude of each participant and their willingness or otherwise to be open to the arguments and perspectives of the other: 'what matters is not so much the conclusions arrived at as the terms within which arguments are conducted. For to talk in new ways is to 'construct' new forms of social relation, and ... to construct new ways of being (of person – world relations) for ourselves' (Shotter, 1993, p. 9). This conversational/dialogic pattern is repeated for Gadamer in any hermeneutic engagement with aspects of our own or another tradition, whether this takes the form of a literal conversation between two individuals or a 'conversation' with a challenging set of ideas, a text or other artefact that one is trying to make sense of.

Gadamer's hermeneutic approach also typically asserts that understanding involves an element of reflection and of self-understanding, concepts to which social work is already actively committed. Understanding is achieved through the assimilation of an alternative viewpoint in terms which make sense to the enquirer. But in exploring the Other's 'world', we also reflect back on the tradition from within which we speak. The dialectic of the process of understanding commits both parties to accepting the possibility of change in their own assumptions and prejudices in relation to their own traditions. Thus an encounter with an Other, and the attempt to seek meaning in that exchange, offer the opportunity to increase our self-knowledge (Marcus and Fischer, 1986). Understanding, then, involves each speaker reflecting on her own tradition and exploring the prejudices she brings to the encounter; it necessarily has a reflexive dimension – an idea that again has currency in social work in terms of the worker's 'use of self'. In relation specifically to anti-oppressive practice, a number of possibilities are opened up: for example, the involvement of a white social worker with a black client offers the possibility of the social worker gaining greater understanding of her own role and place in a largely white-serving bureaucracy and broader white-dominated society – if she is prepared to take the risk of engaging in a genuine dialogue and hearing what is being said to her.

The third crucial point about understanding is that it involves a form of moral-practical engagement; it requires ethical know-how. Moral or ethical knowledge – what Gadamer refers to as *phronesis* – in turn has three main features. I have not the space here to go into these aspects in detail, and therefore state them in necessarily brief form. Phronesis involves i) the ability to make sense of and then apply general normative principles to particular situations; ii) a particular understanding of the reciprocal relationship between means and ends; and iii) a concern with other human beings. In Gadamer's words, with this kind of moral understanding one 'does not know and judge as one who stands apart and unaffected; but rather as one united by a specific bond with the other, he thinks with the other and undergoes the situation with him' (Gadamer, 1979, p. 288).

Each of these points demonstrates the role of application in understanding; ethical knowledge consistently involves an application of general principles in specific, real-life situations. And Gadamer goes on to suggest that all authentic understanding is motivated by the same process – kk the application of a general normative understanding to different concrete circumstances. How relevant, then, is the idea of *phronesis* to social work in general, and AOP in particular? The presumption that social work has a moral base is not new (Butrym, 1976; Wilkes, 1981; Banks, 1995), and a case can be made for a view of practice as practical-moral engagement rather than technique, however skilled (Whan, 1986; Dominelli, 1996). I would like to take the discussion a stage further and consider how the concept of *phronesis* might assist in the development of ideas about anti-oppressive practice.

The goal of challenging different forms of oppression – racism, for example – is plainly morally inspired. But the difficulty of achieving such a goal has left social work in some disarray. What constitutes racism, and by extension anti-racism, cannot always be specified in advance. The emphasis of the idea of *phronesis* is that understanding arrives only in conjunction with application; that is to say, that moral decisions depend on an interpretation of the particular features of an individual case, and its identification as an example of a particular moral dilemma or situation; following such identification, an appropriate course of action must be adopted. Social workers daily find themselves in, and must make sense of, situations of 'uncertainty, uniqueness and value conflict' (Schon, 1983, p. 49). Not only must they 'make sense' of these situations, they must also *act* – and this will involve the application of general normative principles (social work values) to specific concrete circumstances.

Having recognised a situation or behaviour as racist, a range of possible responses may be appropriate; whether a particular behaviour or action can be described as 'anti-racist' will depend on the context in which it is called forth. Consider again the second point concerning moral knowledge: means / ends rationality. Within social services departments, increasing the number of ethnic minority staff is often held to improve services to ethnic minority clients and to show a commitment to anti-racism. But an increase in the number of members of a particular group need not *in itself* be proof of anything very much. Change can remain at the technical level, without fundamentally affecting the claimed end – for example, to decrease racism within social services departments. Unless there is a reciprocity between means and ends, such that 'the consideration of the means is itself a moral consideration and makes specific the moral rightness of the dominant end' (Gadamer, 1979, p. 287), attempts to change the moral focus of social work in this way will be of limited use.

Concern for others and commitment to another's good rather than to maximising personal benefit clearly fit with the aims of anti-oppressive practice. Indeed it is hard to conceive of social work without at least some acknowledgement of the idea of concern for others – though of course the form in which this concern is expressed and the action deriving from it will vary considerably, depending on the prejudices, in Gadamer's sense, of the social worker.

Shotter's account of the 'rhetorical – responsive' version of social constructionism links the latter two features of hermeneutics discussed above – namely that understanding is constructed through dialogue and that such understanding has an ethical dimension – and social work. The arguments he presents in *Conversational Realities* suggest that different ways of talking can help us to construct different kinds of social relationship, and point to a potentially more inclusive mode on interaction that accords respect and 'civility' (1993, p. 15) to *all* conversation participants.

Adopting a hermeneutic approach to understanding would involve an openness on the part of the social worker to the Otherness of the client whose perspective on and understanding of his / her own situation would be of equal standing with the social worker's own. The potential exists within this framework to develop ideas of partnership, respect for persons, and sharing of expertise, and to promote reflective practice. While we cannot expect every social work encounter to conform to the conversational standards that mark a true hermeneutic experience of understanding, the dialogic model offers a useful regulative ideal. It puts the onus for successfully achieving understanding as much on the social worker as on the client. Individual practice and broader systems and procedures can all be critically examined to ascertain the degree to which they promote or inhibit genuine participation in the conversations of social work.

The Limitations of a Hermeneutic Approach

Hermeneutic understanding 'fits' comfortably with humanist, client-centred approaches to social work and such an approach clearly offers an opportunity to achieve greater understanding of the Other, and thence of ourselves as culturally and historically situated individuals. But it does not lead inevitably to empowering or anti-oppressive practice. Criticisms can be raised about hermeneutics' possible contribution to the development of anti-oppressive practice on two grounds – the first is its treatment of the question of power; the second is its emphasis on the role and normative authority of tradition: how does this square with a politics and practice that is committed to challenging some of the basic inequalities sustained by and structuring existing dominant traditions?

The distribution of power becomes relevant because dialogue can simply become another means of control if it fails to take account of power imbalances between the conversation partners. Do the participants in a dialogue contribute equally to the exchange? Or is it rather the case that those with more power, whether as representatives of a dominant culture (white rather than black, able-bodied rather than disabled, middle class rather than working class) or institutional tradition (social worker rather than client), can control a dialogue and ensure that it is constrained within 'acceptable' boundaries? If this is not acknowledged, then there is a very real possibility of the 'conversation' being replaced by 'the monologue of the powerful to the powerless' (Eagleton, 1983, p. 73).

Arguably, the moral – practical imperative underpinning 'authentic' dialogue would take account of such structural imbalances and ensure that the participants strove to minimise their effects. While this may serve as a useful regulatory ideal, however, the lack of attention to issues of power and domination clearly leaves a significant problem for anyone trying to theorise AOP from a hermeneutic perspective. Serious objections have been raised to Gadamer's approach, most notably by Habermas[3], however the emancipatory possibilities of a dialogic approach have also been taken up by other writers whose work directly confronts the structural inequalities and power imbalances that philosophical hermeneutics can disguise. I turn to a consideration of some of this work in the last section of this paper.

The idea of tradition requires more detailed examination, because it is Gadamer's reliance on the normative power of tradition that opens hermeneutics up to critical questioning again and casts doubts on its possible contribution to the development of AOP. Even allowing for the possibility that both parties are willing and able to take on the challenge of a genuine conversation and are prepared to change, how does one deal with the negative aspects of a tradition? Gadamer presents a tradition as 'a linguistic body of commonly shared assumptions' (Kearney, 1986, p. 223) to which we accord a normative authority. But there is no guarantee that our tradition is intrinsically benign. What is one to do if the tradition from within which one speaks is fundamentally flawed, characterised by multiple oppressions – for example, by racism, sexism, homophobia? As Habermas has indicated, 'tradition' may shelter all manner of ideological distortions and repressions and still claim authority over us. Also, there appears to be a fine line between being 'located' within a tradition and being 'entrapped' (Shotter,1993, p.116) within it. This, I think, is Gergen's point when he describes the 'hermeneutic impasse' (1994, p. 256).

A hermeneutic approach does not require blind acquiescence to all aspects of a tradition; indeed, it could be argued that the attitude of moral-practical engagement that underpins authentic dialogue clearly requires the ability to recognise 'illegitimate' prejudices. Within such an approach these pernicious aspects of tradition – racism, sexism, homophobia, ageism etc. – may be understood precisely as examples of unwarranted prejudice that we are ethically obliged not simply to recognise, but then to question, critique and challenge. Hekman, writing from a clearly defined feminist perspective, makes a point that can translate usefully into other areas of anti-oppressive practice: 'A Gadamerian definition of tradition is one that can serve feminism well. It involves seeing tradition as the necessary ground of our understanding and as an open-ended and potentially critical medium that we can employ for our own purposes. 'Tradition' in Gadamer's sense provides us with the tools that we can use to criticize and reflect on our discourses; it is opportunity not enemy'(Hekman,1995, p.133).

It may also be the case that to refer even to a tradition as if it were monolithic and entirely homogeneous is misleading and sets up a false expectation in relation to its authority. The fragmentation associated with ideas of 'postmodernism' suggests that it may be more productive to see 'tradition' as 'an on-going dialectic of continuity and discontinuity made up of different rival traditions, internal crises, interruptions, revisions and schisms' (Kearney, 1992, p. 61). This allows us to move away from the idea of tradition as a kind of cultural and intellectual straitjacket and points to the possibility of there being a multiplicity of intersecting and cross-cutting strands within traditions. Dialogue may then be possible within and between these, as the conversational field expands to include a broader and more heterogeneous range of voices. We each speak from different locations within the overarching framework of a tradition and take up conversational positions which are informed by complex and sometimes competing or contradictory cultural, historical, social and political forces. AOP may be promoted by social workers' willingness to hear these different voices and work constructively to empower their speakers.

Dialogue and Emancipatory Practice

'Dialogue implies talk between two subjects, not the speech of subject and object. It is a humanizing speech, one that challenges and resists domination' (hooks, 1989, p. 131).

Hooks' definition of dialogue clearly resonates with the hermeneutic position outlined in the earlier sections and points towards an acknowledgement of the emancipatory possibilities of dialogue which are the subject of this last section. I turn to feminist theorising, specifically black feminist theorising, to ground the following discussion, for it is here that critical voices have been raised, questioning the right of dominant traditions to exclude and fail to hear them. Much feminist writing has been characterised by the use of metaphors of speech and voice with both black and white feminist writers affirming the importance of 'finding a voice' and of 'being heard' (cf. Hekman, 1995; Henderson, 1992; Hill Collins, 1991; Mama, 1995; Taylor et al, 1995). They suggest that engaging with and representing Otherness is a complex and often fraught activity (Wilkinson and Kitzinger, 1996), but it is also apparent that difference cannot be ignored, or put to one side until a more politically comfortable way of dealing with it emerges. Some provisional ways of acknowledging and working with difference need to be incorporated into social work theory and practice.

Commitment to a dialogic approach takes on the intensely practical and political purpose of including voices that traditional frameworks for the creation and validation of knowledge exclude: people who have been marginalised and silenced on different grounds. Discourses, and the traditions within which they function, are not monolithic: 'There are weak points, places where they may be attacked, and points at which other discourses pose a real threat. ... Where there is power there is also resistance' (Burr, 1995, p. 75). The force of Burr's point is echoed by other writers who note the particular vantage point 'offered' by the often painful experience of marginalisation, and the opportunity it affords to articulate alternative perspectives.

So these voices and the analyses they produce operate as important sites of resistance to the prevailing dominant discourses; they create a space in which to promote a politics of empowerment and offer a framework for emancipatory practice. As Sampson points out, 'The purpose of feminist analyses ... is to create a space in which the long-silenced other can be heard in its own terms, and so participate in the dialogues that shape both self and other' (Sampson, 1993, p. 25). Literally interpreted, this is perhaps what happens when 'the client speaks' and can contribute her definition both of her own circumstances *and* of her understanding of the social work system with which she is dealing. The client, as Other, does not only 'speak for herself', but can also use her perceptions to shed new light on the self-understanding of the social worker within her personal and professional setting.

This approach does not suggest that either 'social worker' or 'client' is a homogeneous category. Neither does it imply that power is distributed such that all social workers are equally powerful while all clients are equally powerless. What it does do is invite reflection on how each of these categories is made up, and how we are differently positioned within them by virtue of 'race', gender, age, sexuality, class, religion, educational background, and so on. In this way, the concept of 'difference' is opened up – it applies to 'us' just as much as 'them', and acknowledges the ways in which 'differences' are structured into inequalities and complex patterns of oppression.

Attempts to start a dialogue about / with difference assist the process of recognising and reflecting on the oppressive elements within a dominant (white, male, heterosexist) tradition and ensuring that dialogic space is made available for the range of different voices that speak from within the broad categories of both 'client' and 'social worker'. 'A feminist politics of difference ... is a politics in which differences among women are confronted and theorized rather than ignored. ... As we begin to explore the variety of power relations that script the lives of women, we are discovering that these scripts differ by class, race and culture' (Hekman, 1995, p. 161). Problems of exclusion undoubtedly still exist (Spelman, 1990) but the dialogic approach is suggestive of a change in orientation towards difference, and one which 'fits' well with the aims of AOP. As Maynard suggests, 'Thinking through and imagining beyond labels such as 'race' and gender, for those in a position to do so, is one important way of challenging both their legitimacy and their efficacy', but, she continues, 'A reworking of language alone ... does not make them go away' (Maynard, 1994, p. 19).

Dialogue, as presented here, is not just about talking to – or even hearing – lots of people; it has profound implications for how we think about, create and use 'knowledge' and 'truth'. Where does 'professional' knowledge or expertise come from? How is it produced and validated? Whose interests does it serve or represent? The point I want to make here is that the *process* by which such knowledge is produced has a fundamental contribution to make to AOP. Writing about the possibility of developing an Afrocentric feminist epistemology, Hill Collins explores 'the use of dialogue in assessing knowledge claims' (1991, p. 212), and highlights its particular role and importance: 'For black women, new knowledge claims are rarely worked out in isolation from other individuals and are usually developed through dialogues with other members of a community' (1991, p. 212). Dialogue in this sense then also supports and informs a sense of connectedness: a community (however this is defined) is the place where truth claims are made and tested. Knowledge and truth are not the province of particular individuals but a community resource and responsibility – and source of power.

An ethical commitment is clearly implied in this form of knowledge creation which resonates with the notion of *phronesis* explored earlier in relation to hermeneutic understanding. It depends on participation, and assumes a fundamental reciprocity between the participants. 'Dialogue is critical to the success of this epistemological approach, the type of dialogue long extant in the Afrocentric call-and-response tradition whereby power dynamics are fluid, everyone has a voice, but everyone must listen and respond to other voices in order to be allowed to remain in the community. Sharing a common cause fosters dialogue and encourages groups to transcend their differences' (Hill Collins, 1991, pp. 236-7). This is perhaps what Gilroy identifies in the idea of an 'ethics of antiphony' (Gilroy, 1993, p. 200).

How then does this relate to social work? I would suggest that, by accepting the logic or validity of this antiphonal process of knowledge creation, and moving away from an 'expert' model of quick fix, technical solutions, social work can start to put partnership into practice. Clearly, this requires more than lip-service to the idea that the client is now the 'expert' on her/his own situation. Ahmad (1990) conveys a sense of how social work might operate if this dialogic approach is taken seriously. Although she is specifically addressing issues of 'race' and racism, the idea of empowerment that she explores has much to offer a broader anti-oppressive practice and connects with the model of knowledge and understanding that has been discussed in this paper.

Ahmad does not use the language of hermeneutics, but her case studies can be read as examples of the application of a dialogic approach. For example, in one case study (1990, p. 36f), each participant allows herself to engage fully with the 'conversation' that the social work intervention process has become. No viewpoint is ultimately privileged, though each person's particular (and necessarily partial) contribution is respected. The social worker's view certainly does not get priority, though her access to specific pieces of specialised knowledge and information about Social Services' procedure is acknowledged. Neither is the client, elevated to a point where her interpretation of events is unchallenged simply *because* it is her view. Each participant takes a risk – that her previous way of looking at the world, at colleagues, friends and 'professionals', may need to be revised. No-one is asked to abandon her previous prejudices (even if such a thing were possible), but rather to put them into play with and against those of the other dialogue partners. One result of this exercise is that each party in the process ends up on new ground: each has learned something about the world of the Other and, further, can use this experience to inform her ways of thinking and making judgements in the future.

AOP, as I suggested at the beginning of this paper, depends on a commitment to an ethically-informed dialogue with Otherness which acknowledges and respects difference. Writing about the problems of trying to represent Otherness, Griffin (1996, p.101) effectively summarises the challenge facing those who are trying to develop AOP: 'We all have to find a way of acknowledging (the political implications of) our differences without representing each other as 'different from' (the norm) or 'Other than' (the norm)'. By looking outside mainstream social work theory then, it is possible to identify an alternative framework which helps make sense of the project of anti-oppressive practice in social work. An ethically-informed dialogic approach to understanding, drawing on the insights particularly of black feminist theorising, makes space for different ways of seeing and knowing and opens up possibilities for empowering practice.

Notes

1 See Macey and Moxon (1996) for a trenchant comment on the need to develop theoretically informed practice in an area where, they suggest, it has been seriously lacking. Social constructionist ideas have not perhaps had much currency within British social work and related theorising but do seem to offer a broad framework for analysis at a number of levels. I do not offer here a general account of the usefulness or otherwise of social constuctionism (for this, see Franklin, 1995 and Craib, 1997) but focus specifically on one version – that of Shotter (1993) – which links into the more detailed discussion of hermeneutics pursued through the chapter.

2 Although I would argue that there is much within hermeneutics that is positive and helpful in conceptualising AOP within a broadly sociological social constructionist framework, it is clear that there are also limitations to this position, some of which I discuss earlier in this chapter. At this stage, though, it is worth noting the view of Gergen (1994), writing from a social psychological perspective. His account moves beyond the perceived constraints of hermeneutics to develop a relational approach to understanding.

3 See Habermas, 1970a and 1970b. Also of relevance here is his theory of communicative action which appeared in 1981 as *Theorie des kommunikativen Handelns*, (translated into English as *Theory of Communicative Action*, the first volume was published in 1984, the second in 1987).

Without attempting a full exposition of the theory, which would place it in the context of the wide-ranging and often eclectic writings about critical social theory that have appeared during a period of over thirty years, I draw attention to Habermas's work to the extent that his criticisms highlight possible problems with the hermeneutic framework sketched out in this paper. So here I will note the Habermas's analysis of the impact of ideology on communicative practice, and his consequent challenge to the dialogic approach proposed by Gadamer. This is not to say that he abandons the commitment to dialogue in toto, but rather that he presents the unconstrained dialogue of Gadamer's hermeneutics as an *ideal*, not as existing practice.

There is an extensive secondary literature providing exposition and critical discussion of these ideas; see, for example, Bernstein (1983), Thompson (1983), McCarthy (1984), Rasmussen (1990), Holub (1991) and Honneth and Joas (eds) (1991).

For discussions that explore Habermas's ideas specifically in a social work context, see Henkel (1995) and Blaug (1995).

An earlier version of this paper entitled 'Hearing voices, talking difference: a dialogic approach to anti-oppressive practice' appeared in the *Journal of Social Work Practice*, (1997), vol. 11, no. 2, pp. 115-126.

Bibliography

Afshar, H. and Maynard, M. (eds) (1994), *The Dynamics of 'Race' and Gender: Some Feminist Interventions*, Taylor and Francis, London.
Ahmad, B. (1990), *Black Perspectives in Social Work*, Venture Press, Birmingham.
Banks, S. (1995), *Ethics and Values in Social Work*, BASW/Macmillan, Basingstoke.
Bernstein, R. J. (1983), *Beyond Objectivism and Relativism*, Basil Blackwell, Oxford.
Blaug, R. (1995), 'Distortion of the Face to Face: Communicative Reason and Social Work Practice', *British Journal of Social Work*, vol. 25, pp. 423-439.
Bleicher, J. (1980), *Contemporary Hermeneutics: Hermeneutics as Method, Philosophy and Critique*, London, RKP.
Burr, V. (1995), *An Introduction to Social Constructionism*, Routledge, London.
Butler, J. and Scott, J. (eds) (1992), *Feminists Theorize the Political*, Routledge, New York.
Butrym, Z. (1976), *The Nature of Social Work*, Macmillan, London.
Connerton, P. (ed) (1986), *Critical Sociology: Selected Readings*, Penguin, Harmondsworth.
Craib, I. (1997), 'Social Constructionism as a Social Psychosis', *Sociology*, vol. 31, no. 1, pp. 1-15.

Dallmayr, F. and McCarthy, T. (eds) (1977), *Understanding and Social Inquiry*, University of Notre Dame Press, Notre Dame, Indiana.

Dominelli, L. (1996), 'Deprofessionalizing Social Work: Anti-Oppressive Practice, Competencies and Postmodernism', *British Journal of Social Work*, vol. 26, pp. 153-175.

Eagleton, T. (1983), *Literary Theory: an Introduction*, Basil Blackwell, Oxford.

Franklin, C. (1995), 'Expanding the Vision of the Social Constructionist Debate: Creating Relevance for Practitioners', *Families in Society*, vol. 76, no. 7, pp. 395-406.

Gadamer, H-G. (1979), *Truth and Method*, Sheed and Ward 2nd English Edition, London.

Gergen, K. J. (1994), *Realities and Relationships: Soundings in Social Construction*, Harvard University Press, Cambridge, Mass.

Gilroy, P. (1993), *The Black Atlantic: Modernity and Double Consciousness*, Verso, London.

Griffin, C. (1996), '"See Whose Face It Wears": Difference, Otherness and Power', in S. Wilkinson and C. Kitzinger (eds), 1996, pp. 97-102.

Habermas, J. (1970a), 'Systematically Distorted Communication' from 'On Systematically Distorted Communication', *Inquiry*, vol. 13, pp. 205-218. Reprinted in P. Connerton (ed), 1986, pp. 348-362.

Habermas, J. (1970b), 'A Review of Gadamer's *Truth and Method*', in F. Dallmayr and T. McCarthy (eds), 1977, pp. 335-363.

Hekman, S. (1995), *Moral Voices, Moral Selves: Carol Gilligan and Feminist Moral Theory*, Polity Press, Cambridge.

Henderson, M. G. (1992), 'Speaking in Tongues: Dialogic Dialectics and the Black Woman Writer's Literary Tradition', in J. Butler and J. Scott (eds), 1992, pp. 144-166.

Henkel, M. (1995), 'Conceptions of Knowledge and Social Work Education', in M. Yelloly (ed), 1995, pp. 67-82.

Hill Collins, P. (1991), *Black Feminist Thought: Knowledge, Consciousness and the Politics of Empowerment*, Routledge, New York and London.

Holub, R. (1991), *Jurgen Habermas: Critic in the Public Sphere*, Routledge, London.

Honneth, A. and Joas, H. (eds) (1991), *Communicative Action: Essays on Jurgen Habermas's The Theory of Communicative Action*, Trans. by J. Gaines and D. L. Jones, Polity Press, Cambridge.

hooks, b. (1989), *Talking Back: Thinking Feminist, Thinking Black*, South End Press, Boston.

Kearney, R. (1986), *Modern Movements in European Philosophy*, Manchester, Manchester University Press.

Kearney, R. (1992), 'Between Tradition and Utopia', in D. Wood (ed), 1992, pp. 55-73.

Macey, M. and Moxon, E., (1996) 'An Examination of Anti-Racist and Anti-Oppressive Theory and Practice in Social Work Education', *British Journal of Social Work*, vol. 26, pp. 297-314.

Mama, A. (1995), *Beyond the Masks: Race, Gender and Subjectivity*, Routledge, London.

Marcus, G. E. and Fischer, M. M. (1986), *Anthropology as Cultural Critique: An Experimental Moment in the Human Sciences*, Chicago University Press, Chicago.

Maynard, M. (1994), '"Race", Gender and the Concept of "Difference" in Feminist Thought', in H. Afshar and M. Maynard (eds), 1994, pp. 9-25.

McCarthy, T. (1984), *The Critical Theory of Jurgen Habermas*, Polity Press, Cambridge.

Rasmussen, D. M. (1990), *Reading Habermas*, Basil Blackwell, Oxford.

Rojek. C., Peacock, G. and Collins, S. (1988), *Social Work and Received Ideas*, Routledge, London.

Sampson, E. (1993), *Celebrating the Other: A Dialogic Account of Human Nature*, Harvester Wheatsheaf, Hemel Hempstead.

Schon, D. (1983), *The Reflective Practitioner: How Professionals Think in Action*, Temple Smith, London.

Shotter, J. (1993), *Conversational Realities: Constructing Life through Language*, Sage, London.

Spelman, E. (1990), *Inessential Woman: Problems of Exclusion in Feminist Thought*, The Women's Press, London.

Taylor, J. M., Gilligan, C. and Sullivan, A. M. (1995), *Between Voice and Silence: Women and Girls, Race and Relationship*, Harvard University Press, Cambridge, Mass.

Thompson, J. (1983), *Critical Hermeneutics: A Study in the Thought of Paul Ricoeur and Jurgen Habermas*, Cambridge University Press, Cambridge.

Warnke, G. (1987), *Gadamer: Hermeneutics, Tradition and Reason*, Polity Press, Cambridge.

Whan, M. (1986), 'On the Nature of Practice', *British Journal of Social Work*, vol. 16, pp. 243-250.

Wilkes, R. (1981), *Social Work with Undervalued Groups*, Tavistock, London.

Wilkinson, S. and Kitzinger, C. (eds) (1996), *Representing the Other: A Feminism and Psychology Reader*, Sage Publications, London.

Wood, D. (ed) (1992), *On Paul Ricoeur: Narrative and Interpretation*, Routledge, London.

Yelloly, M. (ed) (1995), *Learning and Teaching in Social Work*, Jessica Kingsley, London.

14 Negotiating Constructions: Rebridging Social Work Research and Practice in the Context of Probation Work

KIRSI JUHILA AND TARJA PÖSÖ

Social constructionist studies focusing on social work have occasionally been criticized for their overtly theoretical nature: they have seemed to offer very little for actual social work practice. It is a common concern in all social work debate that research in this area is not producing applicable results. However, several attempts have been made to rebridge the gap between social work research and practice, and new definitional approaches such as talking about research-minded practitioners (Everitt et al., 1992) have been introduced. This present paper addresses these issues as well, but from the point of view of empirical social constructionist research.

Our empirical data (suitability assessment interviews) come from the Finnish Probation and Aftercare Association. This is a public association carrying out assessment interviews, as part of a procedure destined to assess the suitability of certain clients for community service. We have two main foci in our study of these interviews. First, we want to illustrate our theoretical and methodological starting points, which are to be found in discourse analysis on one hand, and in joint ethnographic data (re)analysis by and between social workers and researchers on the other hand. Second, we want to demonstrate on the basis of our data how suitability for community service is constructed in the practices of probation work. On a very general level, this paper is about applying social constructionism into empirical research and about the practical self-reflection of social work practitioners and researchers.[1]

Assessment Interviews for Community Service

The assessment interviews we focus on are carried out by social workers in the probation office, and they form part of suitability assessment for community service. Community service is an alternative to custodial sentence, consisting of regular unpaid work. We will not, however, look at community service or suitability as such but at the constructive processes concerning suitability assessment. These processes provide us with an example of social problems work, in other words, how social problems and clienthood are produced in social work practices (Holstein and Miller, 1993; Miller and Holstein, 1991; Jokinen et al., 1995).

The assessment interview, obviously, is not the only important constructive event in the process of establishing community service, which has begun much earlier, in the definition of a certain act as criminal. It is by no means transparent which acts constitute a crime and which do not; there are always constructive processes that make a crime 'exist', as is the case with any other social problem. As Kenneth Gergen (1994, p. 72) has pointed out 'whatever is, simply is, but once we attempt to articulate what there is, we enter the world of discourse'. Even when we seem to be merely observing acts and reporting what we have observed, we have already entered the realm of construction. Facts about acts are created in linguistic actions (Potter, 1996, pp. 20-22.) And once we start seeing an act as potentially criminal, we enter a different world of constructions. There follows a sequence of documents: first the statements by the offender and by 'eye-witnesses'; prosecutorial reviews, assessing the seriousness of the offence and the necessity of charging the offender; and, finally, deliberations about the possible sentence. It means that prior to the professional-client encounter, where community service and the client's potential suitability are discussed, there has been a chain-like sequence of events, choices, selections, interpretations and division of labour, involving the activities of the defendant, police, prosecutor etc. And once the encounter between the social worker and the client is over, the interpretative process continues – for example when the court proceeds to look at the matter.

Our study focuses on the phase in the constructive process where the authorities (the police and the prosecution) have acted on the crime and made it exist, so that it comes under the jurisdiction of the legal system. The prosecutor has assessed the status of the crime and it has been pronounced a convictable offence. At this stage, the community service option stands available for some of the offenders: it is an alternative to custodial sentences of eight months maximum. In such cases, the prosecutor may ask the Probation and Aftercare Association to prepare an assessment report about the offender's suitability for community service.

From the offender's point of view, assessment interview for community service means an obvious change in the process he (for most often it is a he) has been going through: the discursive world where he and the criminal offence are situated in the interview is a different one from the previous, legal world. Instead of the assessment of the act and of its evaluation within criminal legislation and its norms, the focus is now on the offender as a person and especially on his suitability for community service.

From the social worker's point of view, suitability assessment is a rather new practice in Probation and Aftercare Organization. Community Service Act was passed as recently as 1996, after the idea had been tested out in a number of local-level pilot schemes since 1991. At present, the management of community service takes up a considerable part of the employees' time. This state of affairs has led to a lengthy debate about the role of probation work: has the focus of the work changed towards more juridical-administrative probation work from that of providing social support services. In any case, suitability assessment is most often done by people with training in social work, who have not been issued with any detailed, legally defined set of criteria for assessing suitability. Social workers are simply asked to assess whether the client is capable of carrying out community service or not.

The interest for us researchers lies in the fact that suitability assessment is all done through language. In the encounter between the social worker and the client, talk constitutes the most important activity; indeed, talk is such a self-evident component in social work that it is seldom seen as a professional practice requiring specific skills; neither is it seen as difficult to capture in research (Baldock and Prior, 1981; Rojek et al., 1988). Talk does not, however, conform to expectations: the client's or the professional's positions do not in themselves determine the course or outcome of the conversation (Stenson 1994). Yet, talk at the professional-client encounter is not ahistoric. Both the client and the professional come to the encounter equipped with their previous knowledge from earlier encounters, their expectations concerning the present encounter, and their assumptions about what it will or should lead to, and it is these knowledge, expectations and assumptions that are being fished out, negotiated or held back in the interaction (Oranen 1997; Rostila 1997).

In some social work encounters – as is the case in the community service assessment we are currently exploring – a very important function of talk is that of eliciting information for writing out a report. We assume that documents – written reports – make sense of and organize encounters and clienthood: by displaying a series of preformulated conditions and restrictions, they influence the kind of information that is elicited about the client, and how this information – about the clients and from the clients – is reconstructed in the document (Spencer, 1988; Zimmerman, 1969). Their actual influence, however, cannot be known simply by drawing on the existence of these factors (Atkinson and Coffey, 1997; Prince, 1996).

Furthermore, these assessments carry a considerable weight: research findings suggest that suitability reports play an essential role in the decision-making process of the court (Takala 1993, p. 108). Therefore, we also share a practical motivation to study the actual encounter and its transformation into a report.

Combining Discourse Analysis and Ethnography

We will look at the encounters where suitability for community service is assessed in two steps. *First, we will analyse the local conversations between social workers and their clients. Second, these local conversations and their analyses serve as data for a different kind of encounter: in the discussions between researchers and social workers. Methodologically the research is thus moving on two analytical stages: on the discourse analytical and on the ethnographic stage.*

This combination of discourse analysis and ethnography is not far from David Silverman's ideas about the role of 'how' questions and 'why' questions in the study of institutional interaction (Silverman, 1994; 1997; Silverman and Gubrium, 1994; see also Maynard, 1989). Silverman sees these two different types of questions as two (often thought of as competing) ways of understanding the concept of context. In the 'how' questions that conversation analysis normally asks, the context is created by the participants in interaction by their talk: institutions and institutional roles live in talk and can be located in talk. Ethnographic research, for its part, understands context in a wider sense. This is why understanding local conversations, or answering the 'why' questions, presupposes a certain amount of ethnographic data from the organization that is being studied. Silverman believes in the possibility of combining 'how' and 'why' questions even within one single piece of research, as long as the questions are asked in this order. In the present article, *we apply this idea of combining the two analytical traditions, but we also test and reappraise it.*

Our discourse analytical interest focuses on *how suitability is produced locally as an interactional accomplishment in professional-client encounters.* When analysing how the conversational participants of these encounters produce descriptions about suitability we combine content-based analysis with analyses sensitive to talk organization (Antaki, 1994, pp. 120-137). This ethnomethodologically informed way of understanding discourse analysis emphasises that words have no abstract or disembodied meanings, separate from everyday language use and interaction (Garfinkel, 1967; Edwards, 1997; Edwards and Potter, 1992; Heritage, 1984; Holstein, 1993; Potter, 1996; Potter and Wetherell, 1987; Widdicombe, 1995; Jokinen and Juhila, 1996). Instead, meaningfulness is always found in connection with local practices that generate reality. The focus is on actual settings, on participants' conversational actions. Harold Garfinkel (1967) named this phenomenon indexicality: meanings of words are to be understood by reference to where and when they occur; sense is dependent on a combination of words and context.

The local construction of suitability for community service in our data is done by both the professionals and the clients. We do not share the view that there exists some underlying reality about the clients' suitability on the basis of which the participants construct alternative representations (cf. Woolgar and Pawluch, 1985). Rather, it is our understanding that the participants produce the reality of suitability during the course of the conversation. When negotiating suitability, some aspects of the client's mundane life are construed as topics for discussion. What also happens is that some aspects of that mundane life are named and treated as problems; deviance is distinguished from normalcy. What is essential here is how these problems are assessed by the participants: are they seen as constituting risks for the successful carrying out of the community service, or is the client defined as resourceful enough as to succeed?

When doing this assessment business the participants constitute themselves in certain roles. On the one hand the professional constitutes herself in the role of a social worker, mapping potential risks and resources by asking certain kinds of questions from the client. The client, for his part, constructs himself as a client when providing the professional with such information that might be regarded as essential in this mapping (Edwards, 1998). The client does not merely report facts about his life: this reporting is a highly context-bound activity. Facts are constructed in interaction (Potter, 1996).

From the discourse analytical stage we proceed to the ethnographic stage, which also means a transition to another negotiation context. In this context we sit down with the professionals and discuss the course of the professional-client encounters. When analysing these conversations, the focus is on the question *how professionals construct institutional and cultural accounts about local practices in professional-researcher encounters.* Our main interest at this analytic stage is to arrive at formulations about the social workers' professional and organizational action: how the issues at the professional-client encounters are to be understood and explained. With these data, we aim at writing an 'ethnography of institutional discourse' (Miller, 1997).

The main bulk of the ethnographic data consists of conversations and analytical sessions with the workers of Probation and Aftercare Association. These data were being complemented during the research process with additional observational and documentary data (which are not dealt with in this article). Unlike conventional ethnography, our data are not overtly observational (e.g. Emerson, 1988). What we do share with conventional ethnography is an interest in the repeated and in the shared. The repeated and the shared in community service assessment goes beyond the professionals' individual experiences. This is why we propose that the ways the professionals understand and explain issues in professional-client encounters have something to do with local culture in this particular organization (Gubrium, 1989) – perhaps they have something to do with the professional culture of social work in general. It is our understanding that because these cultures are jointly talked into being by the professionals, it was not possible for us to capture their nature simply by exploring the general tasks of the organization, or the community service suitability assessment; or the structure of the clientele, or the educational background of the professionals.

Certainly, our own participation in the professional-researcher sessions has been an important factor in the overall process. On one hand, we present findings of our analyses of professional-client encounters and introduce and sum up topics for conversation. In doing this we also participate in creating the understanding why professional-client encounters get constructed the way they do. The position that we take in this sense can be defined as interpretative partnership. Yet, on the other hand, our position is that of a target audience in the conversations (Sarangi and Hall, 1997, p. 9). We are outsiders to whom the practices of the professional-client encounters have to be explained. In this sense the negotiation context is in itself the kind of an arena where shared institutional and cultural accounts are likely to emerge.

There are, therefore, two kinds of interpretative resources at play in the conversations between the professionals and the researchers. As researchers, we provide the data and discuss our discourse analytical findings. The professionals, for their part, use their interpretative resources about social work profession in general, knowledge about the institutional constraints of their work, knowledge about the structure of the clientele, and so on. As the conversation goes on these interpretative resources inevitably get exchanged and mixed; they become less and less the property of only one group. Hence, one of the key issues produced by this sort of research formula is: *does a researcher's active involvement in the social workers' interpretative resources make for a better analyst of professional-client interaction? Or is it the other way round?*

This article follows sequentially the stages of the actual research. We will first report on the discourse analytical stage, explicating our findings with extracts from the data. We then move on to ethnographic data and to our interpretations thereof. To conclude, we discuss issues related to the technique of combining two sets of data and to carrying out the analysis by stages. In this, we draw on our own – often critical – observations throughout the research process.

When the Client and the Professional Meet: Constructing Suitability in Local Practices

The data on which the discourse analytical part of this article is based on consist of ten tape-recorded assessment interviews and their formulations into written reports. All clients except one are male, and their age varies from 25 to 45 years. The duration of the interviews varies from 30 to 65 minutes. The setting of the interviews is one particular Probation and Aftercare Association regional office. Altogether five social workers are involved in the interviews.

The encounters under study have a clear institutional task: to elicit information for a written suitability report. The social workers have at their disposal an assessment form, the headings of which specify a number of points on which information is to be elicited (cf. Takala, 1993, p. 80). These topics include, first of all, the usual background information (name, address, social security number, profession, mother tongue, and the information sources used in the assessment, among other things); then education or training, employment history, job situation at the moment, economic situation, family, social relations, hobbies, housing, health, drinking habits, the need for support services. At the end of the form there is space for the professionals to describe the clients' self-assessment. There is also a space for 'additional information'.

In our data, all assessment interviews conform to the topical structure of the form. All topics set out in the form are discussed in the encounters, with hardly any exceptions. It is clear, however, from our data that even if the 'frame' for the interview is always the same, the microlevel of the encounters is always construed differently. On the level of local interaction, there is no standard formula for the social worker to act on: a formula which would, as such, be transferred to and drawn upon from one encounter to another.

We focus here on those instances of the professional-client encounters where topics concerning social relations and financial situation are discussed. Through these topics we illustrate how suitability is produced locally as an interactional accomplishment in professional-client encounters. Our focus on social relations and on the economic situation was not a conscious choice. The lack of such a conscious decision from our part is due to our conviction that any one of the themes of the interview is a valid object for research as they all relate to suitability.

When the social worker introduces the topic of social relations, she normally asks questions about the client's marital status and the length of the relationship, or about the client's friends; she asks whether the client has children; whether his parents are still alive, etc. These questions are usually answered by plain 'basic facts'. In the case of the economic situation, the social worker usually starts by inquiring about the client's main source of income. This, in most cases, is unemployment benefit, which fact is already known to the social worker, who moves on to ask about the client's debts and fines. The clients participate by giving answers, but very few give any additional information.

We have chosen the following four extracts for closer analysis in this article since they display a more thorough involvement in the issues of social relations and the economic situation than is usual (two of the extracts

282 *Constructing Social Work Practices*

focus on social relations, and the other two on the economic situation of the clients). Furthermore, these topics seem to become problematized in the course of the discussion. The social worker is very detailed in her approach, and the clients participate actively instead of just giving short answers. However, the pattern is different in the discussions. By *comparing* discussions focusing on one specific topic but constructing them in very different ways we hope to be able to show something essential about the ways of producing suitability.

The four extracts are from two interviews, with two different male clients (clients 1 and 2). The first client is in his twenties and the second client in his late thirties. The clients are being interviewed by a female social worker; the same person in both extracts.

Social Relations

(In the extracts, SW stands for social worker, C1 and C2 stand for clients)

Extract 1

1   SW: What sort of people do you know, friends or so?
2   C1: Well I have all sorts of friends
3   SW: Tell me a bit more precisely what that means – all sorts of?
4   C1: Well I have some mates and
5   SW: Yea, are they connected to your criminal background?
6   C1: Well
7   SW: You have mates with whom you hang around in these
8   C1: Yes and no
9   SW: But you do have such friends too who do not have a criminal
10   background, do you have such friends too?
11 C1: That sort of friends, yes, most of my friends are like that
12 SW: Most of them, well that's fine
13 C1: Or this one chap, who's my best mate really
14 SW: Yea
15 C1: Well he made it to community service, and he went through with it
16 SW: Oh yes, yes, so you know something about community
17   service through him then
18 C1: Mm
19 SW: How do you see, how closely are you connected with these friends now
20   or how much time do you spend together?
21 C1: Well we do keep together quite a lot
22 SW: How do you see – are you able to fend for yourself in that group?

23 C1: How do you mean?
24 SW: I mean that if they say that now let's go and do this
25   or that or let's go and have a beer, can you say no, that you won't go?
26 C1: Well that's sort of ambiguous
27 SW: In what way is it ambiguous?
28 C1: Well I can't really explain it, it's not often that one is like that,
29   at least I'm not, and my friends neither, they are not like that,
30   that now you have to do this and that, on the spur of the moment
31 SW: Okay let's leave this
32 C1: I don't even, I don't even understand that logic,
33   that someone could imagine that something is
34   just decided like that and then out you go and do it
35 SW: Are you saying that you have not come across this kind of thing,
36   when you were young, even if you have
37 C1: Well yes I've come across it, but still I don't understand
38   that kind of logic that someone hides behind the backs
39   of others or something

Extract 2

1   SW: Obviously you have now – at least this is what I have understood –
2   you have become more independent, so that you do not necessarily,
3   do not necessarily – those friends that you have, do they keep together
4   very closely, how do you see
5   C2: No, it is me it is me who decides, if I do go somewhere or do something
6   SW: Yea
7   C2: that I am not committed to them in any way
8   SW: Yea, that's what I have understood, that it is not such a close group,
9   and of course it will change throughout
10 C2: No it isn't no
11 SW: the years, it's when you're young, you're hanging out together with the
12   group, and later on, the links to those friends become more loose
13 C2: Yes, one does not have the energy any more (laughing)
14 SW: Yep, and you could see while you were working that once you keep up
15   the work, get up at seven every morning and go to work, then you're
16   sort of master of your own life, otherwise you cannot make it
17 C2: No you cannot make it
18 SW: No, you cannot
    (conversation about other topics)
19 SW: What sort of relations do you have these days with the people
20   you met in prison? Do you still keep seeing them?
21 C2: First I did, but now I haven't had anything to do with them,
22   not for several months

```
23   SW: You have like become estranged just like that, as it goes,
24          or have you worked at it deliberately?
25   C2: I do try
26   SW: Yea, yea
27   C2: to keep a distance myself
     (conversation about other topics)
28   SW: I think it's really great that you have thought about it that way,
29          and even better if you've been successful in it, how would you see,
30          what things have helped you most in that you've succeeded
31          in breaking those links?
32   C2: There's nothing particular, but I've just decided that it's no use me
33          hanging around with that gang and messing around
34          when you know what comes in the end
35   SW: Yea
36   C2: that it is no good hanging around there, not for anybody
37   SW: Yea, yea, quite so, and I keep noticing that you've been thinking
38          and in a way you've understood the danger in it
39   C2: Mm
40   SW: You get on with your life in an ordinary way and with ordinary people
41          as far as I've understood, you've got your family and your relations to
42          them and to your other relatives are okay, and that surely will help you
43          and support you from now on
44   C2: I hope so (laughing)
45   SW: Absolutely
```

In both examples, the form of the interaction is characterized by the interview format, where the social worker and the client are aligned as questioner and answerer (Peräkylä and Silverman, 1991; Silverman, 1997). The format is common not only in social work but in all help work that uses discussions as a tool. In an interview situation, the speech acts of both parties are essential. Culturally, we share a conversational rule that states that when asked a question, you must answer. There are, however, several ways of answering; as well as asking. Obviously, one can abstain from answering altogether, but in such cases both parties in conversation are likely to account for this abstaining (Tainio, 1997). Although the interview format in the two examples is the same, it is characterized by different overtones.

If we look at the first extract, we can see that the client gives evasive and vague answers when asked about his friends. He says 'well I have all sorts of friends' (line 2) and 'yes and no' (line 8). These answers are followed up by the social worker's elaborating questions: 'Tell me a bit more precisely what that means' (line 3) and 'Are they connected to your criminal background' (line 5). After that the client volunteers a number of details concerning the quality of the friendships and the closeness of the group.

Collaboration ends, however, when the social worker asks a controlling question 'How do you see – are you able to fend for yourself in that group?' (line 22). The client answers with a counter-question 'How do you mean'. Even after the social worker has explained, the client does not give a direct answer, but says 'Well that's sort of ambiguous' (line 26). In the rest of the discussion, the client abandons the role of the answerer. He continues to talk about the matter, even when the social worker is already in the process of closing off the topic, saying 'Okay let's leave this' (line 31). At the end of the conversation the client starts to counter-argument the social worker's accounts on the matter. The conversation about this topic ends thus in a sort of disagreement, when the client re-argues in the last turn that he does 'not understand that kind of logic that someone hides behind the backs of others' (lines 37-39).

The conversation in the second extract advances rather differently. The social worker packages her questions with a number of candidate answers. She already seems to have formulated an interpretation about the client's friends. For instance, in the opening turn the social worker states that 'Obviously you have now – at least this is what I have understood – you have become more independent' (lines 1-4). Another packing of candidate answers is to be found on lines 23 to 24, where the social worker asks whether the client has become estranged just like that, or has he worked at it deliberately. The client aligns with the social worker, accepting the favourable candidate answers. He says 'No it is me, it is me who decides' (line 5) and 'I do try' (line 25). Consequently, the social worker supports the client's choices (there are several expressions displaying acceptance: yea, yep, really great, quite so). A general impression of this extracts is that the participants here construct a strong mutual understanding.

What is interesting here is that rich social networks are generally considered positive in social work practice, as these are seen as resources for the client. In our examples, however, networks are not seen as purely positive – as a matter of fact, quite the contrary. To understand the processes of assigning meanings to social relations, let's look at these conversations, starting from the closing-off sequence of the second example:

```
40   SW: You get on with your life in an ordinary way and with ordinary people
41        as far as I've understood, you've got your family and your relations to
42        them and to your other relatives are okay, and that surely will help you
43        and support you from now on
44   C2: I hope so (laughing)
45   SW: Absolutely
```

In this sequence, the social worker formulates some of the properties of 'acceptable' social networks: they involve ordinary people, preferably relatives, who offer their help and support to the client. But there are other kind of networks as well: deviant networks, unacceptable friendships. How, then, is deviancy defined in these encounters? One essential point seems to be the linking of these networks to a certain life-stage. In the first example, this stage is 'criminal background'; in the second, youth. Another property of problematic networks seems to be the interdependency of its members. Most problematic is the group where everything is done together – a group whose members cannot act independently.

In response to the social worker's interpretation about harmful networks the two clients take up different positions. The first client constructs both himself and his friends as independent actors who decide for themselves and are not easily manipulated, whereas the second client aligns with the social worker, admitting he has realized the danger. In the first extract, the professional expresses strong doubts about the independence of the client and the discussion is ended on a note of disagreement. The second client's orientation, however, is supported by the social worker. It is our understanding that as regards community service, *the first client is defined in the course of the conversation as constituting a risk, being a problematic case because of his social relations, whereas the second client is defined as a person with more resources.*

The social worker has formulated her conclusions about the clients' social relations in the written suitability reports. The risks and resources have been constructed in the reports as follows:

> X's life and social relations have been characterized by a certain restlessness and unplanned changes. (Client 1)
> X tells that he has some former school friends of his, with whom he has been spending some time. He says he mainly stays at home. (Client 2)

Negotiating Constructions 287

Financial Situation

Extract 3

```
1    SW: What about your debts – have you got any arrears,
2        or does the bailiff's office have a record of your debts?
3    Cl: I've got some arrears, yes
4    SW: You've got some arrears – what is it,
5        a bank loan, or a record in the bailiff's office?
6    Cl: Yes I've got a record, I reckon all my debts are there
7    SW: What is it, unpaid fines or what?
8    Cl: Well there's not a lot of fines
9    SW: Aha
10   Cl: There's only one fine of about six hundred marks or so
11   SW: The rest would then be what? Payments or were you sentenced
12       to pay compensation or what?
13   Cl: Well yes compensation, and then there's something silly
14   SW: Is it fixed costs, bills coming in regularly or what?
15   Cl: Yes
16   SW: Yea
17   Cl: But it's not really bills either, that's not the main thing
18   SW: Do you have any idea how much you are in debt?
19   Cl: Maybe something like two hundred thousand, probably,
20       I don't really know (laughing)
21   SW: You just said that it's not that much (laughing)
22   Cl: Well that's not an awful lot, is it
23   SW: Well what you think is that
24   Cl: Since a lot of it is already outdated
25   SW: Yea, I just thought, maybe that's what you were thinking,
26       what are you going to do with them
27   Cl: Well I don't know there's not much you can do
28   SW: Have you been in contact with the bailiff's office
29   Cl: No I haven't
30   W: Well you haven't really done much about the matter?
31   Cl: No I haven't
32   SW: But obviously, one must admit, there's not a lot you can do about it
33   Cl: Mm, there's not a lot I could do about it, without money
34   SW: Yea
35   Cl: (laughter)
36   SW: Yea, yea
37   Cl: With nothing in the wallet, it's a bit difficult to pay off
38   SW: Yea when it concerns sums that are this big. That's all very true, but you
39       could give these issues some thought and think whether it would make
```

40   sense to go and see these people and talk things over, about your
41   situation, and see how much arrears you have
42 C1: Yea and there's an interest of sixteen per cent, running all the time
43 SW: I know
44 C1: Don't much care to think about how much I'm in arrears (laughter)
45 SW: So you think that you don't dare go there
46 C1: (laughter)
47 SW: Yea. Sometimes it might be a good idea to look the truth in the eye
48   and see where you stand and think about things like your possibilities
49   of paying off those debts
50 C1: But what is the use of asking, if I cannot pay anyhow
51 SW: Well I was thinking that what do you think the people at the bailiff's
52   would say if you would just go there and talk things over with them
53 C1: The ladies there, they'd just laugh and say, well
54 SW: I thought that maybe they'd say look here, the guy has come to his
55   senses
56 C1: Well
57 SW: Well joking apart, this is a serious matter and
58 C1: Well of course I could go and ask where to get the winning lottery ticket
59 SW: Yea, but anyhow, it might be a good idea, if you tried to check it out,
60   even if there's not a lot you can do, but certainly they would understand
61   that if you're on unemployment benefit and that's all you have, then
62   obviously you won't be able to settle those arrears, but that would at
63   least show them that you have some sense of responsibility, however,
64   and that you want to look after your own affairs, maybe that would
65 C1: But if I cannot even pay the interest it looks to me it's pretty
66   useless going there
67 SW: Well yea you think about it and it's up to you then to decide what
68   you're gonna do about it

Extract 4

1 SW: Do you have any – what about the compensations, do you have,
2   were you ordered to pay, do you remember, or have you had the energy
3   yet to look at these matters?
4 C2 As a matter of fact I don't really know how much I'm in arrears,
5   I don't have any idea how much debt there is
6 SW: They would know in the bailiff's office. They haven't phoned you then
7 C2: They have sent me (unclear) it's like two hundred marks a month,
8   it's kind of purely symbolical settling it that way, but anyhow
9 SW: The main thing is that you keep paying if off, keep it going
10 C2: Yea
11 SW: That sounds good, two hundred marks per month

```
12   C2: Yea
13   SW: Yea I think it's a good thing that you've got the situation under
14       control now, and when you want to find out about it,
15       I'm sure they'll be glad to tell you
16   C2: Yea
17   SW: How do you feel about your economic situation then?
18   C2: I've got this car but I bought it with money from the bank
19   SW: So you took a loan to get a car
20   C2: Yes
21   SW: How much is the monthly payment?
22   C2: It's a thousand marks a month
23   SW: That'll reduce it pretty fast, you'll get it off your back pretty soon
24   C2: Well what was it, how long a time, I don't remember,
25       it was twenty one thousand marks, the loan, anyway
26   SW: Yea, yea
27   C2: How long will it take then, eighteen months or a little more
28   SW: Yea and you've already been paying for some time now
29   C2: Yes I have
```

Here, too, the social worker uses the interview format based on questions and answers. The social worker starts in both cases by asking about debts in general (lines 1-2 in extract 3, lines 1-3 in extract 4). The questions get more and more detailed while she elicits information on the nature and amount of the clients' arrears. The clients answer her, but their answers are rather general.

In the third extract, the social worker needs to ask several follow-up questions before the client comes up with an approximation. The first follow-up question is on lines four and five: 'You've got some arrears – what is it, a bank loan, or a record in the bailiff's office?'. The second and the third ones are on lines seven and eleven: 'What is it, unpaid fines or what?', 'The rest would then be what? Payments or were you sentenced to pay compensation or what?'.

In the fourth extract, the client immediately says that the exact sum of his debts is unknown to him (lines 4-5). But this answer has already been made understandable by the social worker in her previous turn. A candidate account – stress – is implied in her turn 'have you had the energy yet to look at these matters?' (lines 2-3).

In both extracts the social worker and the client seem to agree that the amount of the clients' arrears is such that it is not possible to pay them off while being on unemployment benefit. This is not to say, however, that the social worker is suggesting a complete abandoning of the debts programme either; quite the contrary. An example of the emphasis on the importance of a regular payment schedule can be found in extract 4 (lines 9 to 12). The social worker displays her warm approval of the client's regularity in paying off his debts, be it with rather small monthly payments.

The sequences concerning the amount of debts and the debt programme are followed in both cases by a provision of advice to the client. In extract three, advice-giving starts from line 38:

```
38   SW: Yea when it concerns sums that are this big. That's all very true, but you
39       could give these issues some thought and think whether it would make
40       sense to go and see these people and talk things over, about your
41       situation, and see how much arrears you have
```

And in extract four, advice is given after the social worker's supporting statement:

```
13   SW: Yea I think it's a good thing that you've got the situation under
14       control now, and when you want to find out about it,
15       I'm sure they'll be glad to tell you
```

The message in these two pieces of advice is very similar: it is important to keep in touch with the authorities and to find out exactly what the situation is. There, the first client is on the wrong tracks, because he refuses to accept the advice. The social worker repeats the advice three times: 'Yea. Sometimes it might be a good idea to look the truth in the eye and see where you stand and think about things like your possibilities of paying off those debts' (lines 47-49), 'Well I was thinking that what do you think the people at the bailiff's would say if you would just go there and talk things over with them' (lines 51-52), 'Yea, but anyhow, it might be a good idea, if you tried to check it out...' (lines 59-64). The social worker gets a similar refusing and rejecting response for her advice each time. She closes off the discussion by presenting her advice for the fifth time, but by leaving the final decision to the client (lines 67-68).

In contrast, the second conversation follows quite a different pattern after the provision of advice. The client accepts the advice by a 'yea' (line 16). The social worker proceeds with a general question about the client's economic situation: 'how do you feel about your economic situation then?' (line 17). The client does not give a direct answer; instead, he provides information implying a bank loan for the purchase of a car (line 18). The social worker orients towards this information from the perspective of responsibility, asking 'how much is the monthly payment' (line 21). In the ensuing conversation, the client's answer ('It's a thousand marks a month', line 22) is interpreted as a confirmation that the situation is under control: the client has thought out a payment schedule (lines 24-29).

We have already seen that the two clients' social relations were constructed differently as regards their degree of problematicity. We see the same thing happening with the clients' economic situation. Even if neither of them is, by all likelihood, able to pay off their debts, *only the first client's situation is constructed in such a way as to imply that he has a problem in controlling his finances*. The written suitability reports verbalize it as follows:

> There is a number of unpaid fines, restitution to make, and bills, running to a considerable sum. He has no plans concerning the settling of these sums. (Client 1)
> The client has arrears, which he keeps paying off monthly. (Client 2)

Social relations and economic situation are only two examples of the different aspects of the clients' lives, discussed and considered in the interviews. The ways in which these issues are handled, however, influence for their own part the final definition of suitability. The first client's assessment report was negative – the one whose social relations and economic situation were constructed as problematic in the course of the interview – while the second client was given a referral to community service.

When the Professionals and Researchers Meet: Constructing Institutional and Cultural Accounts for Local Practices

The second half of this article, the ethnographic study, focuses on the institutional and cultural accounts given by the social workers on local assessment practices. These accounts were made available by presenting extracts as well as parts of written suitability reports (among them the episodes cited above) to a group of social workers from the office where the tape-recordings had been done. In these meetings, some of the participants were actually the social workers whose assessment interviews had been analysed. We have so far had four meetings and the number of professionals present at each session has been from four to ten. Normally, we have first shown extracts of assessment interviews to the participants, and then simply asked them what they saw in the extracts and why it was like that. Often we did not even need to pose any 'why'-questions as the social workers were eager to comment and explain the extracts. The meetings constituted a kind of joint analysis and re-analysis of the data, with the view to make institutional and cultural accounts visible.

In the following, we will outline the most commonly given accounts, presented during the early stages of the joint analytic sessions, on the reasons why the interviews between the social workers and the clients function the way they do. We will pick out themes with compact descriptions on the institutional nature of assessment reviews and on the reflection of occupational culture in them. These are accounts given by social workers in order to make the different shades, emphases and nuances of assessment interviews understandable for us researchers. Social workers seemed to share something that needed to be told to us, who were outsiders. This was evident in the sessions, for example we were permitted to ask time and again about very simple facts of the different turns the interviews took and of the possible aims of the interviewers, and we were always rewarded with answers that were kindly, ample and given in a constructive atmosphere. The social workers usually shared the same views among themselves or at least ended up agreeing on things.

The ethnographic part of our article is based on the notes taken during the sessions and complemented afterwards, on our impressions, and on individual discussions with the social workers. During a number of researcher-professional discussions, we elaborated our interpretations and made them more specific. The way we do analysis and report on it attempts at a presentation of the shared and the repeated, manifest in the different ways of decision-making, sense-making and producing explanations. We have a central role in selecting and picking out these ways – as is always the case in ethnographic writing.

'Invisible' Codes and the Use of Intuition

To our surprise (especially during the first joint sessions), the social workers read from the interview transcripts or from the written reports much 'more' and different things from what we saw in them. They had not, however, recognized individual clients from the extracts, but what happened was that their working community had developed specific, *'invisible'* ways of coding suitability.

As an example of this coding, let's look at the following sentence from a written report: 'it is not possible to organize social support measures'. For us, it only read as a comment on the inadequacy of resources, while the social workers understood it as code for the client's non-committed attitude towards social support. To our perplexed questions concerning the statement that 'the family house is on the wife's name', the social workers answered that the economic situation of the interviewed client was good, but there probably was tax evasion or some other form of white-collar crime. Several of the social workers explained to us that it was impossible to write it down in this form; there were no grounds for claiming that the client evaded taxes. However, it was quite possible to use a coded language understand by the court as well. A similar discussion concerned a report on a client who usually drank Koskenkorva (cheap Finnish vodka) and beer. Why was it necessary to mention what kind of alcohol was consumed? The workers found this self-evident: drinking Koskenkorva and beer is a direct reference to a working class male hard drinking model, the kind where the only objective is to get drunk. The description implies that the client is a heavy drinker, but this has not been problematized in the course of the interview to such an extent that it could actually be written down. This, according to the social workers, was another shared code with the court.

Apart from this coding system, the social workers emphasised the existence of another 'invisible' element in the assessment reports. We were reminded that an interactional situation is the site for other kinds of exchange than the purely linguistic, which is the only one visible in our transcriptions. *The workers emphasised intuition*, criticizing our language-centred approach. We had some lively discussions on intuition during the first two joint sessions.

An agreement was reached in the discussions that the first ten to fifteen minutes of an encounter are decisive. It is these ten minutes the social worker needs to build up an intuitive idea of the client and of his suitability for community service. Especially the most experienced probation workers emphasised the importance of intuition, but they also agreed on the point that the interview exists to check up on the intuition: professionalism is not grounded on intuition only, and the social worker specifies her image of the client by interviewing him. The professionals also made it clear that this is how it should be. Intuition, in the professionals' talk to us, was referred back to experience: intuition is not arbitrary or shallow; it draws on the dozens or hundreds of interviews that a professional has conducted during her career.

There are, however, situations that tend to weaken this intuition: among them are assessment interviews carried out in prison. This point was topicalized in a number of joint sessions as part of our data was tape-recorded in prison. Prison interviews are judged more demanding than the ordinary ones made at the social services office. The client's whole being in prison changes: it does not give out enough hints for the social worker to construct an intuitive view. Clothing in prison is uniform; cleanliness standards hide differences in style; the client's lifestyle just cannot be read out of his or her being. The prison also sets a certain frame of reference to discussions. In prison, clients tend to stress their motivation and commitment to community service more than they normally would; and, most importantly, the professionals were of the opinion that this should not be taken at its face value. The emphasis on intuition thus hides a potential contradiction: on one hand, intuition is regarded as important and impulsively constructed, on the other hand, the professionals also control it and reflect upon it.

Suitability Criteria 'behind' the Topics of the Assessment Form

A wide range of topics is discussed in the assessment interview when dealing with the topics specified on the form. The social workers wanted to make it clear, though, that the assessment of suitability is not primarily determined by this information as such (knowing about the client's social relations, financial situation or substance abuse). It is *'behind'* these topics, through discussions about them with the client, that a picture of the client's suitability begins to be formed.

What, then, are the suitability criteria that the professionals seek and construct 'behind' the topics? Our analysis seems to point towards identifying and categorizing at least the following four criteria: regularity, commitment, life control, and attitude towards criminal lifestyle. These were constantly referred to and they were used by the staff as kind of orientation when they interpreted bits of interviews. During a later stage of the research process it turned out that these were factors that the Probation and Aftercare Association had since long been paying attention to when training their workers. The client's position as regards criminal career was the only factor that did not figure among the instructions given to the social workers. Obviously, it was the workers' practices and discussions that had moulded it to appear as an identifiable factor behind suitability.

According to the professionals, both the interview questions and the professionals' interpretations of the clients' answers are largely motivated by the task at hand, that of assessing whether the client is able and willing to lead a regular enough life for the successful carrying out of community service. *Regularity* is checked on a number of fronts. This is why the professionals so often during the course of the interview check on the duration and regularity of things (how long the client has lived in this town, how often he or she sees his/her parents or friends, how long he or she has been married etc.). The social workers explained that it is not important as such to know where the client resides or whether his parents are alive or not. The important thing is that by talking about these and related issues, about changes in relationships or their permanence, the professionals pick up important information. The two extracts concerning the economic situation of the clients (extracts 3 and 4 in this paper) are examples of testing the regularity criteria: the client who was paying off his debt in monthly instalments was allocated 'suitability points'. The social workers were very clear about this, and made the following comments:

> The amount of debt is not important as such – what is important is whether the client is trying to do something about it
> The willingness to take care of one's money matters is a sign that this is a decent fellow
> What counts is what the client has done to pay off his debts; regularity is important

There were no counter-arguments to this view, even though it was mentioned that it is hard to live with such large debts.

Commitment is another criterion for suitability: the social workers said that they need to be sure about the client's commitment to community service. Like signs of regularity, signs of commitment can be read from many different areas of the client's life – again, paying off at least part of one's debts was seen as such a sign. The staff also explained that commitment to community service actually means disengaging from such commitments that can endanger one's community service. And vice versa, commitment to a certain kind of social relations – to friends with a criminal background, as in the fourth extract – is interpreted as not committing oneself to community service.

Parallel to regularity and commitment, and closely connected to them, is the client's ability to *control his own life*, which the social workers try to figure out. For example, does the client try to do something about things he finds difficult? Does he try to pay his fines; does he try to negotiate on the conditions of his loan, or does he just leave the matter as it is? Is the client able to act independently, without being dominated by his or her friends (this was the issue in the social relations extract)? If he is substance abuser, can he control his drinking? When alcohol consumption is taken up in the interviews – the amount of alcohol consumed, when and with whom, and for how long (up to what point) – the workers say that what they are after is the client's ability and readiness to limit/curb his drinking when necessary. It is not important to find out whether the client is a problem drinker but to assess whether he can limit his drinking so that he is able to carry through the community service.

The fourth central criterion, as assessed by the professionals, is the client's *attitude towards criminal lifestyle*. Criminal lifestyle is not checked out by questions about crimes – as a matter of fact, talk about crimes in our data is almost non-existent – but by finding out about the client's social relations. To an outsider, the discussions about the job or about friends and family might come as a surprise – at least this is what happened to us, the researchers. They were not arbitrary, though, as explained to us by the workers. The nature of social relations, their meaning and content in the client's life are factors through which the client's links with crimes and criminal behaviour are charted. This is the reason for asking (like in our example) a 36-year old man about his friends, how he spends his time when he is with them, where he meets them, and how independent he judges himself to be in relation to them and their doings. It is not essential for the social worker to know where exactly the client stands with his friends, but this information serves the social workers when they try to figure out the client's attitude to offending as this is directly related to criminal career.

Criminal career was a concept the professionals shared: it constituted the basis for assessing the client's situation. We have already seen how it underlay the professionals' action in social relations example. The social workers overtly expressed their view that many criminal offenders commit crimes as a kind of a continuum, a career, where certain regularities can be observed. In its most fervent phase, dependence on friends is at its greatest. This phase often occurs when the person is young or a young adult, but does not necessarily end in adulthood. Biological age, therefore, is not the only explanation. Furthermore, the social workers explained, it is essential to recognize when the offender is starting to be tired of his or her criminal career. Community service can now be one option in supporting disengagement from criminal career. The concept of criminal career also presents new challenges to the social worker: he or she must be able to foresee future developments, too.

The concept of 'criminal career' clearly constitutes a theory, built up in practical work about the object of the work, and this theory is actively related to and interpreted in relation to the theories built up in criminological research. The social workers often referred to a study by Juha Kääriäinen (1994), which consolidated the concept of 'criminal career' in Finnish criminological discussion. The study had sparked off a lot of discussion, legitimizing talk about the different stages of criminal career.

If we look at the ethnographic data as a whole (meaning here the discussions and joint analytical sessions with the social workers), we find that there are two outstanding thematic dimensions. First, the data are characterized by the interpretive nature of suitability assessment work. A recurrent theme in the discussions is how social workers interpret the information they get from the clients and the facts about the client's life situation, and the necessity of these interpretations in view of the suitability assessments. The very core of the work thus lies in active interpretation, and professionality depends on how grounded, non-arbitrary and shared these interpretations are. Second, the specific communicative practices of suitability assessment are central to these ethnographic data: interpretation is tied to the shared occupational culture and experience. Expressions, conversational techniques, metaphors etc. are part of the work done in this specific organization: this is why they do not automatically open up for study by social work teachers and researchers, like us. It is not, however, merely a feature of this organization only: some of the specific communicative practices are shared with other institutions working with criminal offenders, such as criminal courts. The specificity of work practices stems thus from clientele as well as the collective work community and shared experiences.

Conclusions

Finally, we would like to summarize some of the findings of this project concerning social constructionism and social work research. We strongly argue that both practical and analytical relevance can be gained from combining discourse analysis and ethnography in the study of the suitability assessment practices. From the *practical* point of view, a close look at social work practices seems to provide a great variety of new views on work – or suitability assessments – done. The social workers involved in this project suggest that the analysis of professional-client encounters make them more aware of their basic scheme of working, of their habits and also of their power. In other words, discussing client encounters with other colleagues and researchers made the general and local work practices visible and noticed – we were not the only ones who were occasionally at a loss with the actual practices of social work in certain situations.

In this analysis, both discourse analysis and ethnography were used in order to make work practices visible and noticed. Discourse analysis focusing on the encounters between the social workers and their clients explicated the local and interactional categorization of clients as suitable or not suitable. The discussions concerning the social relations and the economic situation of the clients, analysed in the article, illustrate this production of suitability. This visibility made the social workers reflect upon the power of their own talk in interaction. The findings of the ethnographic stage had a similar effect: even if the workers described for us the 'invisible' elements and 'hidden codes' of suitability assessments, these interpretations were constructed on the basis of the clues from interview extracts. The institutional and cultural interpretations, shared by the social workers, can thus be thought to be an integrated part of the interviewing practices – not just forces guiding the process before it actually starts or accounts explicating it afterwards.

One result of this 'making visible and noticed' – according to the social workers involved in this project – was that the project challenges them to rethink several aspects concerning the assessment of suitability. Some aspects concern the interaction between the client and the social workers as such, but the practical relevance does not seem to be limited to face-to-face work only. The findings of the project suggest that there might be new ways of managing the structural organisation of suitability assessments: a 'reorganization' of the roles of the written report and the interview. What is more, the analysis and re-analysis seem to challenge the social workers to express their concerns on the role of suitability assessments in our criminal justice system. As a matter of fact, the practical relevance seems to stretch quite far. The project has so far shown also that social workers are both willing to carry out and very skilled in doing constructionist analysis.

In terms of practical relevance, the position of the client in suitability assessment is one of our biggest concerns. As the analysis has shown earlier, the professionals follow a certain agenda in the interviews and employ certain criteria for assessing suitability. This agenda and set of criteria are not, however, openly specified to the client. The question is, now: should the client be told about them as they seem to be so strongly rooted in the practice? The client's possible agendas merit more attention, too. All this constitutes quite a task for the research. Take, for example, our extracts. The two clients seem to be differently positioned as to the official agenda. Could we possibly find support for an interpretation that the first client, the one who argues with the social worker and is consequently assessed as not suitable, only follows his own agenda, and the incompatibility of his agenda with the official one seals his destiny?

When talking about the *analytic* relevance of the research, several challenging and at the moment partly open questions arise from this kind of methodological approach. The core question is what the relationship between the discourse analytical and ethnographic data and their analysis is. Actually, we have three different kinds of encounters here. First, we have the naturally occurring conversations between the professionals and the clients. Second, we have the discourse analytical interpretation process of those conversations. And third, we have the professional-researcher encounters where the social workers provide institutional and cultural accounts.

During the course of our research, the institutions of assessing clients' suitability for community service were talked into being in two arenas. These two arenas produce different and parallel spaces of knowledge about suitability assessment practices, that is the discourse analytical interpretations of local conversations and the collectively produced accounts of the professionals. These two different kinds of knowledge have a very complicated connection to each other. What we want to emphasise is that the relations between them are definitely not hierarchical. During the research process we were not moving towards a more and more complete or not even a complementary understanding about the practices of assessment interviews. We were not triangulating our data in order to get at an overall 'truth' (Silverman, 1993, p. 156-158).

David Silverman's (1994; 1997) idea of asking successively conversation analytical 'how' and ethnographic 'why' questions was an important methodological starting point. We ended up, however, asking the how-questions both in discourse analytical and ethnographic research. We had two reasons for this. First, the ethnographic data simply did not yield answers to the 'why' questions. As researchers we did try to ask the social workers 'why' questions on the data, but their way of producing shared answers made us analyse them as cultural and institutional accounts ('how' accounts). Second, as the research moved along, it proved to be singularly difficult to keep the two sets of data and two analytical methods apart in a way that would have been necessary for carrying out a two-stage question process. This ties up with an issue we took up when reflecting upon the practical relevance of the research: *not only do the institutional and cultural accounts explicate or make understandable the issues at hand in the professional-client encounters: they are also inextricably bound to these issues.*

We would like to conclude this article with a few open remarks on an issue arising from the combination of different kinds of data and analytical traditions, of crucial importance to the analytical relevance of our research. It is the question about the researcher's position. As researchers, we have the possibility of dealing with both sets of data independently, asking different questions and limiting the context. The attempt at their combination raises at least the following questions: What happens to the researchers' ways of looking at local data in the future, when they have discussed with the professionals and have heard their institutional and cultural accounts concerning the assessment interviews? Can this 'insider' knowledge be defined as a resource in the forthcoming analysis or should it be counted as a risk? If so, in what way?

Even if we decided to carry on with the discourse analytical framework only, concentrating on professional-client encounters, there would always be a need for taking into account the discussions we have had with the social workers. Likewise, focusing on purely ethnographic data is impossible since what we know now about the interactional moves in professional-client encounters may either strengthen or question the discussions we have had with the social workers. The different kinds of data will inevitably be part of the analysis, even if we tried to keep them separate. This is a critical issue for the researcher, who cannot choose not to see something that has become evident from the other type of data or method even if he/she would like to. On the other hand, all researchers have at their disposal some kind of interpretive resources. It is often not reflected upon, however, or it is only mentioned in passing. One concrete benefit from combining discourse analysis and ethnography might be that they force the researcher to reflect and analyse his/her own interpretive resources in the analysis.

Despite all these challenging questions – as a matter of fact, mostly *because* of them, we have found it important to study several kinds of encounters in social work and the different kinds of knowledge they produce. Social work actualizes in a number of widely differing arenas, ant its study cannot be limited to encounters of one type only. In addition, the social constructionist view on social problems does not solely mean looking at how the constructions of problems are created in different arenas: it also means negotiations about those constructions.

Note

1. The present paper is part of an extensive research project focusing on the construction of clienthood and social problems in social work in different social welfare and therapy organizations. The research project 'Institutions of Helping as Everyday Practices' is being carried out in the Department of Social Policy and Social Work at the University of Tampere and in the Department of Psychology at the University of Jyväskylä. In addition to the authors of the present paper, three other researchers are involved in the project: Arja Jokinen, Eero Suoninen and Jarl Wahlström. The project is funded by the Finnish Academy.

Bibliography

Antaki, C. (1994), *Explaining and Arguing: The Social Organization of Accounts*, Sage Publications, London.

Atkinson, P. and Coffey, A. (1997), 'Documentary Realities', in D. Silverman (ed), *Qualitative Research: Theory, Method and Practice*, Sage Publications, London, pp. 45-62.

Baldock, J. and Prior, D. (1981), 'Social Workers Talking to Clients: A Study of Verbal Behaviour', *British Journal of Social Work*, vol. 11, pp. 19-38.

Edwards, D. (1997), *Discourse and Cognition*, Sage Publications, London.

Edwards, D. (1998), 'The Relevant Thing about Her: Social Identity Categories in Use', in C. Antaki and S. Widdicombe (eds), *Identities in Talk*, Sage Publications, London, pp. 15-33.

Edwards, D. and Potter, J. (1992), *Discursive Psychology*, Sage Publications, London.

Emerson, R. M. (1988), *Contemporary Field Research. A Collection of Readings*, Waweland Press, Prospect Heights.
Everitt, A., Hardiker, P., Littlewood, J. and Mullender, A. (1992), *Applied Research for Better Practice*, Macmillan, Basingstoke.
Garfinkel, H. (1967), *Studies in Ethnomethodology*, Polity Press, Cambridge.
Gergen, K. (1994), *Realities and Relationships: Soundings in Social Construction*, Havard University Press, Cambridge.
Gubrium, J. (1989), 'Local Cultures and Service Policy', in J. Gubrium and D. Silverman (eds), *The Politics of Field Research: Sociology Beyond Enlightenment*, Sage Publications, London, pp. 94-112.
Heritage, J. (1984), *Garfinkel and Ethnomethodology*, Polity Press, Cambridge.
Holstein, J. (1993), *Court-ordered Insanity: Interpretative Practice and Involuntary Commitment*, Aldine de Gruyter, New York.
Holstein, J. and Miller, G. (1993), 'Social Constructionism and Social Problems Work', in J. Holstein and G. Miller (eds), *Reconsidering Social Constructionism*, Aldine de Gruyter, New York, pp.151-172.
Jokinen, A. and Juhila, K. (1996), *Merkitykset ja vuorovaikutus - poimintoja asunnottomuuspuheiden kulttuurisesta virrasta* [Meanings and Interaction: Analysing Cultural Talk on Homelessness in Different Settings], Acta Universitatis Tamperensis 510, Tampere.
Jokinen, A., Juhila, K. and Pösö, T. (1995), 'Tulkitseva sosiaalityö' [Interpretative Social Work], in A. Jokinen, K. Juhila and T. Pösö (eds), *Sosiaalityö, asiakkuus ja sosiaaliset ongelmat. Konstruktionistinen näkökulma* [Social Work, Clienthood and Social Problems. A Constructionist View], Sosiaaliturvan Keskusliitto, Helsinki, pp. 9-31.
Maynard, D. (1989), 'On the Ethnography and Analysis of Discourse in Institutional Settings', in J.A. Holstein and G. Miller (eds), *Perspectives on Social Problems*, vol. 1, Jai Press Inc, Greenwich, pp. 127-46.
Miller, G. (1997), 'Building Bridges. The Possibility of Analytic Dialoque between Ethnography, Conversation Analysis and Foucault', in D. Silverman (ed), *Qualitative Research: Theory, Method and Practice*, Sage Publications, London, pp. 24-44.
Miller, G. and Holstein, J. (1991), 'Social Problems Work in Street-level Bureaucracies. Rhetoric and Organizational Process', in G. Miller (ed), *Studies in Organizational Sociology*, Jai Press Inc, Greenwich, pp. 177-99.
Oranen, M. (1997), 'Semmonen pikkunen huoli. Diskurssianalyyttinen tutkimus lastensuojelun arviointikeskusteluista' [Only a Little Worry. A Discourse Analytical Study on the Assessment Discussions of Child Protection], *Janus*, vol. 5, no. 1, pp. 3-25.
Peräkylä, A. and Silverman, D. (1991), 'Rethinking Speech-exchange System: Communication Formats in AIDS-counselling', *Sociology*, vol. 25, no. 4, pp. 627-51.

Potter, J. (1996), *Representing Reality: Discourse, Rhetoric and Social Construction*, Sage Publications, London.
Potter, J. and Wetherell, M. (1987), *Discourse and Social Psychology*, Sage Publications, London.
Prince, K. (1996), *Boring Records? Communication, Speech and Writing in Social Work*, Jessica Kingsley Publishers, London.
Rojek, C., Peacock, G. and Collins, S. (1988), *Social Work and Received Ideas*, Routledge, London.
Rostila, I. (1997), *Keskustelu sosiaaliluukulla* [Talk at Work at the Social Welfare Office: Social Work as Work in Talk-in-Interaction], Acta Universitatis Tamperensis 547, Tampere.
Sarangi, S. and Hall, C. (1997), *Bringing off 'Applied' Research in Interprofessional Discourse Studies*, paper presented in BAAL/CUP seminar on Urban Culture, Discourse and Ethnography, Thames Valley University, London, 24-25 March 1997.
Silverman, D. (1993), *Interpreting Qualitative Data: Methods for Analysing Talk, Text and Interaction*, Sage Publications, London.
Silverman, D. (1997), *Discourses of Counselling: HIV Counselling as Social Interaction*, Sage Publications, London.
Silverman, D. and Gubrium J. (1994), 'Competing Strategies for Analyzing the Contexts of Social Interaction', *Sociological Inquiry*, vol. 64, no. 2, pp. 179-98.
Spencer, W. (1988), 'The Role of Text in the Processing of People in Organizations', *Discourse Processes*, vol. 11, pp. 61-78.
Stenson, K (1994), 'The Social Work Interview as Government: The Dialectic between Orality and Literacy', in S. Hänninen (ed), *Silence, Discourse and Deprivation*, National Research and Development Centre for Welfare and Health, Research reports 43, Helsinki, pp. 28-49.
Tainio, L. (1997), 'Preferenssijäsennys' [Preference organization], in Tainio, L. (ed), *Keskustelunanalyysin perusteet* [Basics in Conversation Analysis], Vastapaino, Tampere, pp. 93-110.
Takala, J.P. (1993), *Rangaistus ja siihen soveltuminen. Yhdyskuntapalvelukokeilun alkuvaiheita ja ongelmia* [Punishment and Suitability for Punishment: Initial Phases and Problems of Finland's Community Service Experiment], Oikeuspoliittinen tutkimuslaitos 120, Helsinki.
Widdicombe, S. (1995), 'Identity, Politics and Talk: A Case for the Mundane and the Everyday', in Wilkinson, S. and Kitzinger, C. (eds), *Feminism and Discourse: Psychological Perspectives*, Sage Publications, London, pp. 106-27.
Woolgar, S. and Pawluch, D. (1985), 'Ontological Gerrymandering: The Anatomy of Social Problems Explanations', *Social Problems*, vol. 32, no. 3, pp. 214-27.
Zimmerman, D. (1969), 'Record-keeping and the Intake Process in a Public Welfare Agency', in S. Wheeler (ed), *On record. Files and Dossiers in American Life*, Russell Sage Foundation, New York, pp. 319-54.

Notes on Contributors

Mimi Ajzenstadt

Dr Ajzenstadt, Lecturer, The Baerwald School of Social Work and The Institute of Criminology, Faculty of Law, The Hebrew University of Jerusalem, Israel. She is studying societal processes leading to the creation and implementation of legal and social policies.
Address: Institute of Criminology
           Faculty of Law and the School of Social Work
           The Hebrew University of Jerusalem
           Mount Scopus
           91905 Jerusalem, Israel
           e-mail: mimi@pluto.mscc.huji.ac.il

Svein Alve

Psychologist and lecturer, Oslo College, Oslo, Norway. He has earlier studied communication patterns in families having members diagnosed as 'schizophrenic' and 'borderline'. At present, he is investigating how social workers construct gender in their work with clients.
Address: Oslo College
           Faculty of Economics, Public Administration and Social Work
           Pilestredet 56
           N - 0167 Oslo, Norway
           e-mail: Svein.Alve@oks.hioslo.no

Elisabet Cedersund

PhD, Associate Professor in the Department of Health and Environment, Linköping University, and Research Associate in the Department of Communication Studies at the same university. Her principal research interests include the study of talk and text in institutional settings, particularly in the social services.
Address: Faculty of Health Sciences
Campus Norrköping
Linköping University
S – 601 74 Norrköping, Sweden
e-mail: Elice@tema.liu.se

Hannele Forsberg

PhD, Hannele Forsberg currently serves as Assistant Professor of Social Work at the University of Tampere, Finland. She has written in the field of family and social work using a social constructionist approach. Her recent doctoral thesis focused on the interpretative practices of family and of the position of the child in social welfare offices and family support centres.
Address: Department of Social Policy and Social Work
University of Tampere
P.O. Box 607
FIN - 33101 Tampere, Finland
e-mail: sphafo@uta.fi

Sally Holland

Tutorial Fellow in Cardiff University. She previously worked as a social worker in South Wales. Her research interests include social work assessment and decision-making.
Address: Cardiff School of Social Sciences
Cardiff University
50 Park Place
Cardiff CF1 3AT, UK
e-mail: HollandS1@Cardiff.ac.uk

Arja Jokinen

PhD, Senior Researcher in Social Work at the University of Tampere. She is studying everyday social work practices, especially client-professional interaction in different social welfare organisations. Her research interest also include the application of discourse analysis and social construction of homelessness.

Address: Department of Social Policy and Social Work
University of Tampere
P.O. Box 607
FIN - 33101 Tampere, Finland
e-mail: sparjo@uta.fi

Kirsi Juhila

PhD, Assistant Professor in Social Work at the University of Tampere. Her research interests include the application of discourse analysis and the social construction of homelessness. She is currently working on a project on social problems work in different social welfare organisations.

Address: Department of Social Policy and Social Work
University of Tampere
P.O. Box 607
FIN - 33101 Tampere, Finland
e-mail: spkiju@uta.fi

Evelyn Khoo

MSW, PhD Candidate, has several years experience in the area of child welfare and worked for five years at the Children's Aid Society of London and Middlesex, in Ontario, Canada. In her current position, she is doing cross-national comparisons of social programs for abused and neglected children.

Address: Dept. of Social Welfare
Umeå University
S - 901 87 Umeå, Sweden
e-mail: ev.khoo@sympatico.ca

Jaclyn Miller

MSSW, PhD, Associate Professor and Director of Field Instruction, School of Social work, Virginia Commonwealth University. She has 30 years of social work experience in mental health and public social services. She teaches social work practice and does research on social work education.
Address: Virginia Commonwealth University
School of Social Work
P.O. Box 842027
Richmond, Virginia 23284-2027, USA
e-mail: jmiller@atlas.vcu.edu

Mary Katherine O'Connor

PhD, Associate Professor, School of Social Work, Virginia Commonwealth University. She has 30 years of child welfare experience and has done research and has written on street children, child abuse and neglect, and the methodological development of constructivist research.
Address: Virginia Commonwealth University
School of Social work
P.O. Box 842027
Richmond, Virginia 23284-2027, USA
e-mail: mrodwell@atlas.vcu.edu

Nigel Parton

Professor in Child Care, and Director of the Centre for Applied Childhood Studies, at the University of Huddersfield, England. A qualified social worker, he has been researching and writing in the areas of social work and child welfare for over twenty years and has a particular interest in the development of social constructionist perspectives in social policy and welfare practice.
Address: Centre for Applied Childhood Studies
School of Human and Health Sciences
University of Huddersfield
Huddersfield, HD1 3DH, England
e-mail: n.parton@hud.ac.uk

Malcolm Payne

Professor of Applied Community Studies, Manchester Metropolitan University, having previously worked in probation and social services and the national and local voluntary sector in Britain.

Address: Department of Applied Community Studies
 The Manchester Metropolitan University
 799 Wilmslow Road
 Didsbury
 Manchester M20 2RR, UK
 e-mail: M.Payne@mmu.ac.uk

Tarja Pösö

Professor in Social Work, University of Tampere, Finland, currently studies social work practices in different welfare organizations. Her main research interests focus on child protection issues.

Address: University of Tampere
 Department of Social Policy and Social Work
 P.O. Box 607
 FIN - 33 101 Tampere, Finland
 e-mail: sptapo@uta.fi

Jonathan B. Scourfield

Formerly a probation officer in South Wales, is now a Tutorial Fellow in social work at Cardiff University. His principal current research interest is the construction of gender in social work practice.

Address: Cardiff School of Social Sciences
 Cardiff University
 50 Park Place
 Cardiff CF1 3AT, UK
 e-mail: Scourfield@Cardiff.ac.uk

Mike Seltzer

Cultural anthropologist and sociologist. He is an associate professor at Oslo College, Oslo, Norway. He has conducted several studies based on naturalistic observation of clients and social workers and is currently studying family therapy practice at a clinic in rural Norway. His doctoral dissertation is based on a participant observational study of merchant sailors at sea and ashore in European ports.

Address: Oslo College,
Faculty of Economics, Public Administration and Social Work
Pilestredet 56
0167 Oslo
e-mail: Michael.Seltzer@oks.hioslo.no

Eero Suoninen

PhD, Senior Researcher and Lecturer in the Department of Sociology and Social Psychology at the University of Tampere. He is one of the authors of the first Finnish text book on discourse analysis and his doctoral dissertation concerns research methodology. He is studying client-professional interaction in different social welfare and therapy organisations.

Address: Department of Sociology and Social Psychology
University of Tampere
P.O.Box 607
FIN - 33101 Tampere, Finland
e-mail: es10343@uta.fi

Danielle Turney

Lecturer in Social Work, based in Professional and Community Education (PACE) at Goldsmith's College, University of London. Danielle Turney qualified as a social worker, and subsequently worked mainly in childcare and child protection social work.

Address: Goldsmiths College
University of London
New Cross
London SE14 6NW, UK
e-mail: d.turney@gold.ac.uk

Susan White

PhD, Lecturer in the Department of Social Policy and Social Work, University of Manchester. Her recent publications concern social theory and its relevance to social welfare and the law; time, temporality and child welfare; and postmodernism and therapeutic discourse and blamings in family therapy. She has just completed a study of young people's narratives of personal distress and is currently part of a comparative research team studying the linguistic practices of child care social workers in England and Finland.

Address: Department of Social Policy and Social Work
Fourth Floor, Williamson Building
The University of Manchester
Oxford Road
Manchester M13 9PL, UK
e-mail: sue.white@man.ac.uk